## Praise for
## The Book of Ruth

"This is a must-read book with many twists and turns as Ruth meets professional and personal obstacles again and again and yet finds her own paths to success. It is imbued with Ruth's strong spirit and determination as she recalls her years of juggling marriage, motherhood, a career (back when mothers were not supposed to have a career) and her art—all while fighting the ghosts that haunted her throughout her life. She battled her ghosts to save North Carolina history, but even more to save her soul."
— **Susan W. Woodson**, Raleigh artist

"This memoir will inspire so many people. Ruth Little is a strong woman who has pursued a life under her own terms, refusing to accept the life that was presented by family and society. Her art career was born from the brave and cathartic act of painting her mother's hoarder house for her first public art show. With her personal resilience in the face of much adversity, she meticulously investigated and protected so many places vital to North Carolina's distinctive cultural character and history."
— **Mary Lambeth Moore**, writer, editor, activist

"Rigorous, observant, colorful, and brave, *The Book of Ruth* weaves threads of social history, family history, and architectural history to create a moving story of a life shaped by people and place. Her example shows us that keeping faith in one's creative, intellectual, and personal aspirations can be precisely the ingredient that sets us free.
— **Brett Sturm**, restoration specialist, NC State Historic Preservation Office

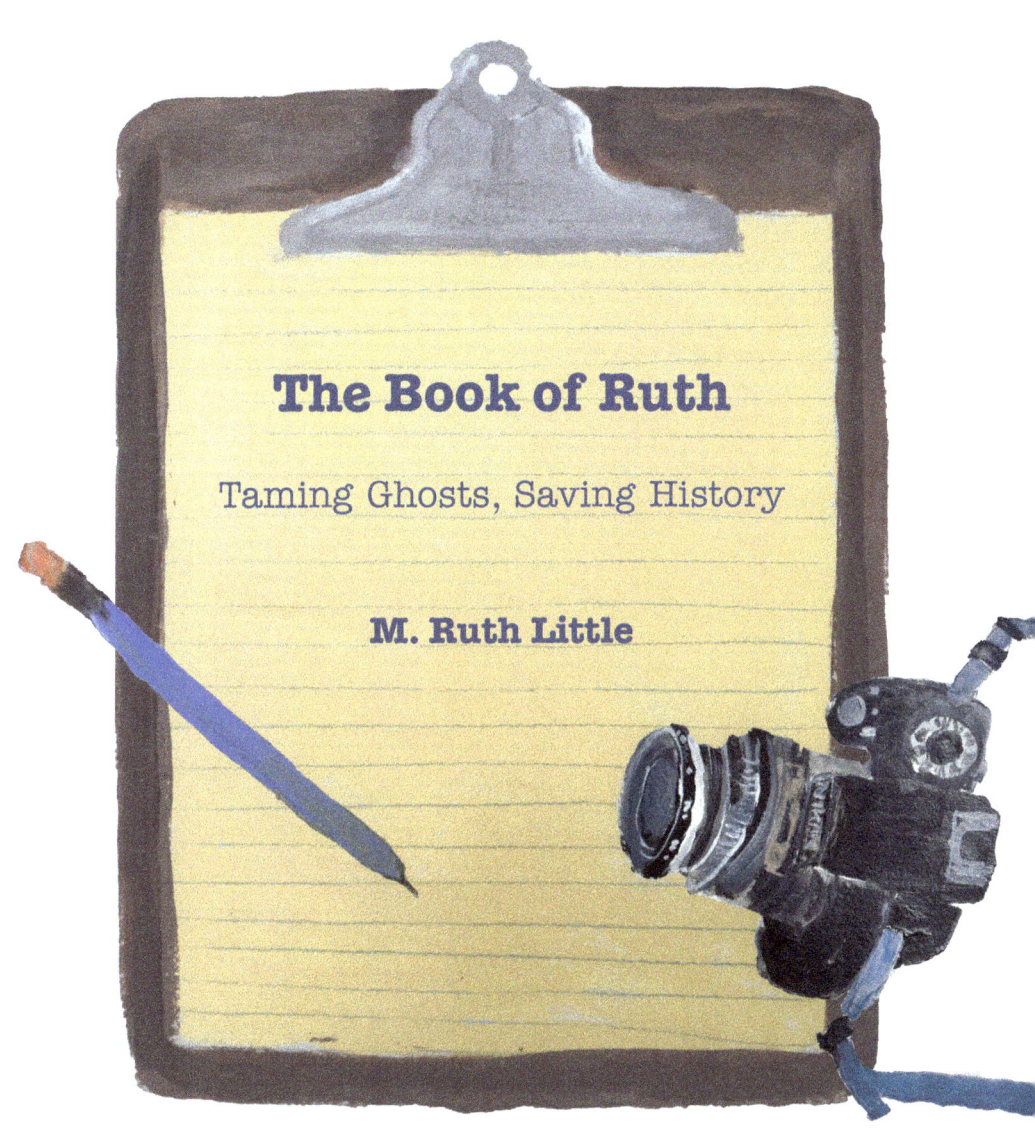

# The Book of Ruth

## Taming Ghosts, Saving History

### M. Ruth Little

LYSTRA BOOKS
& Literary Services

The Book of Ruth: Taming Ghosts, Saving History
Copyright © 2022 by Margaret Ruth Little
All rights reserved.

ISBN print, 978-1-7363055-5-3
ISBN ebook, 978-1-7363055-6-0
Library of Congress Control Number: 2021916718

The contents of this book are the intellectual property of Margaret Ruth Little. Except for brief excerpts for reviews of the work no portion of the text and no image can be reproduced in any form without written permission of the author. Please contact her through the publisher at the address below.

Unless otherwise stated, all photographs are by or in the collection of Margaret Ruth Little. Other photographs are used with the kind permission of Warren Davis, Terry Eason, Ann Ehringhaus, and Carl Lounsbury. All artwork is the property of Margaret Ruth Little.

Excerpts of chapter 1 in *Carolina Cottage: A Personal History of the Piazza House*, Little, Margaret Ruth.. pp. 3–22. © 2010 by the Rector and Visitors of the University of Virginia. Reprinted by permission of the University of Virginia Press.

Excerpt from *Life of Pi: A Novel* by Yann Martel. Copyright © 2001 by Yann Martel. Reprinted by permission of Mariner Books, an imprint of HarperCollins Publishers, LLC. All rights reserved.

Author's photograph by Amanda Olson

Book design by Kelly Prelipp Lojk

Published by Lystra Books & Literary Services, LLC
391 Lystra Estates Drive
Chapel Hill, NC 27517
Lystrabooks@gmail.com

*To the Loves of My Life
Warren Davis, Gia Upchurch, Britton Upchurch*

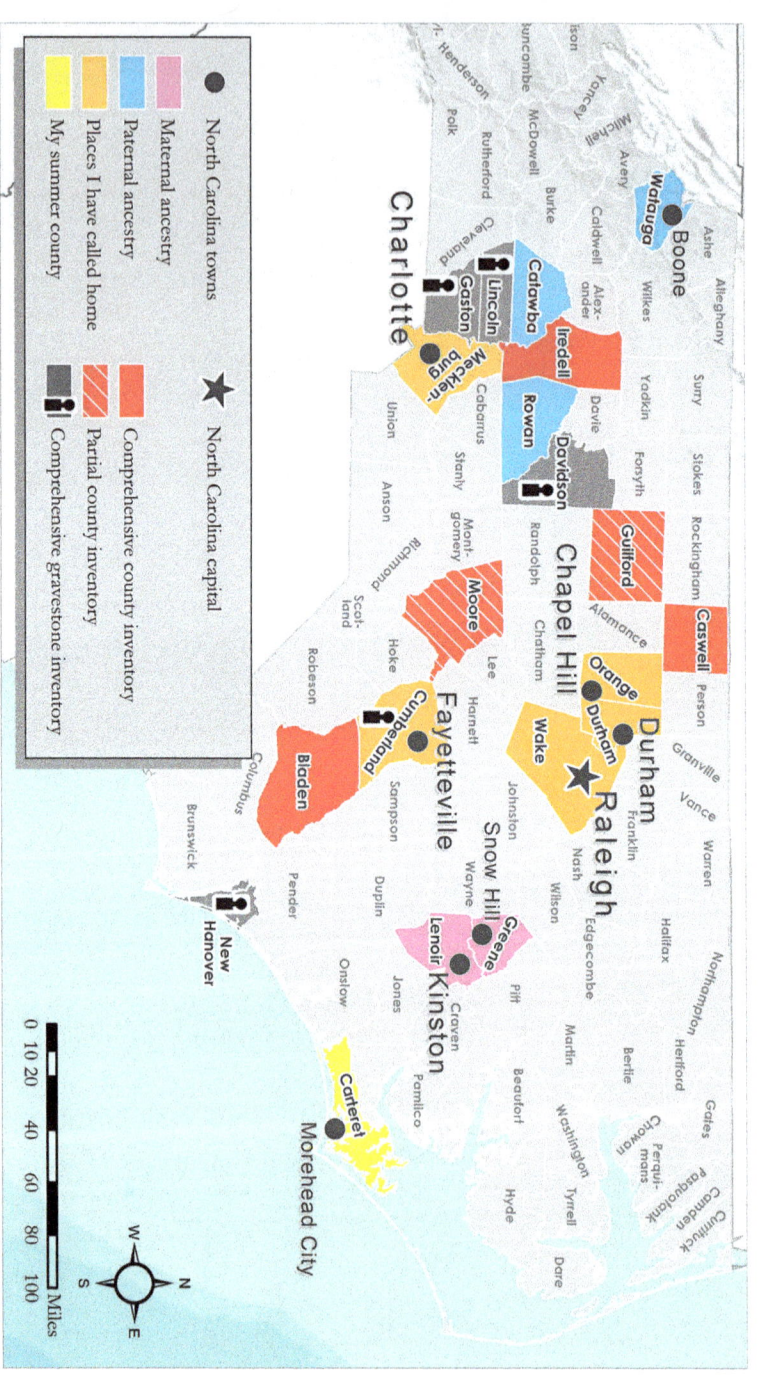

The Book of Ruth geography. Map by Andrew Edmonds, 2021.

## Contents

Foreword . . . . . . . . . . . . . . . . . . . . . . . . . . . . . ix
Prologue . . . . . . . . . . . . . . . . . . . . . . . . . . . . . xi

PART I
**Coming of Age**

   1  Crossing the Threshold . . . . . . . . . . . . . . . . . . .2
   2  A Childhood of Earthy Zaniness . . . . . . . . . . . . . .8
   3  Puberty . . . . . . . . . . . . . . . . . . . . . . . . . . . 18
   4  St. Mary's . . . . . . . . . . . . . . . . . . . . . . . . . . 24
   5  The University . . . . . . . . . . . . . . . . . . . . . . . 33
   6  France, My Introduction . . . . . . . . . . . . . . . . . 39
   7  France, First Love . . . . . . . . . . . . . . . . . . . . . 46
   8  The Telegram . . . . . . . . . . . . . . . . . . . . . . . 53
   9  Grad School and a Career Passion . . . . . . . . . . . 59

PART II
**Launching**

  10  The Dawn of Historic Preservation
        in North Carolina . . . . . . . . . . . . . . . . . . . . 68
  11  Activism . . . . . . . . . . . . . . . . . . . . . . . . . . 75
  12  Marriage and Identity . . . . . . . . . . . . . . . . . . 82
  13  State Work in the '70s . . . . . . . . . . . . . . . . . . 89
  14  First House . . . . . . . . . . . . . . . . . . . . . . . . 98
  15  Charlotte . . . . . . . . . . . . . . . . . . . . . . . . . 106
  16  My Turn to Go Back to School . . . . . . . . . . . . 113
  17  A Two-Hundred-Year-Old Nest . . . . . . . . . . . 120

## PART III
## The Middle Years: Balancing Family & Career

- 18  Marriage No. 2 and Family . . . . . . . . . . . . . . . . . 128
- 19  Longleaf Historic Resources . . . . . . . . . . . . . . . . 136
- 20  Black History Through White Eyes . . . . . . . . . 143
- 21  Projects in Mother's Counties . . . . . . . . . . . . . . 150
- 22  Fayetteville: You Can Go Home Again . . . . . . . 156
- 23  Sticks and Stones . . . . . . . . . . . . . . . . . . . . . . . . 160
- 24  Cape Lookout . . . . . . . . . . . . . . . . . . . . . . . . . . . 163
- 25  Projects Close to Home – 1990s . . . . . . . . . . . . 168
- 26  Liberation . . . . . . . . . . . . . . . . . . . . . . . . . . . . . . 174
- 27  Projects Close to Home – Early 2000s . . . . . . . 180
- 28  Preserving the Recent Past . . . . . . . . . . . . . . . . 187
- 29  Circling Back and Revisiting . . . . . . . . . . . . . . . 195
- 30  Notable Projects After 2010 . . . . . . . . . . . . . . . 204

## PART IV
## Mama Cool Exorcises Her Ghosts

- 31  Roundabout . . . . . . . . . . . . . . . . . . . . . . . . . . . . 212
- 32  Oberlin . . . . . . . . . . . . . . . . . . . . . . . . . . . . . . . . 222
- 33  I Know Who You Are . . . . . . . . . . . . . . . . . . . . 226
- 34  Losing a Cottage, Revisiting Caswell County and Dad's Roots . . . . . . . . . . . . . . . . . . . . . . . . . 232
- 35  Having It All After All . . . . . . . . . . . . . . . . . . . 240

Endnotes . . . . . . . . . . . . . . . . . . . . . . . . . . . . . . . . . . . . 243
Also by Ruth Little . . . . . . . . . . . . . . . . . . . . . . . . . . . 247
More About the Art . . . . . . . . . . . . . . . . . . . . . . . . . . 249
Index . . . . . . . . . . . . . . . . . . . . . . . . . . . . . . . . . . . . . . 250
Acknowledgments . . . . . . . . . . . . . . . . . . . . . . . . . . . 258
About the Author . . . . . . . . . . . . . . . . . . . . . . . . . . . . 259

## Foreword

For years, I've known that North Carolina is literally a different place because of Ruth Little. She has dedicated her career and much of her life to historical preservation in this state. Because of her, we know more about our history and we've kept more of it. I've also known Ruth as a talented artist who discovered a lifelong passion for painting at a young age. After reading *Carolina Cottage*, *Through the Crystal Ball of the Chancellor's Residence*, and now, *The Book of Ruth*, I also know Ruth as a talented writer.

This memoir is imbued with Ruth's strong spirit and determination as she recalls her years of juggling marriage, motherhood, a career (back when mothers were not supposed to have a career), and her art—all while fighting the ghosts that haunted her throughout her life. She battled her ghosts to save North Carolina history, but even more to save her soul.

Ruth and I met when I first moved to Raleigh, when my husband became the chancellor of North Carolina State University. I just feel like our paths were meant to cross. We've had eleven years of adventures together and so many art classes—more than I can count. (I do think we got better!) We were part of a small art gang that rented an old pawn shop across from the university and started the Roundabout Art Collective. All of that has been swept away now, including the "Barrel Monster" that guarded the Hillsborough Street roundabout while it was being built, but we made a lasting impact on Raleigh's art scene.

But I digress. I'm grateful to have this record of Ruth's life, which will be an inspiration to readers and a valuable resource for North Carolina historians. This is a must-read book with many twists and turns as Ruth meets professional and personal obstacles again and again and yet finds her own paths to success. In a life full of many great accomplishments, Ruth's determined spirit may be her crowning achievement.

—*Susan W. Woodson*
*February 10, 2021*

## Prologue

In 1967, at the age of twenty-one, I walked blissfully down a street in Geneva, Switzerland, with a group of new friends. This was our first sightseeing adventure away from the University of Lyon, France. We could do anything we wanted, go anywhere in this strange and beautiful city.

As I scanned the shops ahead, I saw a movie marquee. It wasn't lit, but its advertisement made me stop and stare. In all capital letters, I saw the word *FANTASIA*, a Disney movie I had seen years before. As I stood motionless in the street, my mind froze, and sounds were muffled. Dimly, I was aware of passersby walking around me. I felt a sudden but very real terror and an unreal, out-of-time sensation, almost as if I had left my body.

Within a few minutes, I became aware of my friends around me again, and the sounds of the city resumed at their normal volume. I continued walking. Why would a theater playing a movie that I'd seen in childhood cause an out-of-body experience? Later, it would occur to me that this movie, this reminder of home, was Disney's only cartoon movie of chaos rather than the familiar fairy tale plots of *Cinderella* and *Sleeping Beauty*.

This was my first panic attack, at the beginning of my first year away from home.

A few weeks before, I had arrived in France with a group of students for a year at the University of Lyon. I had physically escaped my controlling mother, but the psychological house-arrest cuff around my subconscious had set off an alarm. By going to Europe on my own, I had apparently ventured too far from home base.

Two years later, I had another moving experience on another

*The four dingbats introducing chapters and sidebars represent favorite architecture, sculpture, and decorative motifs from my career: (from top) the Carolina cottage, a Thomas Day staircase, a compass star, and a discoid gravestone.*

Main Street far from home. Instead of sabotaging my courage, this one gave me my life's work. I had started the master's program in art history at Brown University in Providence, Rhode Island. I walked downtown Weybosset Street to complete my first assignment in an American architecture history class—to take a flattened brown paper bag and a pencil into the city, select a block of buildings, draw a map, and write a paper about them.

My buildings included the Westminster Arcade at 65 Weybosset Street—the oldest enclosed shopping mall in the United States. The Greek Revival-style commercial arcade built in 1828 has an open concourse with small shops along the main floor and recessed shops on the upper floor, illuminated by a sky-lit roof. I could have spent all day browsing the shops, but I drew an image of the façades of my block, took notes on each building, talked to store employees, and wrote a report.

How could this homework be serious work when it was so much fun? I wondered. What was different about this report, what distinguished it from many other papers I had written? The words flowed. As I wrote, I could see each feature I was describing, I could hear the voices of the people I interviewed, and I knew I had found what I wanted to do with my life.

Dr. Bill Jordy's brown bag exercise shifted my focus to American architecture. As an architectural historian, I could walk the sidewalks of ordinary cities with a clipboard, absorbing architectural styles, construction techniques, and history, while interacting with people who used the architecture on an everyday basis. I visualized my future as a researcher, photographer, and historian wandering the world studying cities. But how could I make such a career if my subconscious didn't trust me to explore the world? What made me such a contradiction of curiosity and fear?

*The Book of Ruth: Taming Ghosts, Saving History* explores the four great challenges of my life: an ongoing struggle with panic attacks; the effort to have it all—personal fulfillment as a mother and the creative fulfillment of a career; growing into my identity as an artist; and finding true love. My coming of age played out under a conservative patriarchy in the '60s and '70s that hindered most women of my generation as we fought to have careers and raced our biological clocks to become mothers. After a career of writing about other people's lives, I have researched myself to write about my own life, using many years of my own journals, planners, boxes of letters, clippings, work project files, and 150 years of family photographs.

Part I

Coming of Age

*Fish House, 16 x 20 inch oil on canvas, 2013.*

# 1
## Crossing the Threshold

 In 1999, I crawled through piles of junk and pried open my mother's kitchen door in Fayetteville, North Carolina. The house was unoccupied—we had safely moved her into assisted living in Raleigh. I hadn't been in her house in a decade because she refused entry to her family.

As I looked around, it took time to focus because junk occupied the entire room, sloping from a narrow path through the center up the wall nearly to the ceiling. The top layers were composed of clothing piled on furniture and stacks of magazines. The sink and range and refrigerator were inaccessible. The extra freezer's door hung open and food spilled out of the gap. In the living room, the recliner where she slept at night was surrounded by piles of paper, on which an electric heater was precariously balanced. Her bedroom and master bath were inaccessible. At the door to my old bedroom, I could see no way to enter the room.

Amidst all of this strangeness, I spied two familiar objects. The cuckoo clock I sent her from Switzerland during college still hung on the knotty pine wall. Dad's old console radio sat on the kitchen counter.

Earlier in her life, no one would have imagined my mother living the solitary and secretive life of a hoarder. Virginia "Jenny" Dare White started out as a femme fatale—a beautiful Southern belle from La Grange, a farming town in eastern North Carolina. She finished college with a teaching degree from East Carolina Teachers College in 1936. In her twenties, standing only five feet two inches, she broke men's hearts—Alex, Whiz, Harry, Carl, and many more.

Several of her beaux became army pilots and were shot down during World War II.

Jenny met my father in Lexington, a small piedmont North Carolina town, where she taught first grade. She lived in the Hege Inn, an elegant teacherage that held dances in its dining hall.

My father, Keith Kerley Little, first saw Mother on that dance floor in 1939. He came from the other side of the state, born and raised a mountain man in Boone, North Carolina. Dad owed his profession to the Civilian Conservation Corps (CCC) of the Works Progress Administration government infrastructure program established in 1933—the New Deal that employed men to build public buildings and roads in order to end the Depression. After graduation from high school during the Great Depression in 1932, he lived in a CCC camp in his home county of Watauga and worked with a land survey crew laying out the route of the Blue Ridge Parkway. When the Depression ended, his new skill landed him a job as a surveyor for the NC Highway Commission.

*Times were hard, but Mother and her three older sisters each went to college during the Depression with one dress apiece that they had knitted. Shown here are sisters Virginia (left) and Hazel (right), 1930s.*

After meeting Mother, Dad enlisted in the army in 1941, and they courted during his short, intense breaks from active duty, marrying secretly in 1942 over a weekend furlough in Washington, DC. Mother rode the train to Ft. Blanding, Florida, for conjugal visits before he was shipped overseas to serve with the 62nd Corps of Engineers in Europe and North Africa.

The earliest period of anxiety that I know in Mother's life—and a harbinger of my own lifelong anxiety—happened during her three years of separation from Dad during the war. She lived in boarding houses while teaching in Lexington and, after 1943, in

*Keith K. Little and Virginia White on their wedding day, January 5, 1942.*

Kannapolis, a textile town known as "Towel City" because of Cannon Mills. A doctor friend of her family prescribed belladonna and phenobarbital for her nerves.

My father adored Jenny and patiently tolerated her anxiety, which would gradually blossom into a full-blown disorder manifested as the fear of everything, especially germs. In early May 1945, stationed in France, Dad chose a home furlough for good conduct instead of a promotion. The morning after Mother met his train in Fayetteville on May 9, they saw a newspaper stand in the lobby of the LaFayette Hotel with the headline WAR OVER IN EUROPE. It was V-E Day—victory in Europe. My father never returned to Europe; the Army Corps of Engineers mustered him out of service stateside.

Keith and Jenny finally started their married life together in Silver Spring, Maryland, a suburb of Washington, DC, where Mother's cousin Tut had a barbershop. Dad worked for a civil engineering firm, and they lived with Tut and his wife May until they rented an apartment in downtown DC, where I came into the world in 1946. Before Mother was released from the hospital, she had a test for heart irregularities, probably due to her nerves.

By 1948, they received a VA loan and built a Cape Cod house in Silver Spring. My brother Keith, whom we called Keet, was born the next year, and then Mother had two children to protect from a frightful world. The District of Columbia was too urban and hectic for my parents. In 1951, they told everyone that "Washington has too many one-way streets," and they moved back to their home state—to Lexington where they had so many friends.

*Keith K. Little at work in a 62nd Corps of Engineers office somewhere in Europe during World War II.*

Unlike many teachers of her generation, Mother wasn't totally traditional. She did not retire when she had children. She loved teaching and organized knitting classes after the regular school day, and she saved all of her classes' group photographs for each school year. As a social extrovert, she was a natural performer and incorporated songs and games into reading and writing instruction. She pursued teaching, despite her anxieties, until her retirement the year I went away to college.

Although Mother loved being a teacher, as a parent she seemed locked in teacher mode. Whenever I tried to reason with her, she would say angrily, "Don't sass me!" She had a short fuse: if I didn't mind her, she would grab a wooden yardstick and swat my arms or legs. While I often sat as a little girl with my father reading the funny papers aloud, I have no childhood memories of sitting with her while she read to me or comforted me. Instead of showing love, she showed anxiety.

Mother was not a homemaker: our house was generally a mess unless company was coming. Before I started school in Lexington, she hired a Black nanny named Mamie who cared for us while she taught. Mamie was a young woman who made us corn pudding, and her gentleness soothed me. She showed me the attention and consistency that Mother was always too anxious to offer.

*Me (Annie Oakley) with my brother Keith (Hopalong Cassidy), at home in Fayetteville, NC, 1953.*

In 1952, our family moved to Fayetteville, a military town that acquired the nickname "Fayettenam" during the Vietnam War era of the 1960s because Fort Bragg's personnel were so active in the war.

At first, we rented a house down the street from a big new suburban Baptist church, Snyder Memorial, in the Haymount neighborhood. In 1954, we built a new brick Ranch house near the church. At Mother's insistence, the builders added a two-bedroom rental apartment at the end, giving her the security of having another family close when my father traveled on business.

## Fayetteville

*My hometown of Fayetteville has the most historically layered Central Business District in North Carolina, a unique gem of town planning and architecture. I became a historic preservationist because I grew up in this downtown, participating in parades and civic events; shopping in department stores; my first retail jobs; watching movies; and eating in restaurants before suburban shopping centers drained its life. I learned to drive the two-lane roundabout that circled the Market House at its center: once in the circle, I had right of way at the four streets that intersected the center of the four sides.*

I grew up a left-handed, shy, bookwormish tomboy who ran with the boys instead of playing with dolls. The real me didn't even want to be a girl—I tried endlessly to kiss my elbow, because the saying went "if you can kiss your elbow you'll turn into a boy." I dreaded everything to do with becoming a woman, especially having a period and the bondage of wearing a bra. I loved the jungle gym, which we called monkey bars, and doing cartwheels and handstands, and roller-skating hour after hour with my skate key tied to a string around my neck. One of my favorite comic books series was Wonder Woman. (I learned as an adult that Gloria Steinem grew up reading them too!) I loved the Nancy Drew mystery stories. She was a spirited heroine, a girl detective with a blue roadster.

Our '50s suburban neighborhood swarmed with kids—the Joneses next door and the Greek Vurnakeses and Lamproses and Lebanese Fadel families down the street. Greek, Lebanese, and Jewish families operated the best clothing stores and restaurants in Fayetteville. When playing with the neighbors, being a tomboy was just fine. We played softball in each other's backyards, danced in our bathing suits in the rain, shot competitive marble games in the dirt, roller-skated, bicycled, climbed trees, and dammed up the creek in the woods where the scary hermit lived. Until we all went off to high school, our neighborhood gang stuck together, playing badminton, hide-and-go-seek, basketball, softball, kickball, and kick-the-can.

Dad started his own land surveying company and spent weeks away from home, laying out large housing and military complexes at Fort Bragg Army Base and Pope Air Force Base near Fayetteville. Fort Bragg ramped up to meet the Cold War challenges, becoming the largest army base in the world by the early 1950s. When Dad worked out of town, Mother's fear led her not only to lock our front door at night but also to barricade it with furniture to keep out burglars. No barricade was ever enough; there was always something else to fear.

# 2
## A Childhood of Earthy Zaniness

My family had a waterfront lot in Morehead City in the Promise Land area on Bogue Sound, but they didn't *build* a summer cottage there—they found a ready-made one. True to their Depression upbringing, they bought a surplus World War II Marine dwelling at Cherry Point Marine Base, moved it to the lot, set it up in the air on top of a garage, and then constructed a big wraparound front porch overlooking the water. Such surplus military houses were moved all over Carteret County in the 1950s and reused as private homes. We named it "Little Leisure" as a pun, playing off our surname of Little and our lack of vacation time.

That little cottage provided a coastal retreat throughout my childhood; in fact, I consider Morehead to be my second hometown,

*"Little Leisure," the family beach cottage on Bogue Sound, Morehead City, NC, about 1960. Keith holds his boat's gas tank; Jenny stands on the porch (right).*

my summer town. I have many memories of the cottage, but one early incident stands out.

Purchasing the beach property required legal advice, so in 1959 I went with my parents to visit Judge Julius Duncan at his home in Beaufort. When we arrived, the judge invited us to sit down on his porch. Even now, I can see the long white porch with its green floorboards and four wooden rocking chairs in a row facing the Beaufort harbor. The grownups discussed the real estate transaction. My parents were seeking legal advice from the judge on buying the Morehead City lot with riparian rights to ensure that their land would remain on the water—that no more land could be created in front of their property. We sat with the judge and his old hound dog on his porch at the end of Front Street. The view was beautiful, overlooking the point where the Newport River and Taylor's Creek intersect, but what riveted my attention was the long porch and rocking chairs. During that visit, sitting quietly while the grownups talked, I had an intimation of my future career—I wanted to save places like this when I grew up.

I had no way of knowing it at the time, but I would one day help preserve the places where many of my mother's relatives lived. We saw my father's mountain relatives less often. They lived in Boone, North Carolina, and Roanoke, Virginia, and we visited with them mainly at funerals. Dad did not tell stories about his childhood or family, so I lacked knowledge of his roots. Most of our reunions involved Mother's family: sisters, husbands, and cousins in La Grange, Kinston, Goldsboro, and Snow Hill in eastern North Carolina.

As a child, I spent Thanksgivings, homecomings, and vacations in these small towns in the company of Mother and her older sisters. The aunts had family nicknames: Appless, the oldest, was "Sister;" Willie, second oldest, was "Sissie." The only boy, Herman, was "Bud." Hazel and my mother Virginia, the youngest, went by their given names. My father called my mother "Jenny."

The aunts and their families were all storytellers. Hearing their Lenoir County stories gave me a window into the lives of my maternal relatives before my birth. Mother never tired of telling stories about her grandfather John Rouse, "Fool John," who fought in the Confederate army. At the end of the war, John was walking home, saw Union troops riding toward him, and grabbed some peanut vines and sat in the door of a packhouse. As they rode up, he stuffed peanut shells into his mouth, crossed his eyes and babbled, "Have some goobers," over and over as they tried to question him. Finally one of them said, "Aw, he's nothing but an old fool. Leave him alone," and they rode away. Forever after folks called him "Fool John," knowing that he was foolish like a fox.

John buried three consecutive wives after raising families with each of them and was finally outlived by his fourth wife. At one of the huge Rouse family reunions that included descendants of three of John's wives, Mother read the doggerel poem she wrote about Fool John, which began:

> *Fool John was my grandpa, and you can believe*
> *He had all sorts of tricks up his sleeve.*

I was named after Fool John's youngest child, Ruth Magdalene Rouse, who grew up near LaGrange and married John Hughes White, known as Hugh, of Jones County. He co-owned Inscore & White's Livery Stables in Kinston, and around 1916, they built a bungalow in the Mitchelltown section of Kinston. Owning a bungalow, a modern house with an open floor plan and a conveniently located kitchen, had been "Mama" Ruth's dream for years.[1] My mother and her sisters told stories about the 1918 flu epidemic in that house, where Mama Ruth ran up and down the stairs tending to her sick children until she finally collapsed with the flu herself. Everyone survived, which is why I'm alive today.

Mama Ruth died a few months before I was born, but she passed on two important things to me: her name and her love of "pizers," the local term for a piazza—a porch.[2] Mama Ruth would announce to her family after dinner, "Well, I'm going out to the pizer and blow a little." She meant that she was going to sit where the evening breeze would cool and relax her. I wish she could know how "pizers" became one of my professional obsessions long after she was gone.

My mother's sisters played a big part in my life, too. Aunt Appless, a lifelong schoolteacher, earned a graduate degree at Columbia University and changed her middle name to Hancock after her genealogical research suggested that she descended from John Hancock, the Massachusetts patriot of the American Revolution. She spent her married life in Snow Hill, the county seat of Greene County, adjacent to Lenoir County. Her grand Queen Anne-style frame house at 109 East Greene Street had been built about 1885.

I spent childhood Thanksgivings at a big family feast in Aunt Appless's dining room. No matter how many times we were forbidden, we children couldn't resist sliding down the long, elegant stair railing that graced a twelve-foot high hall. My favorite space was the detached kitchen, connected by a breezeway to the main house. Many years later, when Aunt App's belongings were auctioned at an estate sale, I would acquire two treasures: an eighteen-inch handmade biscuit board and a damaged oil still life, a watermelon painted in the mid-1800s that had hung over the dining room sideboard.

Aunt Hazel, our favorite auntie, lived in Fayetteville. She had boys and spoiled me as her only girl niece, letting me have dance parties in her recreation room in junior high school. Hazel was the tomboy aunt whose fishing boat was named the "Happy Hooker."

Sitting around a living room or a porch with the aunts, the dirty jokes would fly almost like a competition, salacious music to my innocent ears. These relatives had an earthy zaniness that permeated and grounded my childhood. Aunt Hazel borrowed my parakeet and wore him in a cage on her head for a crazy hat contest. Mother had her earthy side, too. Once, she framed a photo of her friend inside a toilet seat as a birthday joke. Another time, she baked a chocolate cake for a club luncheon that cracked into three sections when it came out of the oven. She fastened it together with toothpicks and made a "Dammit Cake" sign for it.

The four sisters were close and vacationed together on the North Carolina coast at Atlantic Beach and Morehead City, bobbing and gossiping together in the ocean in their rubber bath caps. These vacations involved nonstop talking and an abundance of good food. We had mountains of boiled shrimp bought from the boats that docked in Beaufort, as well as special snacks like Aunt Sister's jelly nut sandwiches and rice crispy treats.

The sisters were continuing a tradition of beach trips that had been started by their mother. Mama Ruth sometimes took a Sunday excursion train with her church group to the Atlantic Hotel in Morehead, built by Durham tobacconist Julian S. Carr and other investors at the rail terminus in 1880. It immediately became the "summer capital of the state," a title inherited from the previous Atlantic Hotel in Beaufort that had been destroyed by a hurricane in 1879. Wealthy families brought their trunks to stay for weeks in the three-story, exuberant Victorian frame hotel, with its 223 guest rooms, grand ballroom, large boardwalk, bathing houses, and bowling alley. The railroad ran the hotel until World War I; it burned in 1933.

Ruth and her church friends took day trips to Morehead to access the beach. They probably took the "Money Island Ferry" from the hotel to Money Island, now Atlantic Beach, the barrier island across from the hotel where a swimming pavilion stood. In a changing room at the pavilion, they put on their swimsuits and bathed in the ocean and ate their picnic lunch.

In later years, Mama Ruth told her children a funny dream that indicated her love for these coastal trips. On her way to Morehead, she got off the train in New Bern to use the restroom. Returning to the track, she discovered that the train had left without her. She was so determined to get to the coast that she sprouted wings and flew all the way. When she woke up from the dream, she was more tired than she had ever been in her life. Flying, even if only in a dream, was hard work!

**Above:** *Ruth Magdeline Rouse, age 16, 1898.*
**At left:** *Ruth Rouse White (left), Hazel White (right), and Virginia White (lower right), fishing at Walters Mill Pond, Lenoir County, NC, about 1928.*

## Getting to the Beach

Until the 1920s, when the Model T Ford gave ordinary families their own private transportation, the railroad was the way to travel all the way to the coast. Horse-drawn wagons or buggies didn't have the speed to travel that far. Morehead City was accessible to families across the state, from Charlotte to the coast, via the North Carolina Railroad, allowing even middle-class folks like my grandmother to spend a day at the beach. The only other coastal resort in North Carolina accessible by railroad was Wrightsville Beach, connected to nearby Wilmington by a streetcar built by the electric company. On the beach, the company (Consolidated Railways, Light and Power) built a grand dance pavilion, the Lumina, brilliantly illuminated by electric lights, a novelty at that time.

*Me, age 10, at home, 1325 Woodland Drive, Fayetteville, in my church baptism dress, 1956.*

Another central place in our family life was church, where I encountered Baptist fire and brimstone that instilled religious anxiety into my impressionable subconscious. I was elected secretary of my Sunday school class at age ten, the same year I wrote in my diary, "Today I went up in church and made a profession of faith. I stated that I was a sinner and accepted Jesus as my savior." The next Sunday, I wrote, "Today I joined the church. After church I stood up in front of the church and about half the church shook hands with me." I bragged the next year that I hadn't missed Sunday school in a year and a half.

In the Sunday evening church class, known as "training union," we played a competitive Baptist children's game called "Bible drill," standing in a line holding our Bibles while the teacher called out a book and verse. The first to find it in their Bible won the drill. Another game, called a "sword drill," was to recite the books in the Bible from memory; whoever knew the most won. I enjoyed the recitations and could rattle off the sixty-six books by memory until middle age. In March 1960, my church had a weeklong revival, and on the last day, 300 people made a rededication of faith, including Mother and me.

My religious training influenced my childhood profoundly, vividly imprinting the idea of a vengeful God that would punish me if I strayed. This concept stayed with me well into adulthood. At age twenty-two when I encountered the God is Dead theological movement, I gradually transitioned away from organized religion into a flexible moral code with a strong emphasis on justice, mercy, and a life goal of making the world a better place.

The mother of my childhood was an active woman with a wide array of interests. She charmed her wide circle of friends with her energy and passions for plants, genealogy, and history. She had her hair washed and curled each week at the beauty shop. She loved history, writing poetry, antiques, old houses, and saving old family photos, all interests she bequeathed to me. She collected and hoarded old things—a sideboard with a missing drawer, a chaise longue with ratty horsehair upholstery, old cast iron bedsteads, a cast iron clothes rack from a department store, an old-time wall phone with black earpiece and metal ringers. She thought that each old book she bought was a "first edition." To store all her "treasures," she erected a pair of frame storage sheds in our backyard.

Mother overprotected and restricted me physically and socially. One reason might have been a health concern that she never discussed with me. When I was seven or eight, I overheard either Mother or the pediatrician say my heartbeat was abnormally fast. I was worried that I had a bad heart but was too afraid to even ask anyone about it and carried the dread for years. For whatever reason, Mother anxiously worked to tame my tomboy tendency by dressing me in frilly dresses or skirts and blouses and keeping my straight brown hair carefully curled. In adolescence, I endured permanents to ensure that the curls lasted. Appearances were very important, and she made it clear that, in her eyes, my looks were lacking. She criticized my glasses, my hair, and my laughter, saying, "Don't laugh so loud. It's not ladylike." Spoken or unspoken, these critiques were aimed at making me more attractive to the opposite sex. Her stories about how many marriage proposals she had turned down when she was young seemed like they were meant as a putdown.

My brother and I had a close relationship throughout childhood and presented a united front against Mother's excessive supervision. We learned to hide our cuts and scrapes from her because she would obsessively fuss over them. She lined the toilet seat with paper when we used a gas station bathroom on road trips to keep us away from "germs." Because she was afraid of everything, we delighted in tormenting her. We caught the black widow spiders that were so plentiful outdoors in glass jars and left them in her bedroom. I kept a rubber spider on my bedside table to scare her away at night. When I left the house on an outing, she called out "Be careful!" instead of the more optimistic "Have fun!"

In the five-year diary that I used from the fifth to the ninth grades in the 1950s, I confided my insecurities. It wasn't a secret diary—Mother used it as an event calendar, writing in the dates of my tap and ballet classes. I wonder what she thought when she read, "Mother tries to make me go to bed at 8:30 and I am fourteen! Then she finally let us stay up to see a program and then made us go to bed before it was over." Another day: "We went to Southern Pines for a visit but Mother's nervous system is upset and she feels awful." The next day she checked into a hospital for several days for tests that diagnosed vertigo.

Another significant entry in my diary-calendar noted that "Mother hit me and I got real mad. I was planning to go to the library. She wouldn't let me go." I don't remember that particular incident, but it's easy to imagine my distress at being barred from the library. Our little public library in downtown Fayetteville was a magical destination where I devoured armfuls of books during elementary school, especially stacks of thick old fairy tales, and thrilled to the child heroes of violent stories. Carolyn Sherwin Bailey's *Miss Hickory* (a character who is literally a nut), published the year of my birth, 1946, devastated me because a squirrel ate spunky, tart-tongued Miss Hickory's nut head at the end. Re-reading the book recently, I finally understood it—Miss Hickory's twig body grafted itself onto a tree trunk and grew a new tree, representing the life-death-resurrection cycle of nature.

Because my knack for drawing developed early, I felt destined to be an artist when I grew up. I always found it easier to draw a picture of something rather than describing it through words. Elementary and junior high school teachers asked me, along with other artistic students, to paint murals of each season with tempera paint on the bulletin board at the back of their classrooms. From a young age, we would often draw while listening to classical music. I especially recall the frightening scene I drew of craggy rocks and gnarled tree branches, inspired as I listened to Mussorgsky's "Night on Bald Mountain." I found the dark dissonance of the music thrilling. In the sixth grade, I was asked to draw a mural on the cork display board about the Middle Ages, and in eighth grade, I was assigned to create a mural about the Fayetteville Arsenal, a massive armory constructed in the 1800s to provide the US military with better access to weapons.

I excelled in school and felt confident in the classroom and with a paintbrush in my hand. It was a time when I was growing and becoming more independent in many ways, but Mother, knowingly or not, discouraged me from going too far from her sight. As she got older, she did not mellow. She didn't trust me to use tweezers to groom my eyebrows as I entered adolescence, because she said someone ruined her brows by plucking them when she was a teenager and they never grew back. When she went through menopause in the late 1950s, she often stayed in bed all day. If I made plans to go out, she would shout at me as I passed in the hallway. "Don't leave me, Ruth, I am dying!"

"Don't leave me, Ruth." Those words would echo in my head for hours after she spoke, and without my realizing it, they stayed there for years to come, rushing back when I ventured too far, still carrying the fear that she bequeathed to me.

# 3
## Puberty

Puberty was in the air when I was eleven years old, a sixth grader in 1957. Every Friday we pushed back our desks at school and danced to rock music at the end of the day. I fell in love with rock 'n' roll. One afternoon that year, visiting in Snow Hill, my older cousin Lyman played a 45-rpm record, Fats Domino's version of "Blueberry Hill," on his portable record player.

In an instant, listening to Fats sing "I found my thrill," my senses sharpened. I felt alive in a different way—between the legs. I developed an interest in clothes and saved my allowance to shop at The Vogue shop in downtown Fayetteville that sold Ladybug blouses and Weejuns, slip-in leather loafers. I grew embarrassed at carrying my old violin case, with the pawnshop violin I had played since elementary school, to junior high school because only nerds took violin lessons.

That same year, next-door neighbor Cathy and I tried to settle the mystery of how babies are made. She spirited out a big medical book with illustrations from her parents' bookshelves, and we pored over it in my tree house high in a chinaberry tree. But the drawings of the man's penis and the woman's vagina didn't offer any clues as to how the two might fit together. We remained mystified until whispered exchanges in the girls' bathroom at school provided more specific information.

My diary sparkled with adolescent confessions. "I danced with Chris, Bobby, David and about 4 more boys." "I danced with Hank! He's dremy [sic]. Karen and I like him. We have to dance mostly slow dances." "Karen and I are real chums. We have started a club.

Diane, Martha, Sandra, Karen and I are members." "Our club took in 2 new members, Jo and Rhonda." With a Christmas gift of ten dollars, I went to Fleishman's Big Store and bought a whole wardrobe—white shirt, sports shirt, blue skirt, and blue sweater.

The twin themes of achievement in school and failure with boys dominated my seventh, eighth, and ninth grade years at Alexander Graham Junior High, the old high school building at the foot of Haymount Hill and Hay Street. We girls wore layers of petticoats—the more the better—under our dresses. It was torture to keep the petticoats from drooping below our hemline, which drew mean-girl taunts of "your slip is showing!" After school, Karen and I walked over to Hay Street, stepped into the ten-foot-wide City News Stand to read comic books, and then bought cream puffs at the bakery that we ate very slowly on the city bus that dropped us off near our homes just off Bragg Boulevard.

In eighth grade as I was about to turn fourteen, I finally got my period, later than most other girls. Mother had never talked about it, but a small printed booklet handed out at school prepared me. Not knowing when it would arrive, on February 8, 1960, I wore my favorite skirt—a fitted pink sheath skirt that I thought quite sophisticated. There I was, trapped at school with blood stains on the back of my skirt, which I hid with someone's sweater tied around my waist.

Mother wouldn't allow me to shave my legs because she was afraid I would hurt myself. This resulted in an incident that became the most humiliating day of my adolescence, worse than having started "the curse" at school. When I was fourteen, I worked for weeks to put together a special Easter outfit to wear to church. On March 26, I wrote in my diary that I had bought a green Easter dress with a crushed cummerbund and matching head band with tan flowers at Belk for ten dollars. I picked it up on April 2 after it had been altered to fit and also bought some white "flats." On Easter Sunday, April 17, with great excitement, I put on my dress and my first nylon stockings to wear with my new flats. Then I looked in the mirror and was horrified. The nylons smashed my leg hair flat, creating dark, hairy lines beneath the transparent material. My anticipation of looking so pretty in my new outfit was spoiled. I flung myself on my beloved cast-iron bed in my finery and cried my heart out.

If I couldn't make myself cute, I could at least earn straight A's and be inducted into the honor society. I was selected to draw the cover of the student directory. I bragged to myself about getting high grades on exams. I worked almost all night on a ten-page history report and told my diary that "I had to read my history paper today. I was scared to death and I know I look awful." Boys I had crushes on—Jimbo and Hank—liked me but didn't ask me to the dances. Jimbo nominated me to represent our homeroom in the teenager-of-the-year contest but asked Nancy McDuffie to the dance.

In ninth grade, March 1962, I turned "sweet sixteen and never been kissed," the ultimate humiliation. One day that summer, a bunch of us went to ride the motorized toy cars at the Go-Kart track. Later, I sat on the bleachers with my slightly older neighbor, Dickie Byrne, a husky blond boy that I had a crush on, and the magic event happened! Now I could enjoy being sixteen.

My academic achievements continued, but no matter how well I did, Mother worked to minimize my success in school. In ninth grade, we took the Iowa Test of Educational Development, and I scored in the ninety-ninth percentile in six of the eight subject areas. Using her status as a teacher, Mother interpreted my test results as average. She would have agreed with the 1953 study, *Women in the Modern World*, written by a woman who noted:

> [The] best adjusted girl is intelligent enough to do well in school but doesn't make straight A's, able to stand on her own two feet and earn a living but not so good a living as to compete with men, and capable of doing a job well but not so identified with a profession as to need it for her own happiness.[3]

Another success in the ninth grade was writing a weekly column, "Ruth Reports," in the "Teen Times" page for the *Fayetteville Observer*. I stayed out of the spotlight—I was a workhorse, each week reporting names of the show ponies who attended parties to which I wasn't invited, and those who won sports events, had birthdays, and were seen at Teen Club dances. I described a "romper room skit," a pep rally where cheerleaders impersonated teachers and insurance agents, and a beauty pageant skit where they impersonated Little Red Riding Hood, Grandma, and other wacky characters. How I envied their spunky bravery to act on stage.

High school was more of the same; I was anything but Nancy Drew, the dashing detective. I tried to escape my nerdy glasses by wearing contact lenses to attract boys.

We girls also wore a girdle—like a long Spanx, but even more uncomfortable because it was stiff elastic with clips attached to keep up our hose, or garter belts, a shorter version of a girdle. (This underwear was uncomfortable but no more so than the hateful panty hose and tights that came along in the 1970s and 1980s.) Another form of female torture was overnight hair rollers. To improve our sex appeal, we slept every school night in rock-hard rollers to create the '60s Flip—mid-length long hair flipped up on the ends like Annette Funicello, one of the Mouseketeers on the 1950s *Mickey Mouse Club* TV show. Soft rollers came later, but in the early '60s rollers were hard plastic with a cover that locked the roller in place.

Although the biggest social issue of the early 1960s was civil rights, my classmates and I lived in a white-skinned bubble. Fayetteville High School integrated in 1963 during my junior year, but I had no contact with the two token African American students. I gave African Americans little thought, since I lived in a white suburb and had no Black friends. Mother employed Black maids who never seemed to please her. Any Blacks I might have come into contact with were domestics or yard workers.

My most vivid high school memory occurred on November 22, 1963, while I labored over a measured drawing in mechanical drawing class. The loudspeaker rasped out the announcement that President John F. Kennedy had been assassinated. That night my junior girls "powder puff" team played touch football against the senior girls to raise charity funds, although all of us, students and adults alike, were zombies, dazed by the assassination. JFK had been my idol since junior high school—his death cut me to the core.

That year, 1963, is also when Betty Friedan published *The Feminine Mystique*, an exposé of the oppression of American women. If I had read that book a little sooner, I might have been prepared for the pitfalls that lay ahead. Friedan opined on how the patriarchal culture brainwashed women into becoming wives and mothers instead of fulfilling their innate talents. After being essential in the workforce during World War II, women who were fortunate enough attended college, and then they were shunted into their assigned homemaker role. Women who wanted to be poets or physicists were considered neurotic, unfeminine, and unhappy. Universities were skeptical in the 1950s and 1960s about the value of a professional investment in female students, no matter how apparently able and ambitious. Girls learned not to get caught up in a career or intellectual passion, not just at home but from their college professors.

My parents had radically different expectations for me. My father, a gentle soul, assumed I would have a career and hired me to work part-time in his engineering office. After he met the first female architect he'd ever encountered, he suggested that I consider becoming an architect, but I told him that I could never handle the math. (I never actually "got math" until I earned a real estate broker's license at the age of thirty-seven.) Yet he also expected that I would marry and be financially dependent on a husband, so when he bought life insurance, he named only my brother as his beneficiary.

Mother expected me to be a schoolteacher like herself; she also expected that I would be a virgin until marriage, a lady who would attract the right husband and have children. Although her vision for me was limited, she provided me an ahead-of-her-time model of a working woman.

The Vietnam War was escalating as I finished high school in 1964. Growing up in Fayetteville, near Fort Bragg Army Base, the conflict not only threatened my male classmates but accentuated the problem of being a female because we all grew up too soon. The war triggered a rush to the altar. Of the dozen girls in my high school homeroom my senior year, all but two were engaged or married by the time we graduated. Only my friend Susan and I were headed to college, then she married over the summer and did not go. In retrospect, I see that I dodged my own bullet by not marrying as young as most of my peers. Fortunately, at that time marriage was the last thing on my mind.

# 4
## St. Mary's

I couldn't wait to go to college and leave my stifling home environment. During senior year, I polished my writing skills with weekly theme papers for advanced composition, taught by Mrs. Carruth, a tough English teacher. My parents could afford college tuition, but their prejudices restricted my choices. I announced my intention to apply to William & Mary College in Williamsburg, Virginia, but was told that "you need to attend college in North Carolina so that you will make friends and meet a husband from here." Next, I chose Duke University in Durham, North Carolina, and was informed that "Duke girls wear cashmere sweaters and pearls, which we can't afford, and we don't want you in school with Northerners and Jews."

My parents' opinions weren't the only barriers to selecting a college. In the early 1960s, the patriarchy sheltered white women and subjugated all women to varying degrees. I couldn't enroll in the University of North Carolina because females could only study there as junior or senior students unless they were studying nursing. In fact, longer than in other areas of the country, virtually all Southern colleges prohibited underclass women from admittance.[4] UNC and NC State University did not admit underclass female students until later in the 1960s. The University of Virginia kept its main campus exclusively male by opening Mary Washington College in Fredericksburg in 1944 as its women's undergraduate division. A 1960s civil rights lawsuit forced it to commingle the sexes in 1970.

As a result of these restrictions, many young women in North Carolina started out by attending junior colleges such as Peace

College or St. Mary's College, both in Raleigh, or a four-year girls' school such as Meredith College, also in Raleigh, or the University of North Carolina at Greensboro. Graduates of the junior colleges could then transfer to UNC-Chapel Hill for the final two years to earn a bachelor's degree.

I followed this pattern by attending St. Mary's, a two-year junior college that for a century had sheltered young women from affluent North Carolina families. The tall brick main building with flanking stone dormitories sat on a circular drive behind a grove of old trees along Hillsborough Street, a few blocks from the North Carolina State Capitol. Many of my classmates in this beautiful birdcage were legacies, meaning older women relatives had also studied there. It was considered a "finishing school" where a young woman would meet a husband of her social standing and gain enough education to be an asset to him.

To meet the right husband, the traditional "debut" was a time-honored social coming out for the daughters of prominent upper-class families who had reached the age of maturity and were ready to marry. The Terpsichorean Club of Raleigh, founded in the 1920s, selected the girls to be included in the North Carolina Terpsichorean Ball held each September. Many St. Mary's girls debuted the summer after their freshman year.

As an avid social climber and stage mother, Mother began a campaign to have me tapped as a debutante. In 1965, she tirelessly wrote letters to her well-connected relatives and friends to ask them to sponsor me. This list included my father's cousin, the mayor of Blowing Rock; her cousin, the mayor of Pine Level; and her friends in Lenoir County. She wrote debutante officials and even politicians, including our US congressman, asking that I debut in fall 1965. Mother cited her lineage as a member of the Daughters of the American Revolution and the United Daughters of the Confederacy. She told them that my father's grandfather had served in the North Carolina legislature.

In the end, all her hard work was for naught. She should have started a year earlier, when the deb list was compiled and invitations were sent out. All the fuss embarrassed me, of course. Rather than making my social debut to the first families of North Carolina, I aspired to be an artistic and literary debutante. I wanted to make a difference with my life, not simply to marry into society.

In spite of friction with my parents during college, I didn't want to hurt them. I wrote them faithfully and called regularly. I often wrote Mother, my primary reader, in a sweet, tender tone and sent her "surprise" presents. I let her know exactly where I was, where I traveled, whom I was with, and when I was coming home because I knew how much she worried about me.

The two years at St. Mary's passed in a whirl of academics and competition to have a date every weekend instead of staying on campus. The most desirable dates were fraternity brothers because fraternities provided built-in social circles and frequent parties. A classmate who was going steady with a frat boy often recruited other classmates as blind dates for her boyfriend's pals. When a young woman and frat guy were serious, she often wore his fraternity pin and she was considered "pinned." The social system depended on a dense web of family and geographic connections.

Sometimes I dated boys at the UNC fraternity pledged by students from the Snow Hill area, in the network of small towns where my mother grew up. I also dated NC State University guys whom I met working in the St. Mary's dining hall, where meals were served family style. Strapping State guys would carry giant trays to each table, laden with platters and bowls. My job, serving the food, was a fun way to earn spending money.

Young men from NC State, UNC, and Duke invited St. Mary's girls for weekends of football games and fraternity parties, necessitating an elaborate ritual to preserve the damsels' purity. We stayed in chaperoned overnight guest houses, kept by genteel widows as a means of paying the taxes on their large homes on commercial corridors such as Hillsborough Street in Raleigh or in downtown Chapel Hill or Durham. Unless our parents signed us out with

Miss R. and Miss I. T., older, unmarried deans whose office occupied a corner of the "parlor," a responsible adult had to send a permission letter to the school for us to spend the night away from campus. Thus, the guest house hostess would send a letter to the deans, allowing us to sign out for the weekend.

The boys that we dated had an independence that we could only imagine: Our birdcage protected our virtue and our wings were clipped. We had to wear dresses or skirts, as pants weren't ladylike and couldn't be worn off campus. Even though we had driver's licenses, we weren't allowed cars or motorcycles. It was unthinkable that we might drive to Durham to walk on the wild side in night clubs and dance halls. When not spending the night away, we had rigid curfews. Our dates would deliver us to the parlor by 11 p.m., then meet each other at an all-night diner for breakfast or burgers to sober up.

In spite of the *in loco parentis* vigilance, I had a pure blast. College students in the Raleigh-Durham-Chapel Hill area in the 1960s chose from music venues that attracted big names. We escaped our prison on weekends at Duke or UNC, attending concerts by soul, rock, and folk music singers like The Temptations, Otis Redding, and Janis Joplin. Peter, Paul and Mary played at Reynolds Coliseum at NC State. My favorite group, the Rolling Stones, didn't appear until the early 1970s.

One weekend, with a group of Duke guys and their dates, I partied at a speakeasy in the basement of Gregory's Barber Shop in Hayti, the Black Durham business district. This neighborhood was later bulldozed by the urban renewal project that built NC 751, the Durham Expressway. We knocked on the rear basement door of the barbershop on Main Street, Gregory peeped through the keyhole, the Dukies uttered the secret password, and the door opened. We played the juke box and drank hard liquor, then legally sold only in ABC stores in North Carolina, not in private retail establishments. The low-ceilinged room had a colored light in the ceiling, high-backed wooden booths, and a bar that served liquor and bags of pork rinds. On another Duke weekend, we partied at the Stallion Club on Highway 55 in Durham. The music and dance club in a big prefab metal building had a predominantly African American clientele, along with a cult following among white college students. Soul groups and singers like Otis Redding played there.

My awakening to the value of the Black experience came slowly as an adult. Until I researched this memoir, I had been unaware that an early morning bombing severely damaged the Stallion Club a few years later (*Carolina Times*, April 20, 1968). The article failed to mention that the unsolved crime was probably a Klan attack. I knew about the Klan because of seeing one or two burning crosses in front yards while driving with my parents at night, but I sailed through childhood naively unaware of racial tensions in North Carolina.

My only contact with Blacks were Mother's household help; I have warm memories of Mamie, our nanny when I was a little girl. Later in childhood, I was embarrassed by Mother's insensitive treatment of the women she hired in the afternoons to do the ironing. Once in a supermarket in a Black neighborhood, I witnessed a young Black woman berate Mother after overhearing her ask a clerk for "niggertoes," the racist name for hazelnuts.

As indicated by the debutante campaign, important components of Mother's social status and club life were her memberships in the Daughters of the American Revolution and the United Daughters of the Confederacy. She and her sisters did painstaking genealogy to prove their lineage to ancestors who had fought in those wars. When I refused to join the organizations because I considered them irrelevant and the UDC actively racist, she was displeased. "You'll be sorry later, Ruth, that you didn't take advantage of our connections."

Attending a small women's college located near NC State, which was a large, mostly male university, had its perks. One November evening in 1964, there was a loud commotion outside my dorm. When we residents looked out our windows, we saw hundreds of young men from State surrounding our tiny building, chanting "Pan-ties...pan-ties...pan-ties." It was a panty raid, which was an American ritual of the 1950s and 1960s. Raids functioned as humorous protests against curfews and restrictions barring male visitors from women's dorms, especially at colleges that started admitting large numbers of women after World War II.

Instead of being frightened by the raid, we were thrilled by the attention. Following directions from our sophomore hall proctors, we raced to find our prettiest panty, wrote our telephone number on the garment, and flung it out the window. I seem to recall that one or two girls got a phone call from the lucky boys who caught their panties. Later, we discovered that boys had broken into another dormitory, and a girl beat them back with her tennis racquet.

An article in UNC's *Daily Tar Heel* newspaper fed the historic rivalry between UNC and NC State. "Those Nasty State Men; Panty Raids in Raleigh" noted that the raid on the women's dorm at NC State failed, so the mob marched on to St. Mary's, where the reception was considerably more enthusiastic. "The girls cheered 'em on," the article reported. "Most of the men left about midnight."[5]

After school or on weekends, we walked to Cameron Village to buy goodies at a bakery or took a long hike to see a foreign film at the Rialto Theatre at Five Points, a neighborhood about two miles north. Sometimes our parents came to campus on Saturdays to take us to the Angus Barn for a steak dinner, or to eat lunch at Ballantines, the elegant cafeteria at Cameron Village in the office building designed by architect Lief Valand.[6] Most of us attended the Ambassador Theatre on Fayetteville Street, owned by Mayor William G. Enloe, where *The Sound of Music* played for years.

On weekends, students were required to be greeters at Smedes Hall, the main building. One Saturday during my duty, a handsome blond, blue-eyed guy named Tom showed up. He invited me for a ride in his car out to Yates Mill, an old grist mill with a mill pond and dam on a large boulder outcropping. We climbed a chain link fence and crawled over the boulders. That became a regular

Saturday outing for us. I have no idea how I climbed a fence and played on the rocks, as we weren't allowed off-campus in pants. Perhaps I carried them with me and changed somewhere. I always saved a big plate of food from our dining hall for Tom, as he was perpetually hungry. Our bond was strictly friendship, but I remember what a sweet young man he was.

My biggest romance at St. Mary's was with a student I met at the Jewish fraternity at NC State. Richie grew up in New York, the son of a clothing manufacturer, and he suited my taste for more sophisticated, dry-witted, non-Southern men. Of course, he was "forbidden fruit." One weekend when I invited Richie to visit our Morehead City beach cottage and my parents realized he was Jewish, they called St. Mary's and ordered me to be "campused." I was prevented from leaving campus for the remaining six weeks of my sophomore year and never saw Richie again. Like many Southerners in that day and age, my parents were prejudiced against Blacks and Jews.

When I came home from St. Mary's and caught up with my friends in Fayetteville, I learned the news about our classmates in combat in Vietnam. Growing up in an army town during wartime was a harrowing experience. Two of my class of 1964 classmates died in combat: Ken Hosea Albritton (1968) and Jeff Riek (1970). I didn't know Jeff, but Ken was a handsome youth who played in the Fayetteville High School band all three years and also played basketball. It was a painful awakening to realize that these young men died far too soon because of a brutal and unjust war that I opposed.

"Finishing school" or not, St. Mary's dedicated, gifted faculty provided us a superb and well-rounded curriculum in humanities and sciences. They taught us as though our education would improve our lives and as though we were destined for careers. My favorite teacher, Dr. Mabel Morrison, was a stern older woman whose nurse-style shoes made ominous squeaks as she walked down the linoleum corridor to our American history classroom. She called on

*In the faded photo, I sit on a stool in front of seven large canvases, half landscapes and half figural, at my graduation art show at St. Mary's Junior College, Raleigh, 1966. My classmate JoAnne Ferrell's paintings hang next to mine.*

students randomly to regurgitate dates and facts. Terrified at not knowing the answer, I memorized each class lesson and internalized the grand timeline of Western history. Having this historical framework paid dividends throughout my career.

I had other memorable instructors as well. English teacher John Tate captivated our minds and took students on Broadway play trips to New York City. Mildred Stamey's theater program taught me the craft of stage management, and I managed most of St. Mary's plays during my second year. Art teacher Margaret Williams, wife of eminent NC Museum of Art curator Ben Williams, allowed me a non-critical forum to stretch my painting wings. I was asked to draw the programs for our annual May Day dances: dwarves and Arabian queens and Disney characters dancing in a circle for "Beyond the Rainbow" and Peter and Tinker Bell flying into a bedroom for "Peter Pan." Whether we danced at the Terpsichorean Ball in a beautiful gown or not, St. Mary's turned out to be a perfect launching pad for my class of 1966.

*Venus and Veronica—The Old and the New*, 20 x 24 inch oil on canvas, 1966.

My art at St. Mary's explored more than just Walt Disney characters. My only surviving early painting shows a thin young woman in a bikini and high heels facing and touching the armless Venus de Milo statue. Behind the statue are a large bottle of Smirnoff vodka with the word "Hippocrates" on the seal and an oversized pack of Winston cigarettes with the cautionary label "Cigarette smoking may be hazardous to your health." Between the statue and the young woman hangs a pocket watch, the dial labeled "Atropos." Hippocrates was the Greek father of medicine; Atropos was one of the three Greek goddesses of fate. Clearly the young woman is me facing the choice between the Greek ideal of moderation in all things and the temptations of alcohol, cigarettes, and sex.

# 5
## The University

Like many students at St. Mary's, I graduated with a junior college degree and then transferred to the University of North Carolina to earn a bachelor's. Once at the university, out of the confines of a girl's school, the shocking modernity of the 1960s hit me hard and shattered my sheltered world view. I arrived in Chapel Hill seeing myself as an artist, a straight-A student, a law-abiding citizen, a virtuous woman, and a person capable of earning a graduate degree. I did not leave with the same beliefs.

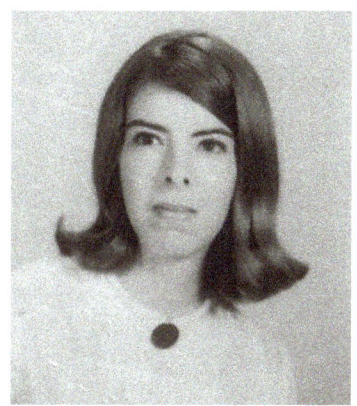

*My junior class yearbook photo, University of North Carolina, Chapel Hill, 1967.*

At UNC, male administrators and professors told me that I couldn't do things that I've lived long enough and had the good fortune to go ahead and do anyway. Several instances of demeaning guidance from male professors at pivotal moments in my higher education remain vivid memories.

My first disillusionment came from an art professor, probably abstract expressionist painter George Kachergis; I'm not certain. Abstract Expressionism ruled the '60s and '70s art world.[7] In a summer school class at UNC, I painted a seascape with a Victorian house perched on a sand dune. We were painting on easels. The professor, full of fervor for his heroic abstract visual mode, walked up to my easel and decided to use my painting to make a point to the class about representational subject matter. I don't remember

33

his exact words, but in no uncertain terms, he demeaned my real-life depiction.

The art professor's criticism so demoralized me that I had an identity crisis over my determination to have a career as an artist. Throughout childhood, art was my special skill and my destiny. I drew and painted unselfconsciously—fairies dancing in circles, cartoon strips with talking dogs, and biblical scenes for Sunday school stories. I painted murals for each season in my classrooms and illustrated covers for school directories, plays, and performances. I remember no frustration in high school art classes or at St. Mary's. In my first art class at UNC, in thrall to the '60s gestural abstraction created by the likes of Jackson Pollock and Willem de Kooning, I came to believe that my illustrative art wasn't "real" art. I swerved from a career as an artist to the study of art history—other people's art.

In the same summer session, I took a math class and encountered the "New Math," a dramatic change in the 1960s after the Sputnik crisis revolutionized American science and math education. The conceptual math that replaced rote arithmetic was Greek to me and shook my self-image as having a good brain. To pass the class, I found a student assistant tutor and memorized the material rather than learning the method and philosophy, as was the goal. Although I had done well in algebra and geometry in high school, this college math class gave me a nearly permanent mathematics phobia.

During my junior year at Carolina, I began to be exposed to politics in action. North Carolinians, including my parents, considered Chapel Hill to be a den of communism, a reputation earned because the civil rights movement of the early '60s was linked in the public mind to communist agitators. In 1963, the conservative North Carolina General Assembly passed the Speaker Ban Law, banning any known communist or anyone pleading the fifth amendment regarding their communist connections to speak on campus. To challenge the law, activist students invited communist-leaning speakers to campus and also filed a lawsuit that overturned the law in 1968.

I considered this political controversy glamorous; my parents thought their daughter was exposed to pernicious influences. For some reason, the Port Hole Restaurant behind the university art building in Chapel Hill had acquired a communist taint, so of course it was one of students' favorite eateries, and the fluffy rolls with butter and honey didn't hurt either. (My favorite restaurant was the Pine Room, the university cafeteria. A boy I was sweet on often bussed tables at dinner time, and I would leave him a flirtatious message written with peas on my plate.)

Like my classmates from St. Mary's College, I pledged a sorority during fall rush in 1966 and plunged into the Greek life, being elected projects chairman of the Panhellenic Council at UNC. During a "Beat Duke" fraternity parade down Franklin Street, I rode on the back of a frat guy's motorcycle. Our photo appeared on the front page of the *Daily Tar Heel*, although I'm barely visible behind him. The sorority alumnae were upset at the negative publicity—I guess it was unseemly for a young woman to be on a motorcycle. Thank goodness I wasn't identified in the photo.

While I was enjoying some aspects of college life, I continued to feel diminished in my academic pursuits. My professors, all male, ranged from old conservatives to young firebrands—and some representing both types put me down in their own ways. The professor of the beginning education class I took to fulfill my art education degree requirements gave me an A for the semester, but the printed grade report checked the box "not recommended for graduate school." It was fine to get a bachelor's degree in art education, but I wasn't PhD material. A radical assistant sociology professor burst another youthful bubble when he assigned a paper analyzing the effect of the police in American life. My conclusion, that police performed an overall beneficial role in society, earned me a grade of C because the prof considered all cops to be corrupt. (Some classes, like geology, taught in a big lecture hall by an eminent professor who had written our textbook, were a joy. I believe I could have become a geologist if I weren't committed to art.)

The final, crushing blow to my ego and spirit at UNC happened during spring break my junior year when I went on a cruise to the Bahamas with two friends. One night, I met a cute guy from Fayetteville, Arkansas. He was a tall, slender, smooth-talking blond-haired charmer, a type irresistible to me. We wandered through dance halls in Nassau, drinking sweet rum punch out of paper cups until he suggested a walk on the beach.

We walked barefooted in the surf under the stars. He became quiet, and the ocean sounded louder to me, as it always does at night. No one else was around. Suddenly, he stopped and kissed me, too hard, and then he pushed me down roughly in the sand and pulled up my skirt. For several minutes I struggled mightily. Finally, I was able to push him away and get back on my feet, but it was too late.

When the cruise ship docked back at Fort Lauderdale, Florida, I found a phone booth and called Mother, who was hysterical with fear because she had dreamed that I drowned. Perhaps that was some sort of mother-daughter psychic message, for I had indeed symbolically drowned. Although I was raped, I felt responsible because if I hadn't gotten tipsy on the rum I might have been able to fight him off. I had the typical "it's my fault" reaction many women of my generation experienced. Because of my religious upbringing, I was emotionally devastated and ashamed of my "sin" and prayed that I wouldn't be punished by getting pregnant.

After an anxious month waiting for the menstrual cycle that never came, a trip to the infirmary confirmed the pregnancy. This date rape and the improbable pregnancy shattered my self-image as a good girl, a virgin, a state I had been preserving carefully for marriage. The pregnancy also undermined any concept I might have had of a gracious and good God; this proved without a doubt that God was vengeful.

I attended the rest of my classes in a fog that spring as I searched for a solution to my condition. My grades plummeted as I dragged myself to class and then back to the dorm room to sleep. Abortion was illegal in North Carolina in most cases. However, the state allowed "therapeutic" abortions in the event of rape or incest if the woman obtained opinion letters from three psychiatrists that having the baby would mentally harm her life. As if the situation were not stressful enough, I had no car and had to depend on a mother from whom I had hoped to separate. Mother was actually quite supportive and of course wanted to keep the whole affair a secret. She drove me to the offices of three doctors who interviewed me and supplied the letters. I don't recall how my father reacted; he tended to leave the parenting to Mother.

After I finished the semester, kind Dr. Christakos performed a legal abortion at Duke Hospital. I was one of the 829,000 North Carolina women who had induced abortions in 1967.[8] As a Christian, raised in the Baptist church, this tragedy confirmed the fire and brimstone lesson I'd learned in Sunday school: God punishes sin.

During this existential crisis, I grasped for a lifeline of hope. I dreaded returning to UNC because the pregnancy had ruined the spring semester and the campus no longer felt like a happy place.

During this low point, I heard about a year-abroad program in Lyon, France, operated by the French department at UNC. I applied as a student for the 1967–1968 school year and was admitted. Mother absolutely refused to allow me the opportunity because she feared for my safety. One of the psychiatrists who enabled my "therapeutic abortion" read her the riot act. "Mrs. Little, if you do not allow your daughter to have this adventure, you are being very selfish." So we bought a trunk, and I filled it with new clothes sewn by a seamstress who lived nearby.

Françoise Gilot, Picasso's mistress, said that "regrets" are only for things we didn't do, what we missed. When you did something, you achieved results, sometimes positive, sometimes negative. If I hadn't been raped and had an abortion, I wouldn't have gone to France for a year. While the course work at UNC stimulated me, when I signed up for a year abroad, I was driven by a sense of adventure and a desire to escape. I had no idea how much this decision would reset my values and change my life. The young woman who started this trip was not the same as the woman who returned.

## 6
### France, My Introduction

In September 1967, my parents drove me in their Chevy station wagon to the New York City dock to join the "UNC Year at Lyon" students on the SS *France* ocean liner to sail to LeHavre, France. Students and parents enjoyed an onboard gala, then the parents disembarked, and our ship slowly pulled away. Mother and Dad stood on the dock, Mother singing loudly over the sound of the engines, regaling me with the chorus of Doris Day's signature 1950s song "Que Sera, Sera." What will be will be—our future's not in our hands.

The song was clearly a blessing of sorts, perhaps meant to comfort herself and quell her own anxiety as much as a farewell to me.

The five-day voyage on one of the most glamorous ocean liners in the world, surrounded by a large group of new friends, looking toward a year of learning the French language and culture, filled my heart with excitement. My primary emotion, however, was gratitude for a second chance to be myself, a new start to create the future that I wanted.

After a quick day in Paris, we arrived by train in Lyon, France's second largest city. In my first glimpses, I saw a city that was smaller but still grand, with tree-lined boulevards along two rivers. The University of Lyon resembled the Louvre, and its imposing entrance gates faced the Rhone River. The smaller Soane River lay at the foot of the old Roman city atop the Fouviere mountain, with the medieval cobblestone streets of Vieux Lyon stepping down from the hilltop to the river. The weathered buildings, with no fresh paint, seemed to have changed little since the old black and white World War II movies I was familiar with. Little boys rode home for lunch with a baguette loaf tied to their handlebars. Old women walked home from the butcher with the day's food in string bags. I was not in North Carolina anymore.

After sleeping in a university dorm on the hill in Vieux Lyon for the first few weeks, I rented a room from a marquis and marquise, aristocrats a notch below a duke and duchess, on the two top floors of their apartment building, 22 Quai Tilsitt. Their building on the Soane River faced Fouviere and Vieux Lyon.

The de Leotoings, landed Catholics, owned an ancestral medieval castle in the Cantal Mountains of France, built in the 1300s, which they reluctantly opened to the public in order to pay the taxes. The Marquis Henri de Leotoing d'Anjony, an old banker, and the Marquise, a deaf dowager, may have suffered terribly during World War II like so many others. Their reduced economic situation forced them to rent out the maid's quarters and an upstairs bedroom to foreign students. Instead of paying a servant, their divorced daughter lived with them, a recluse due to the shame she brought on the family through her divorce. She shopped and cooked for the family.

Although it wasn't obvious at first, I was far luckier to live with a French family, quite close to the university, than my classmates in the dorm. I rented the maid's quarter, a small bedroom just off the kitchen at the rear of the apartment, with a toilet across the hall. The accommodations were far from luxurious. Madame issued me one set of sheets and one towel when I arrived and allowed me one shower per week, in the bathroom on the upstairs bedroom level. Once she angrily accused me of carelessness when she found a rip in the top bed sheet. If my French had been better I would have retorted that her sheet ripped because it was rotten. I had no social contact with the family, took no meals with them, and was only allowed to use their telephone in an emergency.

On the plus side, my bedroom had a large double casement window that opened to a side street, with a view of the river, and a bidet for hygiene that helped compensate for the single weekly bath.

Then there was Nancy and her dog Lady, who lived in the upstairs bedroom with a balcony overlooking the river. Nancy was a divorced American medical student studying at the École de Médecin at the university, and we became best friends.

The American students in my classes, all first timers out of the United States, were a tight-knit group who worked hard at school during the week and met on evenings and weekends for dinners. We had Monday-to-Friday morning classes in French grammaire and literature with Mademoiselle Simonet and wrote weekly "expositions" in French under lycée (high school) literature teachers. The French language

*My student ID card, University of Lyon, France, 1967.*

came easily, but previously I had considered myself a crack writer and the famous French logic of simple, clear sentences and paragraphs with topic sentences bedeviled me. My first essays for one French professor, a strict man with a flat-top haircut, earned scores of two and three out of a possible grade of ten. When I received an eight on my last essay, I was inordinately proud.

I thought I was well equipped to travel alone and was excited by all the travel opportunities. Our chaperones from UNC, Professor Castaneda and his wife, organized periodic tours during the year. Just a few weeks after arriving in France, we had a group trip to Geneva, Switzerland, for the weekend. This is where my first panic attack occurred—the incident I described in the prologue—apparently triggered by a theater marquee showing Walt Disney's movie *Fantasia*.

One moment I was walking along with friends, delighted to be in a new city. Then I saw that marquee and suddenly had an intense, out-of-body experience that felt like a death. Because I had the security of being with friends, in a short time I managed to shake off the profound shock of the strange encounter. Why would a theater playing a movie I'd seen during my childhood cause my mind to freeze?

Looking at it in retrospect, this first panic attack came at the beginning of my first year away from home. Although my spirit was free in a new country, and free from the unwanted baby that had been thrust on me, I was carrying the subconscious baggage of my mother's extreme protectiveness, which conveyed that the world must be a threatening place. As noted in the prologue, *Fantasia* was Disney's only cartoon movie depicting chaos instead of the familiar fairy tale plots of *Cinderella* and *Sleeping Beauty*. In that foreign place where everything was unfamiliar, it was also a sudden, jolting representation of home. Mother's fear nearly prevented me from the French year abroad, and subconsciously, I believed I couldn't take care of myself.

After that, I spent most of my time in the company of friends, nearly always traveled in a small group, and recall only one more panic attack until the end of the year. During university breaks we traveled to the British Isles, to Vienna and behind the Iron Curtain to Hungary for Christmas, and to Italy and Greece for Easter. We took trains and boats, and we hitch-hiked. One or two of us purchased cars. We drank our way through the Beaujolais winery country and toured the châteaux of the Loire Valley. Through my friend Nancy, I met a wealthy Lyonnaise family who invited us to elegant lunches at their country home. Traveling to countries with different architectural traditions, from the quaint half-timbering of medieval English houses to the white stucco, arched doors, and red tile roofs of Mediterranean villas, taught me architectural history without my realizing it.

In the afternoons, we took classes of our choice at the university. I especially recall the Byzantine architecture class because I studied and photographed Byzantine churches during my spring vacation in Athens, Greece, for a term paper for that class. The fieldwork was frightening because I worked alone and was trailed by Greek youths who hissed creepily at me. Macho hissing at women on the street was a common form of street harassment to women who dared to travel alone in public throughout the world. I traveled alone—no longer the timid UNC girl who smarted over a bad grade on a sociology paper. In France, I had become a serious student of art history.

My family anxiously awaited my letters all year. I wrote them weekly and received long letters from Mother, typed on airmail stationery with crowded paragraphs on both sides of the paper, about life in Fayetteville. If I hadn't saved these letters, I wouldn't have realized that Mother was relatively normal then, still cleaned the house occasionally and did some cooking, and that she apparently loved me. Sometimes she signed her letters "Moth." On Nov. 7, 1967, she wrote a particularly chatty letter, gossiping about the wedding of my St. Mary's College roommate and including a doggerel poem she had written to introduce a local actor who was to speak at one of her clubs. She mentioned she was scrubbing the kitchen floor with steel wool and had washed and spray-painted the floor vents, preparing to have her bridge club over. She said she wished I could come and help her. "While you were here I would hug you real hard, Honey." She signed it "I love you very much."

That wasn't unusual for most mothers, but until then I had almost never heard "I love you" from Mother. Obviously, my long absence affected her. Some parts of her letters reveal her lifelong obsessions and mental disorders, but they also show that, at age fifty-four, she was still leading an active life full of normal activities. I had no way of knowing how much all of this would change in the future. At the time, our correspondence was a lively exchange of gossip and motherly advice on her end and stories of friends, classes, and excursions on mine. In a November 15 letter, Mother chided me for not being in the photos I had sent her. "We think you are pretty and very photogenic, so please get in more of the photos yourself." At the time, this was a startling request to me, so different from all of her previous criticisms of my appearance.

I heard from my father less frequently, but just after Christmas I received two whole pages of his neat printing that pleased me because he considered me grown-up enough to know the worries he had never shared before. I think my long absence had made us closer. He asked me not to spend too much money on travel. He was concerned about his business and the possibility that my brother might be drafted in the Vietnam War. It is especially interesting in retrospect that he was worried about deferred maintenance on our home, but "Jenny will have to take the initiative if anything is done. I have been stopped too many times when I tried to do something." He reported a two-day visit from Aunt Appless and her son Lyman during Christmas "and you know how those visits are." He closed with, "You write wonderful letters and we enjoy them very much, all my love, Dad." His letter made me feel proud that I merited his confidence.

Mother's post-Christmas letter went beyond her normal frugality as a child of the Depression. She asked me to save all the wrapping from her packages so she could prove to the post office that she sent them air mail and get a refund. She had just received a cuckoo clock I had sent them in November. She told me that they hung it on the knotty pine wall over the kitchen table.

Years later, after Mother had passed away and I was cleaning out her house, I found that clock still on the kitchen wall behind the vast piles of papers and boxes. The cuckoo bird's head was cracked, but the clock was mostly intact. I recalled her letter and later found it:

> We call the little cuckoo bird "Rufus." He is in such a hurry to do his job and get back to his quarters! We can hear him in our bed with the kitchen door closed. And he is on the kitchen wall next to the storage apt. room. We love him! When he calls his

*hour, Daddy and I look at each other and smile—course we are thinking of you!*

It was good to find that clock. At that moment, surrounded by the visible and overwhelming evidence of my mother's mental illness, I savored a moment of remembering there were times when she had energy, times when I felt the love that was so hard for her to show.

## 7
## France, First Love

One February evening, a group of us American students went dancing at a "boite," a nightclub, in Lyon. We sat in chairs along the wall of a dark crowded dance floor, the familiar rhythms of American rock music from a jukebox setting an intimate vibe. Suddenly, a tall, handsome, serious young man named Pierre approached and asked me to dance. He folded me into his arms, and I felt the smooth fabric of his leather jacket on my cheek. The song playing was one I had heard a hundred times, but it sounded strange in a good way. In Pierre's strong arms, the door to heaven opened. It was a coup de foudre—love at first sight—for both of us.

For the rest of the school year, we spent as much time together as possible. He was studying at the École de Médecin, a military medical school at the University of Lyon, to become a dermatologist, which required a regime of onerous courses and demanding exams—all while wearing a khaki military uniform to class. Because I often traveled with my school friends, Pierre and I never had enough time together. Mostly we sat in his Citroën Deux Cheveux (a two-horsepower economy car) on the street in front of my apartment in the dark and whispered and embraced each other as if our lives depended on it.

Our romance unfolded in excruciatingly slow motion because neither of us had access to a telephone, so we communicated by letter. He wrote lovely strings of French words on thin paper with the colored letterhead of the medical school bearing the slogan "Pro Patria et Humanitate" (For Country and Humanity); I wrote in the French I was learning in the cour d'etrangers (French language

*Pierre Galopin, 22 Quai Tilsitt, on the Soane River, Lyon, France, 1968.*

department) at the university. Once or twice, he telephoned me at the Leotoing residence, but I was not encouraged to use their telephone.

On March 3, Pierre wrote that he could not meet me at a planned time because of an anatomy test. But Sunday at 10 a.m. "on pourrait se voir dans la matinee et sortir hors de Lyon pour dejeuner et ne rentrer que le soir." It was signed "Groses Bises Pierre." (We can go to the country for a picnic lunch and return in the evening. Giant kisses.) For this picnic, our first big outing, I used the Leotoing kitchen to cook my Southern idea of a first-class picnic—fried chicken and deviled eggs. We rode into the countryside in his Deux Cheveux and ate on the grass. We pledged our love for each other, and he declared that it was time we made love. I lied, telling him I was a virgin, and said I was reluctant. Because I'd been attacked in Nassau, I still felt pure in spirit and wanted to retain that purity.

That same month, my friend Carolyn Cobb and I hitchhiked to Paris. One short ride we took was with a trucker. Carolyn and I shared the front passenger seat of the truck cab, and the trucker began to masturbate, then reached his hand up my skirt. We screamed at him to stop the truck. He pulled over to the side of the highway, and we tumbled out onto the ground, thankful to have escaped the lecherous driver.

I wrote Pierre when we returned from Paris, but the letter was delayed because I put an incomplete address on the envelope. Finally, he wrote me back on March 26, from the "amphitheatre" (lecture hall) of his class. He hoped I had a fun trip to Paris but "Je n'etais pas tellement tranquille de te voir partir." (I was worried about your trip.) Then he declared his love. "Tu ne peux pas savoir comme j'ai penser a toi pendent ces deux dernieres semaines et comme j'ai hate de te revoir! Je t'embrasse tres tres fort. (You cannot know how I've thought of you these last two weeks and how eager I am to see you. I embrace you with all my strength.) He asked to meet me the following Saturday about four o'clock.

Most of our dates were simple, walks in the country or just riding in his car. I stood countless times in the shadow of the entrance at 22 Quai Tilsitt or sat on the wall along the Saône and waited for his little dirty Deux Chevaux to putter up to the entrance. As many times as I rode in his car (the front right seat kept the contour of my rear), I never decided what color it was—dirty gray, dirty blue, or dirty white. He loved to drive around Lyon after being cooped up in his École St. Militaire all week, then we would drink a beer in a café, all the while talking and talking, always in French. I grew to love the sounds of the words, the feel of the phrases on my tongue, especially when Pierre spoke them.

In April, the student revolution of 1968 closed down the university and the rest of our classes were held in a small public school. Contact with the United States was cut off because the French labor unions went on strike, including the post office. We managed to send letters to our parents by posting them in nearby Geneva, Switzerland. The "soixante-huitards," the striking students, protested against capitalism, consumerism, American imperialism, and France's heavy-handed institutional bureaucracy. We American students heard the sounds of violent demonstrations in Lyon and feared the crisis, since, as Americans, we felt as if we were part of the problem.

*Me with Canadian students at a "Hippy Party," Lyon, France, 1968.*

I had taken an evening art class at Lyon's Ecole de Beaux Arts, the art and design school, which had been occupied by the protesters. At the end of the year, I endured verbal abuse from the student radicals when I braved the students' barricades to retrieve my art work from a locker at the school, but I successfully rescued my art by explaining forcefully in French that I had a right to reclaim my locker contents. Standing up alone to the soixante-huitard revolutionaries, I proved to myself that I was not the same timid Southern girl that had left North Carolina the year earlier. The protests, known as "May 68," resulted in lasting administrative and economic reforms to the old classic French system of education and business.

～

During April, Pierre studied for his semester exams, and a group of us spent our two-week spring semester vacation in Italy and Greece. On April 18, Pierre wrote that he hoped I had a good Easter vacation and asked me to write and tell him when I was getting back. "Je t'attendrai devant chez toi Dimanche 21 Avril vers deux heures de l'apres midi." (I'll be at your place at 2 pm Sunday April 21 and if you haven't arrived by 2:30 I won't wait any longer.) He thanked me for the postcards that I sent and said that I have no idea how much he wanted to be with me on the voyage. He said it had been almost one month since he had seen me, and I had surely had time to forget him a little.

We returned after April 21, so Pierre waited for me in vain. I wrote him as soon as I returned to Lyon. On April 24, he wrote that he would meet me at my building on Friday at 8 p.m. He chided me on my letter, teasing that I had forgotten a lot of French and he would have to work on me a little. No doubt I would be "toute bronze par le soleil Mediterranean" (tanned by the Mediterranean sun). In late April, we took a weekend getaway to another town, signing the hotel register as Monsieur et Madame Galopin. I loved his last name, which in French means tramp, scalawag, or imp.

Classes ended in May for Pierre and me. On May 8, he wrote that he admirably passed his studies but that he had not learned enough biochemistry. On May 10, he wrote to apologize for not being able to see me Thursday because of remedial biochemistry lessons. We had planned a little trip, and he lamented having to cancel it because it would have undoubtedly been "la plus belle semaine de toute l'annee" (the most beautiful week of the whole year). He wished me a good trip to Geneva, where I was traveling next, and said he would see me after I returned.

I remained in Lyon until July to spend time with Pierre and scheduled passage back to the United States on July 12. I felt I had a duty to go back to Chapel Hill to finish my college degree, but the upcoming end of my time with Pierre and my life in France loomed ominously.

Those extra weeks were the perfect final act of my year in France. The most delicious anticipation I ever remember was our rendezvous in San Malo, Brittany, which was an all-day train ride away. Pierre had a commitment in London to attend a friend's wedding, so we agreed to meet in San Malo afterwards, on June 24. After exploring Brittany, we planned to go to Spain.

I arrived in San Malo at six o'clock in the evening and began my search for one of the ten hotels that Pierre and I had copied out of a telephone book. Telephones weren't common, and we had no way to reserve a room in advance. I found one right across from the station and checked in. When Pierre returned from London, he was to call each hotel to discover which one I had checked into.

While waiting, I went to a restaurant up the street and had one of the most delicious meals of my life—a big steaming bowl of moules (mussels), a salad, a steak, ice cream, and a whole liter of hard cider. When I returned to the hotel, the fat little manager bustled over and said a young man had called for me while I was gone. He said he had checked into room 13 and then gone out. I sat in the little bar in the lobby, first with coffee, then a "demi-pression," and waited eighty long minutes. Finally, Pierre sauntered casually into the bar with his big boyish grin and pulled up the chair next to me. After so many obstacles and disappointing cancellations, we were together at last.

Later that night, snuggled in a soft bed in our small chamber, Pierre said, "I was jealous when I watched my pal Patrick marry an English girl. Now I feel like it is us who just got married and are beginning our own honeymoon." I felt happier than at any other moment of my life and thought about how wonderful it would be if we were the newlyweds.

The next morning, we woke up to a driving rain. We walked out on the ramparts of the old fortress guarding the harbor of St. Malo, laughing and griping together in the rain, and saw the iron cross marking the grave of Chateaubriand, the famous Romantic writer and statesman, high on the cliffs overlooking the Atlantic. The second day, we endured a hellish all-day drive through the northern interior of Spain to the Costa Brava, to San Carlos de la Rapine, a small undeveloped Mediterranean town.

Spain was having one of its worst heat waves—115 degrees Fahrenheit. I could hardly breathe in a way that was more than metaphorical. During our entire five days in Spain, I felt a curious sensation I had never felt before, a stark fear like a great weight pressed on my chest, forcing me to breathe in short shallow gasps. It wasn't so much a physical breathing problem as a fear of the unknown, of dying suddenly now when I had so much to live for. I had the desire to scream all the time and controlled myself only by utmost effort.

I'm now convinced that this phantom chest weight was caused by my extreme mental anguish at the imminent end of my time with Pierre and my return to the States. I remember lying in his arms in the early sunlit mornings with a Mediterranean breeze coming through the open window. I knew then that I would never forget these moments, and I never have.

## 8
## The Telegram

On July 12, as the SS *France* pulled out from the port of Le Havre, France, I gazed out at the ocean and thought about Pierre. We had returned to Lyon on the Fourth of July. I stood on the curb in front of my apartment building crying as he handed over my sneakers from his car. We promised to write, and he promised to come to see me the following summer. Sitting on the ship, I wrote in my diary:

*My eyes settled on two objects which seemed to symbolize Pierre—a double-masted sailboat and the lighthouse on the rocky point of the harbor. As I watched the tall white sails billow in the gusty breeze, I realized that I never had the opportunity to go sailing with Pierre. Of all the things that we could do together, this would have pleased me the most. The sails are like Pierre—big, noble, and dignified, yet natural, no pretense. They were alone in the middle of the bay, pitted against all of nature's elements, enjoying the struggle. They remind me of Pierre's stubborn determination to be a doctor who can help where he is needed, i.e. in Africa. I often doubt whether I will ever again meet another boy with such a unique combination—handsome, strong, athletic, intelligent and ambitious, patient and good-natured, deep, faithful, honest and masterful. Sometimes I become terribly depressed that I may never again see Pierre. Even if he comes to the U.S. next summer with his brother George, the chances are remote that we would be able to plan and carry out a life together.*

*There is only one obstacle to marrying him—he is French and I am American. Nancy once asked me if I loved him because of or in spite of his being French. I answered "in spite of." It's not just that it would pain my family if I married and raised a family so far away, but "Would I be able to live happily in France?" I don't believe a person is capable of denying his heritage. I've grown accustomed to the ambiance of America, and my behavior patterns are permanently established.*

My year in Lyon was one of the greatest influences on my life. I changed from a provincial Southern Baptist from North Carolina to a cosmopolitan, budding art historian. I became an adult during that year, in both my parents' eyes and my own. The year abroad and travel throughout most of Europe during class breaks expanded my understanding of the world. Exploring the grand art museums of Europe, studying Byzantine architecture in Greece, the buildings of Michelangelo in Florence, Italy, and medieval castles in France and Spain—all turned my head away from an art career to a major in art history. I swerved from creating my own art because a college art professor belittled my subject matter and style and because I fell in love with historic architecture in Europe.

When I returned to the United States, I measured all ideas and all civilization against what I had seen in Europe. I fell in love for the first time, with a Frenchman who became my emotional stability—the secure person I had never had. Why did I leave him? I told myself it was because I was too American to deny my heritage, but what if it was fear of leaving home and marrying a foreigner?

A letter from my sorority, Kappa Alpha Theta, awaited me when I got home on July 17, 1968. The July 5 letter stated that "it has come to our attention that you were involved in a situation last spring.... we must accept your resignation or terminate your membership." (Thanks, sorority sisters, for your treachery.) I sent the central office a face-saving telegram stating that "I will not have the time in the one semester remaining of my college career to devote to KAT Sorority. Please accept my resignation from a wonderful organization." The sorority shamed me by kicking me out, but they actually did me a favor, because I landed in a much better place than if I had returned to UNC my senior year and stayed in the sorority. I realized that the social pressure of the Greek system had focused me on shallow things. What sweet revenge it is to name them here.

In practical terms, the transition back to school went well. Preparing for my return, my mother bought an old five-bedroom house on McCauley Street near the UNC campus. I moved in and became a landlady, renting out the other four bedrooms to friends. That fall, I focused on finishing my bachelor's degree, a double major in art history and French, while constantly thinking of a reunion with Pierre in the summer of 1969. We exchanged letters every few weeks throughout the year, professing our continued love.

During the spring semester of 1969, I started graduate school at UNC, the path of least resistance to earning a master's degree in art history. One day my Greek art professor cautioned me against the easy route. "You've lived your life in North Carolina. It's time for you to get out of the South and do your master's work in a different region of the country. I recommend Brown University in Rhode Island."

So I applied to Brown and was accepted to enter Brown's master's program in art history in the fall of 1969. In the meantime, I finished the spring semester at UNC. Every day when I walked to the Lenoir Hall cafeteria for lunch or coffee, I watched UNC's Food Workers' Strike of 1968-69. Throughout the year, picket lines of Black food workers circled Lenoir Hall with signs protesting bad working conditions and low pay due to institutional racism. Eventually, the food service shut down. The long strike was finally resolved successfully and non-violently. The political turmoil of the 1960s had first arrived at Chapel Hill, called "the Southern Part of Heaven," with civil rights protests to desegregate its restaurants in 1963-64. The strikes foreshadowed the student strikes I would encounter in graduate school at Brown the next year.

During this academic year in Chapel Hill, I didn't even consider dating other men as Pierre and I corresponded frequently and anticipated our summer reunion. In spite of a year apart, our love remained as strong as ever. But in early June, I received a letter telling me how hard he was working to pass his exams and that he hadn't yet received authorization to travel to the United States from the military school general. He said, "L'ete '69 arrives tres vite" (summer '69 is coming quickly). "You cannot know how much I look forward to seeing you.... We need to go to Istanbul one day when you return to Europe and that will not be very long. Do you want to? ... Don't think if I don't write you often that I don't think of you. It means nothing. You are always present ... I am so tired of studying now. How I would love for you to be in Lyon to give me monstrous clouds of energy. That is your primordial quality. Your presence exhales shining life. I believe that is why I loved you immediately. You can't know how unhappy I will be if I'm not able to see you again."

Pierre's letter instantly made me feel his presence, as if a whole year hadn't passed by. I began to count down the days until he would arrive in July.

In early July, I received a telegram: "Accident. Can Not Come."

I was devastated. I assumed that Pierre had invented an excuse not to come because he wanted to end our relationship, but soon I received a letter that explained the real reasons. On July 8, 1969, he wrote that he had failed his bacteriology exam that he had studied so hard for and also totaled the Citroën.

> *All is lost—the trip—the time I would have spent with you and the care with which I organized and prepared for my trip to the US with 30,000 francs. If it were only the money I would be sad but it is all that is lost this year that is the saddest. This has been the blackest year of my life. I haven't gone out and have economized throughout the year, and then I had an accident that destroyed my car and I failed my exam. The first thing I thought*

*of was you, and how unhappy you would be: that perhaps afflicts me more than the exam results. You know we must have courage! Everything for the voyage was ready—I had bought a big suitcase to hold all my trip stuff. It is useless now and I've hidden it from view. You don't know how sad I am to give you pain. I am truly in pain, providence was not on our side this year. I don't know what else to say because I'm so unhappy, and will get to work to retake the exam in September. Believe me that I'm afflicted to ruin your summer when we would have passed such agreeable moments. I quit by embracing you strongly and hoping that your pain won't be too too large.*

My heart was broken: I had what they called at that time a nervous breakdown, which left me a hollow shell. I lay awake through many long nights. I felt that my heart would stop beating unless I stayed awake to monitor it. When I lost Pierre, I lost my identity as a woman who had found her perfect love. Although Pierre often had to reschedule dates and we never had enough time together, he gave me the security of being seen and loved for who I was.

Unfortunately, at this moment, I had been reading the book *God Is Dead*, and already my lifelong belief in God had slipped away. My childhood faith in a supernatural being who had my back had finally yielded to reason. In one fell swoop, I lost my relationship with my lover and my supreme being.

I had a session with a therapist that provided no comfort, and in desperation I escaped to our family cottage in Morehead City on the Atlantic Ocean, my favorite place in the world. I sailed my little Sunfish "Tramp," named in honor of Pierre Galopin and my favorite Otis Redding song. I swam in the healing ocean. Rock music became my barbiturate. Over and over and over I popped quarters into the jukebox in the Atlantic Beach pavilion and listened to "In-A-Gadda-Da-Vida," the longest rock song ever recorded. The loud rock guitar and drums was the only thing that drowned out the sound of my repetitive, despairing thoughts.

By the end of the summer, I was able to sleep again. My parents again drove me in the station wagon north—this time to Providence, Rhode Island, where I entered a master of art history program at Brown University. As we rode on Interstate 95 and passed New York City, I entered into a long, low-level panic attack because I had never been north of it. I felt like we would fall off the edge of the known world—a crazy fear considering the international travel of my previous year. This was one of many times I would see that panic has no logic.

# 9
## Grad School and a Career Passion

In spite of my broken heart and ongoing panic, I stayed in Providence from 1969 to 1971 and earned an MA in art history from Brown. My class consisted of six women, several of whom were earning PhDs, while the rest of us were master's candidates. We were a band of sisters who have supported each other ever since, reminiscent of the eight women at Vassar in *The Group*, the 1963 novel by Mary McCarthy. I knew then that my own education would not be complete without a PhD, the terminal degree I would need to teach at the university level.

Brown was a much more supportive environment than UNC-Chapel Hill. I left behind the South where women were simultaneously elevated on a pedestal and deprived of agency. I arrived at Brown at a serendipitous moment, as appreciation for American historic architecture was growing with the approach of the country's two hundredth anniversary in 1976. The history of ordinary buildings and places was becoming as intriguing as the Mount Vernons associated with famous people. I had two main mentors, William F. Jordy and Antoinette Downing. Dr. Jordy, a Brown professor and architectural historian, steered me towards the history of architecture, and Mrs. Downing, the chair of the Rhode Island Historic Preservation Commission, gave me a part-time job and a passion for historic preservation.

Other, remote mentors during grad school were Ada Louise Huxtable, *New York Times* architecture critic, and Jane Jacobs, whose 1961 *Death and Life of Great American Cities* established the practice of historic preservation on a grand scale. I read every scrap they wrote in newspapers and books and wanted to emulate them.

My trajectory towards art history was so strong that I buried my self-image as an artist.

Instead, I focused on art created by others. I intended to specialize in medieval manuscript illumination—the miniature drawings and paintings hand-created by the scribes who copied manuscripts. I'd been captivated by the "marginalia" doodled in margins, intimate and sometimes lascivious scenes of contemporary life that I had seen in books as an undergraduate (and of course during childhood in the hilarious marginalia in *MAD* magazine). Several undergraduates I befriended in the art department were artists *and* historians, exotic creatures I could only envy from afar. Their study of the history of art stimulated them to create original paintings and sculpture in their spare time, in contrast to the tight pencil drawings of Georgian and Federal style houses on the College Hill campus of Brown that I made for fun. These were the equivalent of botanical illustrations—my historian training valued clarity, coherence, and representation.

My biggest project at Brown—a handsome exhibition and catalogue of original caricature drawings and prints—taught me that I didn't want a career in art museums. The basic exercise of the Brown University program for a master's degree was that each year's class of MA art history students prepared an original exhibition, from beginning to end, displayed at the Rhode Island School of Design Museum of Art. The renowned art school adjoined the Brown University campus. Our mentor, Professor Juergen Schultz, selected our exhibition, "Caricature and Its Role in Graphic Satire."

We six female students worked throughout the two years to select 110 original caricature drawings from Europe—primarily English, French, Italian, and German from the Middle Ages to the mid-1800s, borrow them from various private collectors and museums throughout the United States and Europe, then prepare a meaty, stylish catalogue, and produce the exhibit. The first winter we sat around Professor Schultz's bed like vestal virgins because he was bedridden with back trouble. We divided up the art pieces and prepared catalogue entries that explored the political or religious intrigue that prompted the satire. The show hung from April 7 to May 9, 1971, as we finished our degrees.

Traveling to collectors' homes and museums in New York and New England and conducting research in hushed museum collections introduced me to the work of art museum curators. I found the ancient, small European drawings and prints to be effete and arcane. I wanted to preserve American art that was endangered, especially architecture, because it is a generally public form of art accessible to ordinary people.

In contrast to the man at UNC who destroyed my passion for painting, at Brown I found a professor who gave me my life's work. Dr. Jordy taught a large lecture class in American architecture. Providence was a "six degrees of Kevin Bacon" sort of place in those days: Jordy's wife was the sister of the famous child-rearing expert Benjamin Spock, and everyone knew the cartoonist Edward Koren, who lived on College Hill. As I described in the prologue, our first assignment in Jordy's class was to take a flattened brown paper bag and a pencil down into Providence's business district and write a paper about a block of buildings. There I discovered the oldest enclosed shopping mall in the United States—the Westminster Arcade at 65 Weybosset Street, built in 1828, with two levels of shops illuminated by a skylighted roof. I could have spent all day browsing in the little shops, but I stayed focused, drew an image of the façades on my block, wrote descriptions of the buildings, and talked to store employees to get some history.

Dr. Jordy's brown-bag exercise shifted my focus to American architecture. If I had become a medieval art scholar, I would have spent my time in manuscript collections, tiptoeing around a library like the J. Pierpont Morgan Library in New York City, carrying a magnifying glass and wearing white gloves, turning the pages of priceless manuscripts slowly under the supervision of a stern curator. As an architectural historian, I could walk the sidewalks of ordinary cities, absorbing architectural styles, construction techniques, and history while interacting with people who used the architecture on an everyday basis. I visualized my future as a researcher, photographer, and historian who wandered the world studying the built environment instead of cloistered in a quiet art collection.

I had accidentally stumbled into one of the two places in the United States—Rhode Island, and Charleston, South Carolina—that pioneered the historic preservation movement in the mid-twentieth century. Antoinette Downing, director of the Providence Preservation Society, spearheaded it with *Early Homes of Rhode Island* in 1937 and *The Architectural Heritage of Newport, Rhode Island* in 1952. Her friendship with Professor Jordy led to a job. Antoinette hired me and other Brown students Alice Hauck and Jack Renshaw for a 1970 summer inventory of the eighteenth- and nineteenth-century buildings of Newport. In addition, our classroom learning led to real-world action to determine the impact of a proposed waterfront urban renewal project on Newport's historic port area. We worked out of the Newport Preservation Society office.

I commuted to Newport from Providence in my Opel Kadett station wagon, a slight mustard-colored tin can that the wind sometimes blew sideways into the next lane as I drove over highway bridges. It was my first car, given by my parents in 1969 soon after I entered Brown. (By contrast, they gave my brother a new Ford Falcon when he was only a freshman at NC State University, because boys needed cars.)

My thesis project at Brown was a "catalogue raisonné," an archival guide to Thomas Tefft's architectural drawings in the archives of Brown and the Rhode Island School of Design. Tefft attended Brown, became an architect, and helped to create the Italianate Revival style. His papers were donated to Brown after his untimely death at age thirty-three from a fever in Florence while on a "Grand Tour" of Europe in 1859. I roamed New England to track down every building in Tefft's drawings, writing descriptions and taking photographs. In addition to Italianate villa house designs, he adapted the Romanesque Revival style for churches and industrial buildings such as train stations and textile mills. In the 1840s and 1850s, cavernous mills with long rows of tall arched windows built from Tefft's designs used power harnessed from Rhode Island's rocky rivers to spin fabric.

After the Civil War, the textile industry moved to the southern United States, and the landscapes of many rural areas are dotted today with what remains of their buildings. These abandoned and neglected mills spoke to a deep psychic need in my life. During my childhood, Mother brought home thrift shop finds and dumpster rescues—things like a "Freud's couch" with horsehair upholstery, a sideboard with a missing drawer, a cast-iron clothes rack from a department store, an antique wall phone—and stuffed them into storage sheds in our back yard. These pieces cried out for restoration, but she was a collector, not a restorer; she thrilled to the hunt, not the refinishing. I yearned to document and evaluate these magnificent palaces of industry as a first step toward recycling them for new uses.

Providence was a magical place for a Southerner like me, with many styles of old buildings, crystal blue skies without the summer haze of North Carolina, and smart, motivated young people attracted by my Southern drawl. Once in a crowded elevator in New York City, I asked someone to "mash the button" for the third floor, and everyone howled with laughter at my colloquial expression. In the northeastern United States, buttons are pushed rather than mashed. In New England, I raised eyebrows when I ordered a "co-cola." "What is that?" they asked. I learned to pronounce the full name "Coca-Cola" when I wanted my favorite soft drink.

When Mother and Dad drove up to Providence to visit me during spring break, I saw a dimension of Mother's anxiety disorder that I'd never experienced. We drove to Montreal, Canada, through a blizzard. When we arrived, Dad and I were eager to see all the sights, but the big-city hustle and modern commercial atmosphere activated Mother's anxiety. She became incapacitated, crying and complaining constantly, and refused to go outside the hotel. Although her behavior weighed on us, Dad and I explored the cosmopolitan city without her. We loved the modern underground shopping mall in Montreal, but she feared the elevators and escalators.

My own anxiety was under control in graduate school, and though I was often lonely, I don't recall actual panic attacks. In the fall of 1969, Pierre continued to write, although I wrote back that I was afraid to wait another year to see him. He replied that he wouldn't write anymore in order to help me forget him.

In January 1970, I wrote telling him that I had tried to forget him but that no matter how hard I studied he would appear in my mind. I dated a lot of exciting men at Brown, but no one turned my heart away from Pierre. I wrote the letter late at night and addressed the envelope. The next morning, I did not mail it. The letter not mailed—the path not taken—ended our relationship. If I had mailed it, I likely would have become une Française, a French woman.

In May 1970, I received the coup de grace. Pierre wrote that he believed that our romance was finished and we would stay only good friends. That year, he had met Genevieve, a sweet medical student in his class. "She doesn't have your humor and energy but we are together."

Possibly, I could have gone back to France and reclaimed our relationship. He was my first and greatest love. He loved me for my tenderness, my spontaneity, my energy, and said I was the only girl for him and was different from all the girls he'd known before.

I never stopped loving Pierre, but we were doomed because I was caught up in graduate school and my first professional job and he couldn't come to the United States because medical school was so demanding.

During the spring of 1971, as I finished up my graduate degree at Brown and mourned the loss of Pierre, I was comforted by a

Lakota Sioux saying: "Sometimes I go about pitying myself, and all the time I'm being carried on great wings across the sky." Those words have lifted my spirits ever since.

## Part II

## Launching

*View from Dix Hill, 24 x 24 inch oil on canvas, 2012.*

# 10
## The Dawn of Historic Preservation in North Carolina

I owe my career to the passage of the National Historic Preservation Act, signed by President Lyndon Baines Johnson in 1966. I belong to the first generation of historic preservationists in the United States. My father found his profession of land surveying through the New Deal's Civilian Conservation Corps. My schoolteacher mother collected antiques and houses, including rental houses and a beach house. I created a career that combined my parents' interests into the new field of historic preservation.

Americans came to an appreciation of their historic buildings and properties very slowly during the twentieth century. In 1935, Franklin D. Roosevelt signed the Historic Sites Act into law, which organized national parks under a National Park Service as another New Deal program to create jobs during the Depression. Under the park service, the Historic American Buildings Survey (HABS) program hired unemployed architects, engineers, and surveyors to survey, record, document, and interpret historic properties. While many early American landmarks were documented by the HABS program, no federal system to preserve these historic properties was put into place until passage of the National Historic Preservation Act of 1966. Post-World War II construction of an interstate highway system under President Eisenhower and urban renewal programs in the downtown cores of cities had destroyed many historic properties. Americans saw negative changes in their cities and worried about losing their national identity.

The 1966 act created the National Register of Historic Places and directed each state to open a State Historic Preservation Office (SHPO) to coordinate a statewide inventory of historic properties, nominate properties for inclusion in the National Register, review the impact to historic properties of all federally funded and permitted projects, and advise and educate the public. This national historic preservation network, under the direction of the National Park Service, created the new field of cultural resource management, in which historians, architects, archaeologists, architectural historians, and others who formerly were employed primarily in academia, teaching at universities or other institutions, could now earn a professional livelihood in government. These careers do not require a PhD, thus opening jobs to a larger swath of professionals to participate in the field.

In September 1971, after finishing coursework for a master's degree at Brown, I drove my Opel Kadett to Raleigh to begin work with the new NC State Historic Preservation Office, established in 1970. It was my dream job: I actually got paid to document historic buildings all over the state! I returned home with a fierce pride in North Carolina, where my father's clan settled in the piedmont and mountains and my mother's clan in the east. I wanted to celebrate the state's architectural legacy by writing a book about it, like my mentor Antoinette Downing had done for Rhode Island.

The State Historic Preservation Office was located on the third floor of the State Archives/State Library Building at 109 East Jones Street in Raleigh. I loved the excitement of working in a building full of cultural agencies and the opportunity to do field work. If medals were awarded for the quantity of buildings surveyed, I'd be on the podium. I traveled throughout the state to document landmarks and give talks to county and city historical associations.

Much of my career has been a repeat of Dr. Jordy's brown bag and pencil exercise—wandering along commercial streets and through neighborhoods with a clipboard and a camera, completing an inventory of the historic structures. I consider a comprehensive architectural survey—documentation of the built environment through notes, sketch maps, photography, and interviews with owners and residents—to be the foundation of all architectural history. My thousands of field reports on historic places and objects that reside in the NC State Archives in Raleigh and the Southern Folklife Collection at the UNC Library in Chapel Hill all started with curiosity, a clipboard, and a camera.

One requirement of my job was to take an independent study course, a North Carolina history class, offered at NC State University. I bought a dog-eared copy of the standard history text, Lefler and Newsome's 1954 *North Carolina: The History of a Southern State*, and read it chapter by chapter in my spare time, taking tests mailed to a history professor. Although dated, the reference book guided me for decades as a general framework for the state's history.

North Carolina is my special place in the world, and the five years I worked for the preservation office in the 1970s were the happiest of my life. That was an era of urban renewal, as government and the private sector raced to raze landmarks and bulldoze highways through old neighborhoods and the countryside. I helped fulfill the preservation office's mission to counter this widespread destruction by preserving North Carolina's historic built environment—grand houses, middling houses, worker housing, old churches and graveyards, old mills and factories, farm complexes, historic districts, and historic parks and landscapes.

I felt as if I radiated light and energy in every place in the state that I traveled. I told people that I got paid for doing what I loved the most—saving our legacy—for the princely sum of about $9,000 a year. Several days a week, I checked out a car at the State Motor Pool, stowed my clipboard, survey forms, and Nikon camera with plenty of black-and-white Kodak film, a few boxes of color slide film, and a bag lunch. Hazards of fieldwork included chiggers, ticks, mosquitos, and snakes. At least once, my camera tumbled off the roof of my car as I left a property, but those old metal cameras were tough. The Nikon negatives that I shot during my career preserve thousands of places and moments in time that have disappeared.

My work wardrobe didn't always meet the norms for proper female dress. When I traveled for fieldwork—walking through a historic district to inventory each building or driving through the countryside looking for historic landmarks—I often wore a denim overall dress because I needed a lot of pockets, did not want to carry a purse, and blue jeans hadn't come into style yet for women. I took notes with a pencil, so kept a spare pencil in one pocket. Another pocket held rolls of film, since I often shot eight or ten rolls of black-and-white film, thirty-six frames each, while doing fieldwork. The car key went into a third pocket.

On days when I stayed in the office, I wore skirts and tops rather than pants. The skirts tended to be short, as was the fashion. When I researched in the state archives, a large portrait of longtime archivist Mary Rogers looked disapprovingly down at me from a high spot on the wall. Once I was called into the office of a female administrator and lectured on the inappropriateness of miniskirts.

In the office, I researched and wrote reports on my fieldwork. I picked up many new skills, including learning to read the flowery penmanship of original handwritten wills and deeds from the 1700s and 1800s in bound ledgers or on microfilm in the state archives. If I hit a wall with a research question, such as about some obscure person or event in the past, I would flag down archivist George Stephenson, a human encyclopedia on North Carolina history, and always find an answer.

I spent much of my first year working each week in Caswell County on the first comprehensive county survey conducted by our agency. During the antebellum era, tobacco farmers of Caswell County, on the Virginia border, had developed the famed "Bright Leaf" tobacco that filled their coffers with money to build splendid antebellum farmhouses. Among the state's one hundred counties, Caswell was selected for the first survey because it was the home county of our agency's head administrator, eminent historian Dr. H.G. Jones.

Architectural historian and county native Tony Wrenn and I drove every Caswell County road and documented every pre-1900 building and significant newer structures with floor plans and site plans, written evaluations, and photography. Many of the farmhouses were abandoned. I drove to the county each week and took room and board at Tony's family home, then returned to Raleigh on the weekends. Evenings in Caswell County, I sat in bed with a German language textbook, studying for the Brown University graduate German exam required to receive my master's degree. I graduated in May 1972.

Under Tony's tutelage, my fieldwork skills and understanding of traditional eighteenth- and nineteenth-century North Carolina building practices improved. Tony's habit of stopping at old family graveyards in farm fields sensitized me to the paramount importance of gravestone inscriptions as historical documents identifying the owners of the old buildings we recorded. More importantly, I acquired an understanding of gravestones as evocative sculpture.

Rural North Carolina in the 1970s was an unspoiled network of family farms and crossroads country stores where men sat on the front porch in the summer and indoors around the pot-bellied stove in the winter. We stopped at these stores to pick their brains about the families who had built the farmhouses, and also ate cans of Vienna sausage and packs of Nabs from their shelves for lunch. Sometimes we found a local restaurant serving a meat and two sides in a buffet line. We judged the quality of the food by the number of pickup trucks in the parking lot.

The oldest houses were often log cabins or small frame houses with doors ajar and windows broken. Picking our way through overgrown fields to survey such cabins, we found splendid black snakes sunning themselves along the joints between logs in the cabin's walls. Nearly every inhabited farmhouse had a front porch with a couple of metal chairs waiting for visitors. The chairs' positions signaled whether the residents were at home. When they left, they turned the chairs backwards and leaned them against the floor or wall.

## Dorton Arena

The Dorton Arena rose improbably from vast acres of cleared farmland west of Raleigh that belonged to NC State. Known internationally as the "Raleigh Building," it was famous because its integration of engineering and architecture created one of the largest open interior spaces in the world. The huge structure consists of concrete and steel parabolic arches, like a pair of curved boomerangs intersecting at the ends, that rise ninety feet high in the center and enclose a space three hundred feet long and three hundred feet wide. These are supported by vertical steel wall piers and interlocked by a saddle-shaped roof consisting of steel cables running in opposing directions. This revolutionary engineering creates an expanse of uninterrupted space that holds 5,500 people in raised seating and 4,000 on the central floor, allowing each spectator a view of the central arena.

*When I moved to Raleigh, the monumental Dorton Arena, a modern icon and performance hall at the North Carolina State Fairgrounds, designed by Polish architect Matthew Nowicki, became one of my favorite buildings. Photo taken in 2018.*

*Although completed in 1953 and too new to be historic, I decided it needed listing on the National Register of Historic Places as one of twentieth-century America's seminal architectural and engineering landmarks. Dorton Arena was one of my earliest nominations. Although the National Register's criterion of eligibility required that a structure be at least fifty years old, the agency allowed the not-quite-twenty-year-old building to be listed under a special category of "buildings of extraordinary national architectural significance." Today when I read my listing report in the NC Department of Natural and Cultural Resources website, the author credit line cites the "Survey and Planning Unit Staff," but a note at the end of the bibliography lists me as a "survey specialist" and the author of the nomination.[9]*

## 11
### Activism

The 1970s were my standing-in-front-of-bulldozers years. Because I lived in the old neighborhood of Oakwood (much more on Oakwood later) and worked downtown, I had a proprietary interest in Raleigh's historic landmarks. However, the urban renewal movement of that time meant that federal and state governments and private owners were building new infrastructure on the ruins of Raleigh's vintage landmarks. One that stands out in my mind was the Vass House, a Victorian villa located at the northeast corner of Capitol Square. The imposing wooden house with Queen Anne-style ornament included a corner tower. The state government destroyed this landmark to build a parking lot. The day the wrecking ball beat down the house, its lifelong owner, the widow, Mrs. Vass, died in a nursing home. Her body must have sensed this loss even if her brain, mercifully, never knew.

In spite of all the renewal projects at that time, Raleigh remained small and sleepy. The downtown barely bulged out of its 1792 core of North, East, South, and West Streets. The "inside the beltline" (ITB) phrase, which later became real estate shorthand for a desirable downtown location, had only half of its current meaning because only the north half of the beltline had been built; the south half was completed in the 1980s.

Working in the State Archives/State Library Building at 109 East Jones Street, I often walked the few blocks to Fayetteville Street and all over downtown on my lunch hour. Old houses still stood on main streets, including the Vass House on Capital Square and houses on Moore Square. The Dorothea Dix Hospital for the mentally ill was in full swing. If we thought we were about to experience an emotional breakdown, we'd joke, "I'm going to check myself into Dix Hill." Most of the state's history and arts organizations, such as the State Literary Society and the Preservation Society of North Carolina, held their yearly meetings the same week in September, known as "Culture Week." We teased that there was so little culture it could all be consumed in a week.

Still, the density of cultural institutions within a compact, walkable area of downtown Raleigh thrilled me. North Carolina's State Capitol had become a museum in the 1970s after the splendid, exotic North Carolina State Legislative Building was built on Jones Street. The liveliest scene on Capitol Square was the lawn facing Fayetteville Street, where the "Peanut Man" sold bags of nuts to feed the pigeons. The legislative building, which included hanging roof gardens, was designed by famous Washington, DC, architect Edward Durrell Stone.

The North Carolina Museum of Art, the first state art museum in the country, operated in an old government office building off Capitol Square and was a lunchtime haunt for me. Ben Williams, the museum's first curator, was the husband of my art teacher, Margaret Williams, at St. Mary's College. As a young American artist living in Paris in the 1920s, Ben had studied under French Post-Impressionist painter Henri Matisse. Ben served as curator from 1956 to 1979.

In 1972, the state proposed a new location for the museum on Blue Ridge Road, in the suburbs near the state fairgrounds. I believed this important cultural amenity belonged downtown and was one of a number speaking at a public hearing in favor of keeping the museum downtown. I told the legislators that "it will leave a hole in the cultural complex of the downtown area if the museum is moved to a suburban location. Problems of parking could be solved by an imaginative architect." Unfortunately, we didn't win that battle.

Working in the 1970s for the state preservation agency, whose mission was to save historic landmarks in North Carolina, was heart-wrenching. State government was one of the worst villains, making me feel like Don Quixote tilting at windmills. One of the targets for demolition was Raleigh's "Fifth Avenue" residential section on Blount, Halifax, and North Wilmington Streets, where bankers, railroad barons, and industrialists built their wood and brick mansions in the late 1800s.

Soon after I moved to Raleigh, I became part of a small group of urban activists who brought the dawn of historic preservation to Raleigh in the 1970s. I found various ways to protest the destruction of historic properties. Perhaps most notably, I literally stood in front of the state bulldozers for the Gaston House, an Italianate design on North Wilmington Street by famed Jacob Holt of Warrenton. Since state government had decreed the demolition, my action was strictly symbolic, but I've never regretted it.

In another action, I wrote an "obituary" for a house at No. 9 Blount Street, demolished in October 1973 by the state government. I bought the entrance lights, the hall light, and some of the hardware after demolition, and Oakwood neighbors Bill Makepeace and Bob Hoadley bought the porch balustrade.

One of our drinking buddies at the Players Retreat bar and restaurant on Oberlin Road across from NC State University was Mike Levister, a demolition contractor known as "Mad Mike." One Saturday, we watched him take apart the "Tara"-style front porch of an early 1900s house in Durham. As a tall, fluted wood column toppled, out swarmed a gigantic hive of angry bees. When the dust settled and the bees flew away, we carried the column home to make some very heavy fern stands.

In the fall of 1971, my friends and I were concerned about the plight of the Dodd-Hinsdale House on Hillsborough Street. The 1874 Italianate red brick mansion with its balconied tower gave Raleigh the vintage class of bigger cities like Richmond, Virginia. The city of Raleigh condemned the abandoned house because it attracted vagrants and looters.

We hatched a plan to draw citywide attention to save the house.

I painted "HELP" in large black letters on a bedsheet, and Tom Erwin, Ardath Goldstein, Linda Harris, and Jan Johnson met me the night of January 12, 1972, at the house with an extension ladder. We climbed onto the front porch and hung the bedsheet message from the tower balcony. Jan, a *Raleigh Times* reporter, had a staff photographer ready to get a picture.

The next afternoon, the paper's front page featured the HELP image. *The News & Observer*'s editorial that day, "Distress Signal Meaning Wider," reported that the "North Carolina Historical Preservation Society—two lawyers, two librarians and a state department employee—hoisted the distress signal."

> The appeal really goes much further than just the Dodd-Hinsdale home.... There are plans for the new modern Capital mall to cover the area north of the present legislative building. Although some of the historic sites may be incorporated into the plan, others such as the old Seaboard railroad building are doomed. A few historic homes are already gone, such as the Dortch and Taney homes and most recently the Vass home. A modernistic mall needs the interesting flavor of late 19th century dwellings. A nighttime vigilante group can't raise the money, supply the effort or provide the initiative alone. Preserving history requires community effort in order to prevent destroying the physical structures representing America's relatively short lifetime.

We vigilantes named ourselves "Capital Landmarks Inc." and, led by attorney Bill Joslin, a member of the Hinsdale family, we began negotiating with the family to save the home. Our board of directors eventually grew to fourteen Raleigh citizens interested in preserving local landmarks. While we were working to raise $25,000 to match a federal grant that we had obtained, the Hinsdales sold the house to Charlie Smith, owner of the Angus Barn restaurant, who planned to convert the house to an elegant French restaurant.

"HELP" banner photo by Janet Howard on the front page of the Raleigh Times, January 13, 1972. Jan Johnson wrote the article, "House Gets 'Help' from Its Friends."

This happy ending for the mansion thrilled us. Even though Charlie died of cancer a few years later, his family carried out his project for the Second Empire Restaurant, now one of Raleigh's finest. I wrote the National Register listing report for the house in 1972.

In 1975, the city condemned the landmark Montague Building on the southwest corner of Moore Square as unsafe. The bank that held the Montague Building in trust for the Montague heirs had convinced their clients to tear down the building for a twenty-five-car parking lot. The 1912 three-story brick building at 128 East Hargett Street had declined along with downtown Raleigh in general. This building became another historic rescue for our revolving fund group, Capital Landmarks Inc. The heirs gave us permission to repair the building's problems cited by the city—broken windows and an accumulation of pigeon droppings and broken glass—if the city would work with us. For six weekends, we showed up wearing gauze masks and shoveled debris into black plastic garbage bags. Finally, we hired "Mr. Chimney Sweep" to vacuum out the remaining debris with a huge suction hose.

In the meantime, we agreed to pay rent to the Montague heirs, but of course we were young adults with no money. One of our members, Fred Whitney, who worked in city planning, pulled out his credit card on several occasions to convince officials that we weren't just penniless agitators. We delayed actually paying rent for many months while we befriended the heirs and convinced them that the property had historic and commercial worth and would be a much better investment if they recycled it rather than destroyed it. When the city of Raleigh hosted the Moore Square Festival for the Bicentennial, Capital Landmarks Inc. decided that the Montague Building needed to be dressed for the occasion. We got a bucket of red paint and painted the rusty cast-iron column at the entrance a bright red color. Eventually, the heirs decided the building was worth saving.

Today the Montague Building has many tenants in its cavernous interior spaces. The oldest tenant is Café Luna, a big Italian restaurant on the corner of the main floor, and the front iron column still wears its Bicentennial red paint. The rear elevation, of red brick with an arcade of arched windows and a walkway along the main floor overlooking a sunken plaza, offers a surprising contrast to the main façade facing Hargett Street. As for Capital Landmarks, we had saved another important Raleigh landmark without having to pay a dime in rent.

Capital Landmarks Inc. functioned as a catalyst for the preservation of a number of important downtown Raleigh landmarks. We convinced Raleigh's small historic preservation community that there was work to be done beyond the boundaries of Mordecai Historic Park. We convinced merchants and commercial property owners that many of their downtown holdings had historical significance. After we preserved the Dodd-Hinsdale House and the Montague Building for adaptive reuse, the city of Raleigh Arts Commission purchased the Sanders Ford Dealership for conversion to Artspace, a studio and gallery space for emerging Raleigh artists. The Raleigh Historic Properties Commission was formed to protect historic landmarks through city ordinances. Through boldness and hard work, our "nighttime vigilante group" preserved two pivotal landmarks that continue to enrich Raleigh's business district.

Our nonprofit status made us a handy conduit for government preservation grants. Ardath Goldstein Weaver, one of the original "vigilantes," described us proudly as "young people taking full advantage of the system." The American Revolution Bicentennial Administration granted $25,000 to Capital Landmarks for publication of *The Raleigh Historical Inventory*, Raleigh's first historic architectural survey, written by Linda Harris with assistance by Mary Ann Lee and published in 1978. The Corinthian capital logo of Capital Landmarks, drawn from the state capitol, graces the book's cover. Our nonprofit organization officially disbanded in 1978 because local government agencies began to carry on the work that our group of vigilantes had begun.

## 12
### Marriage and Identity

One year after moving to Raleigh, I became engaged to a graduate student in history, introduced to me by my best friend. My fiancé was working towards an MA in labor history, then switched to law school a year later. We hit it off intellectually and physically; he had the same tall, lean, graceful body and chiseled features of my big-time music crush Mick Jagger, and we traveled around the state to Rolling Stones concerts. I merged into his circle, which included graduates of the School of Design (now College of Design) at NC State.[10] We spent many of our weekends hiking and tent camping in the Appalachian Mountains of North Carolina.

A few months before the wedding, we moved into the Oakwood neighborhood, one of Raleigh's earliest suburbs with the city's largest collection of late nineteenth-century Victorian dwellings. Our tidy one-story, foursquare-plan house on North East Street stood behind the grand Victorian villa where our landlord, Jimmy Stronach, the best landlord in the world, lived. Next door to us, in a shotgun house (a narrow, one-room-wide worker rental house) owned by Jimmy, lived Harvey Bumgardner, an NC State poultry scientist and a lifelong friend of Jimmy's. Rose bushes purchased by Harvey at the Winn-Dixie grocery bloomed profusely in his backyard.

## Stronach Stables

*Jimmy's mother, Pauline, (1887–1986) ruled his household and attributed her ripe old age to eating a country breakfast, a country lunch, and oatmeal for dinner. Jimmy's great-grandfather, stone mason William Stronach, emigrated to Raleigh from Edinborough, Scotland, in the 1830s to supervise the stonework of the state capitol. Jimmy, born in 1928, remembered riding the trolley that wound through Oakwood on metal tracks to the business district. His father would take him to his grandfather Frank Stronach's horse stable on South Wilmington Street, beside Stronach Alley, where old men sat around an iron stove. The cast metal horse head from Stronach Stables still hangs in Jimmy's back hallway.*

My years in Oakwood were the prime of my twenties, when I established my historic preservation career, married, and realized that I wanted both career and motherhood. Born in the first year of the baby boom, I belonged to the new generation of baby boomers who battered down, partly by sheer population density, the conservative, patriarchal world order in which women kept house and raised children. The year 1972 was a banner one for women's freedom. *Our Bodies, Ourselves* was published, and for the first time birth control pills became legally available to unmarried women.

I devoured my copy of *Our Bodies, Ourselves*, the groundbreaking instruction manual on women's bodies and sexuality by the Boston Women's Collective. It explained in clear laywoman's terms all aspects of the female reproductive system, detailed the pros and cons of different forms of birth control, and demystified female orgasm by teaching how to masturbate. For many years, a dog-eared copy occupied my bookcase. That book was an important part of my growing feminist consciousness.

This, unfortunately, was a few years before another groundbreaking book came out, *My Mother/My Self*.[11] During my engagement to be married, Mother staged a series of hostile actions that I could never forgive. She demanded that my fiancé and I stop living together, so he rented an apartment in Boylan Heights, another Victorian neighborhood adjacent to the business district, but that rental was mostly for show. Shortly before our October wedding, while we were at work, Mother redecorated our Oakwood house to suit her notion of social decorum. She brought in bedspreads, hung curtains, and arranged throw rugs. Both of us considered it another example of her intrusive and willful invasion of our space, and although we maintained a fairly cordial relationship, we hardened our hearts against her.

As our wedding date approached, my ambivalence about marriage was so agonizing that I had a panic attack the day before the wedding. My dear brother obligingly drove around with me as I weighed the pros and cons. My fears centered on losing myself. I didn't want the role of wife, and potentially mother, to blot out my identity as a professional historian and preservationist, an artist, and a woman free to travel and have many different experiences. I believed that marriage was a bad bargain for a woman, but I decided that my life needed to move forward, and marriage was the next logical step. Ultimately, the only protest I managed against losing my identity in marriage was to hyphenate my husband's name with mine as "Little-Stokes." Not only did I not want to lose my maiden name; as a historian I wanted my work to remain accessible to researchers in the future. This was a rebellious act in the 1970s, when women were expected to take their husband's name without question.

Shortly before the wedding, I wrote Pierre, my first love, a letter of closure. I told him I'd been afraid since 1968 that I wouldn't be able to replace his love, but I'd finally found another love with a graduate student in French history, specializing in the nineteenth-century origins of French labor unions. "Perhaps we will visit the Lyon archives in 1973. Promise me you will remember our promise to 'rester toujours des bons amis.' Toujours, Ruth."

In spite of this connection to the past that remained strong, I looked ahead. Our 1972 wedding was a social event involving three Raleigh landmarks. I bought a wedding dress, a tea-colored satin with lace sleeves, on sale on the third floor women's ready-to-wear department of Hudson Belk department store on Fayetteville Street. We said our vows in St. Mary's College Chapel, a mid-1800s wooden Gothic Revival chapel by English architect Richard Upjohn. We held the reception and danced to a string ensemble in the Sir Walter Raleigh Hotel's ballroom. We had so much fun that our wedding license disappeared among the plates down the dumbwaiter to the basement kitchen. We spent our honeymoon night in the Velvet Cloak Inn[12] on Hillsborough Street, a faux New Orleans-style hotel with ornate iron balconies. Unlocking the door to our room, we discovered our best man and best woman lying in our bed, waiting for us with bottles of champagne.

Pierre's letters continued to arrive even after I married in October 1972. He sent me an invitation just before his December 1972 wedding, along with a touching letter from a man about to be married. He wrote that he had thought often of me during the past years. He was sad that I never answered his last letter and thought I was irredeemably angry at him. He continued to profess his love and invite me to come see him and his wife. He wrote that I would always be one of his most special memories. He would save my photos and look at them and remember me when he was an old man. "But before that happens there will be much work, sickness, and people to cure and a whole life to build."

∽

While adjusting to life as a newlywed, I was also immersed in my work. One of my key projects was very close to home: I wanted to preserve Oakwood. Oakwood was the frontier, the place I needed to be and the place I needed to save. At the time, there was a proposal to build a north-south expressway that would have destroyed the entire block between North East and North Bloodworth Streets—a traffic river cutting the 'hood in half.

My goal was to get Oakwood designated as a historic district on the National Register, but the hurdles were daunting. The requirements included compiling a history of the neighborhood, investigation of each house, photos, interviews, and determination of the historic boundaries. In addition, I needed to be able to document the dates when Oakwood's nineteenth-century homes were built—not an easy task. As an employee of the State Historic Preservation Office, I did the fieldwork and wrote the district listing report to protect the neighborhood from adverse effects from federally funded projects such as highways.

Part of the documentation for Oakwood's history came from an unexpected source. I talked Jimmy Briggs into letting me go through the Briggs Hardware account books from the 1850s to the 1880s. I was interested because Jimmy's grandfather, Thomas Briggs, built the hardware store on Fayetteville Street in 1874 and also operated a contracting company and a sash and blind factory in Raleigh after the Civil War. Briggs built many of the Victorian houses in the Oakwood suburb. One of my fondest memories is convincing Jimmy to donate the hardware account books to the state archives—now anyone can access them at 109 East Jones Street.

The value of the account books became very clear to me after I examined them. The books were stored in the high-ceilinged second floor, a single room extending from Fayetteville Street back to Salisbury Street. Broken windowpanes and dust and pigeon droppings littered the upper floors. Reading the account books from 1847 to the 1880s enabled me to find construction dates for the houses in the Oakwood Historic District. For example, the 1851 account book shows Briggs's payment for constructing the Thompson-Allen House, a two-story front-gabled frame at 516 East Jones Street. The house was enlarged and brick-veneered in the early 1900s.

The Briggs Hardware connection to Oakwood continued even in the 1970s. In those days, the main street level of the store was lined with shelves and bins holding all sorts of tools and supplies. At the back, a central staircase led a half-level down to the hardware department. If you restored a house in Oakwood and were missing a doorknob or hinges, you could find exact replacements there because Briggs still carried the same style hardware.

In retrospect, I realize my motivations on the Oakwood project ran deep. This was a time when I was trying to preserve my own individual identity, so preserving the character of this neighborhood struck a chord. Perhaps even more compelling, my intense focus on my work fed a need to separate from Mother. She rescued old things but never fixed them up. By rescuing Oakwood and many other properties and neighborhoods, I was completing her work on a larger scale and paving the way for long-term preservation.

In 1974, when Raleigh eliminated the proposed north-south expressway through the center of the neighborhood from its transportation plan, we knew that Oakwood was safe. Years later, construction of Raleigh Boulevard east of St. Augustine's College helped solved the expressway need. I adapted my historic district research as the first walking tour to celebrate the neighborhood's rescue from a catastrophic highway. A graphic designer neighbor on Bloodworth Street created the attractive brochure with decorative Victorian clip art.

One day in 1975, Jimmy Briggs and I stood in front of his venerable Briggs Hardware. The original granite carriage stone still stood at the curb in front of the store, a remnant of the days before the street was paved. Jimmy swept his arms out to encompass the whole street and said, "Fayetteville Street is going to disappear because they're going to build a mall." Jimmy was correct. The Fayetteville Street pedestrian mall built in the late 1970s, an attempt to make downtown's retail corridor as attractive as suburban shopping centers such as Cameron Village and Crabtree Valley Mall, had the opposite effect. The lack of parking along the street nearly killed commercial activity. In 2006 Fayetteville Street was restored to a drivable corridor that has exploded since then with energy and activity.

Ultimately, my role in the rescue of Oakwood was the creation of the Oakwood National Register Historic District in 1972–1973, the first historic district in Raleigh and one of the first in North Carolina. Oakwood's survival as one of the largest neighborhoods in North Carolina of late 1800s Victorian houses demonstrates how well the state and city's preservation programs have worked. Today, I still have many friends in Oakwood, and this community will always hold a special place in my heart.

## 13
### State Work in the '70s

Oakwood was just one of many projects I worked on in the early 1970s. My five years in the State Historic Preservation Office in Raleigh set the foundation for a lifelong career to preserve the antiquities of my beloved state and enough passions to last a lifetime. Survey fieldwork, historical research, oral history, report writing, teaching groups of students the fundamentals of fieldwork, lectures to county historical societies, and writing the first architectural history of a city published by the preservation office were as exciting as any university teaching position would have offered.

Each "survey specialist" had an assigned chunk of the state. By virtue of growing up in Fayetteville, I had the Sandhills region, a sandy-soil monoculture of vast longleaf pine plantations until it was deforested by lumber companies from 1870 to 1940. Longleaf pines grow slowly and produce tar and turpentine—the "naval stores" used to caulk and waterproof sailing ships. The tall, strong tree trunks were fashioned into ship masts. We nicknamed the Sandhills region the "soft underbelly" because it occupies North Carolina's southeast corner, a section of the coastal plain stretching from my hometown to the coast.

In spite of having an assigned territory, I also worked with buildings and districts throughout the state to document landmarks, place them on the National Register, and work with local advocates to preserve them. Although I had given up my dream of an art career, I often used my drawing skill during fieldwork by sketching architectural features of buildings in my field notes. Some of my most meaningful projects during North Carolina's "dawn of historic preservation" appear throughout the remainder of this chapter.

## Fayetteville

In my hometown of Fayetteville, I had the opportunity to draw attention to the oldest downtown commercial block by listing it on the National Register in 1973. Fourteen two-story brick row stores with shared walls occupied the 100 block of Person Street at the corner of Market Square. Most nineteenth-century commercial construction was constructed of abutting buildings, the walls so close together they were called "party walls." Just four years earlier, I had embraced historic preservation while doing homework in downtown Providence, Rhode Island, so commercial buildings are a special passion.

Fayetteville's Market House, an 1830s English-style city hall set above an arcaded (arched-wall) market, stands at city center, with the four main streets extending outward. I gave the block a unique identity by naming it "Liberty Row," because the triangular point of the block is a cherished landmark known as Liberty Point, where patriots signed the "Liberty Point Resolves" supporting the

*Store on Liberty Row, 100 block of Person Street, Fayetteville, with restored tunnel to Bow Street, 1973.*

American Revolution in 1775. Liberty Row is one of the most cohesive nineteenth-century commercial rows in North Carolina. I determined that the store adjacent to the point, the oldest commercial building in the city, predates 1842. From an 1825 map, I discovered a long-lost street-level tunnel through the center of the row to Bow Street in the rear. The tunnel had been filled in by a later store, but Fayetteville decided to open it back up as a result of my discovery.

### Grove Park Inn

In 1972, I visited the famed Grove Park Inn resort hotel in Asheville in order to list it on the National Register. Completed in 1913, the six-story hotel, constructed out of granite from Sunset Mountain where it was built, overlooks the valley of Asheville. Millionaire E. W. Grove of Tennessee, maker of such drugs as Bromo Quinine, a cold tablet, entrusted his son-in-law, an amateur architect, as designer and contractor. Massive granite boulders laid with concealed mortar form the walls and surrounding terraces. The deep-hipped clay tile roof has undulating eaves and eyelid dormer windows. The grandeur of scale and rustic simplicity of materials repeats the contours of the Blue Ridge Mountains where the hotel nestles. Original Arts and Crafts-style furnishings crafted by Roycrofters of New York and White Furniture Company of Mebane, North Carolina, are still in use.

The hotel management gave me freedom to explore every nook and cranny to collect information for the nomination, including the cavernous basement kitchen. Soon after its listing in 1972, the Grove Park Inn's owners proudly included "listed in the National Register of Historic Places" in its advertising. The four-star hotel is a premier destination in Asheville. I took great pride in recognizing the landmark's significance through this listing, although only I know that I wrote it, since the nomination form identifies the author as "Staff."

## Pinehurst

The golf resort village of Pinehurst, in the Sandhills of Moore County, was designed as a health resort by landscape architect Frederick Law Olmstead in 1895 for soda fountain magnate James Walker Tufts. It became one of the earliest golf resorts in the United States when Scottish course designer Donald Ross designed courses there a few years later, and its courses are now among the most prestigious in the country.

Pinehurst cried out for documentation and preservation, so I wrote the Pinehurst Historic District report in 1973. In my architectural essay, I noted that the light, durable weatherboard and shingled construction of the early houses and hotels reflected the seasonal quality of a resort. Tufts's grandson James Tufts talked with me for hours. He revealed that the family had managed the village for three-fourths of a century and then sold it to the Diamondhead Corporation of New Jersey.

On the ground outside the old Tufts family office, I found a tall mound of account ledgers and files and realized that the Tufts family records were headed to the landfill. I immediately went to the Pinehurst Library to tell the librarian to send a truck to rescue the documents. They were able to retrieve them and preserve them as the Tufts Archives in a new wing of the village library. At that time, Diamondhead was in the process of an ill-advised modernization of the village and golf courses that bankrupted the village by the 1980s. The family documents were worth saving because the ledgers, letters, blueprints, and drawings reveal the creation of the resort of Pinehurst and its pioneering golf courses that transformed the economy of this region of North Carolina during the twentieth century.

## Elizabeth City

One of my last projects before moving to Charlotte in 1976 was the Elizabeth City Historic District, perhaps the favorite of my early career. The thirty-block district included a dense commercial district with the largest concentration of antebellum shops in the state, along with houses built throughout the 1800s. I was amazed at the Pendleton building, a stylish antebellum brick store; the 1897 vaudeville theater on the third floor of the Lowrey Building; and the unusual Virginia Dare Hotel and Arcade of 1927, with a nine-story hotel and flanking commercial arcades.

My muse and guide, local historian Fred Fearing, met me for coffee or lunch each time I visited the city. Fred told fascinating stories and often mentioned his "spiritual advisor." I never met this friend of his but wondered where I could find one of those for myself. I stayed at the "Vicki Villa," a pink 1960s motel where all the historians, archaeologists, and restorationists who worked for the State Preservation Office stayed while working in northeast North Carolina. One night, I ate at a nearby oyster bar and had no cash, so I washed dishes to pay for my oysters. I'd wash dishes anytime to eat oysters!

## Greensboro

As my swan song before moving to Charlotte with my husband, I directed a team of architectural historians in a survey of 172 historic buildings in Greensboro, a bustling commercial city in the late 1800s and early 1900s. I assembled our fieldwork and photographs, researched and wrote an essay, edited the manuscript, and supervised the publication of *An Inventory of Historic Architecture, Greensboro, NC*. Our inventory pre-dated the destruction of much of the city's historic urban civic, commercial, and industrial buildings, so we at least documented them even if we could not save them.

This first inventory of historic buildings published by the State Preservation Office was produced in-house in 1976. It was typeset in the basement and printed and bound with a spiral binding. The cover featured one of my favorite Greensboro buildings—the Jones Brothers Bakery on East Lee Street. The now-demolished bakery featured a striking 1920s Art Deco façade of black and white glass in chevron and sunburst patterns.

My first experience shepherding a manuscript through publication turned into a nightmare. The typesetters made so many errors that proofreading the "blue line," the typesetter's proof, took almost as much time as I spent writing the original manuscript.

### Bladen County

In 1974, my preservation office colleague Michael Southern and I surveyed the entirety of Bladen County, on the Cape Fear River north of Wilmington. This was one of the first thorough investigations of my "soft underbelly counties" of southeastern North Carolina. Several days a week we drove around the county on every paved road and navigated down dirt lanes to identify the oldest houses. As we walked through overgrown paths to reach abandoned houses, what we mostly found were ticks. We were never afraid to knock on a door and introduce ourselves to the inhabitant, then ask if he or she knew the history of the building. Once we encountered an elderly man who was separating locally grown rice from its husks with a pestle in a large wooden mortar. We returned another day to tape an interview with him about the county's long-gone longleaf pine forest economy. He remembered the naval stores era when workers tapped pine trees to extract "naval stores"— tar, pitch, turpentine, and rosin materials used to maintain wooden sailing ships. In his Bladen dialect, he pronounced the elm tree as an "ellem" tree. Only a thin remnant of those ancient noble longleaf pines remain.

## Lane House—First Encounter

There are two key events that happened during this period that I'll always remember. One involved a house and the other a headstone.

Preservation work for the State Historic Preservation Office took me to old farms, schools, industrial buildings, and mills in the countryside. Through my work, I became acquainted with local antiquarian Richard Parsons. Richard lived like a nineteenth-century Raleigh gentleman in an elegant two-story frame townhouse built in 1798, where his children Theo and Julia Bynum grew up robustly healthy with heat from the numerous fireplaces. One weekend in the early 1970s, Richard drove me to the second oldest house in Wake County, out in the country southwest of Raleigh on Jones Franklin Road.

How could I have known what a fateful tour this would be? As we walked to a derelict wood farmhouse, Richard pointed to a short brick stack jutting from the roof peak on the right side. "See that date-brick? It says 1775! This was the plantation house of Joseph Lane, whose brother Joel's land became Raleigh." The house's extreme age was thrilling, but what captivated me most was the porch. Set beneath a swooping angle of the steep roof, it had heavy chamfered posts with some traces of barn red paint and several scalloped boards, like a ruffled awning, edging the cornice.

"Let's go inside," Richard said, "but I'm warning you, most of the woodwork is gone. The best mantel is in one of the owner's friend's houses, and the wainscots and most of the doors are missing."

We entered the main room, and out of the dusty gloom loomed an enormous fireplace, almost big enough to walk into. In the corner beside the fireplace, two steps led to a door to an enclosed stair.

"Look inside here," said Richard, opening another door beneath the stair.

In the side of the brick chimney was an arched warming oven, just big enough for a loaf of bread. I felt like I was in New England or Colonial Williamsburg. I'd never seen a warming oven in a

North Carolina house, although perhaps they can be found in one of Old Salem's eighteenth-century Moravian houses.

Richard explained that the room we stood in was in fact the original main room of Joseph Lane's house. Along with the chimney dated 1775 and three small shed rooms at the rear, this was the whole house. We gazed up twelve feet to the ceiling, formed by exposed joists with handsomely beaded edges. Around the fireplace a raised panel wall rose up to the ceiling. We walked through the back door of the main room into the rear shed. In the corner a petite fireplace was recessed into the side of the main chimney. Then we moved back into the main room and climbed the winding stair beside the chimney to the attic. The stair treads were so small I had to turn my feet sideways. At the top was one long room where we could stand up to full height only in the center. The Lane House felt like a dusty treasure box that had been looted, but its sturdy mortise-and-tenon framework and its floors and walls and ceilings seemed as good as new to me. As we went back downstairs, my heart opened to this house.

Another serendipitous experience that reverberated over many years involved a grave marker. During a field trip in 1974 to an antebellum farmhouse near the Cape Fear River in Buies Creek, Harnett County, I found a tiny headstone in the family graveyard, an encounter that would exert an unimaginable force in my future. It was crudely cut out of thick reddish-brown sandstone in the abstract shape of a human figure, with a large nose and lips, small eyes, and a large heart. I couldn't read the inscription, but the lettering indicated an eighteenth- or early nineteenth-century date. Harnett County, in the inland coastal plain of North Carolina, was settled in the eighteenth century by Highland Scots immigrants. Because of my familiarity with Scottish gravestones, I recognized that the little grave monument was a rare, early Highland Scots artifact. The gravestone would become a rosetta stone for me.

But at the time I was focused on photographing the farmhouse and didn't take a photo of the gravestone. After several weeks of being haunted by the evocative object, I returned to photograph it and discovered it was gone. Someone had removed it, whether to save or destroy it I never learned. It probably disappeared into a private collection. Old gravemarkers were perishable, and I vowed that sometime in the future I would conduct a survey of early graveyards in the state and compile a photographic archive for posterity.

## 14
### First House

I fell in love with the Lane House, which would be a future project, but my first house restoration started in 1973. With the help of my parents, my husband and I bought the Lucy Wynne House in Oakwood, 404 Elm Street. The transaction with the owner, Gavin Dortch, was a classic old-school, front yard negotiation and handshake. Mother prided herself on her bargaining power, and it came in handy. Gavin asked for $10,000, Mother offered him $5,000 cash, and he countered with, "It's yours for $7,500."

I felt a combination of elation and dread. Mother loved being involved in my life in Raleigh, but we had a complicated dynamic in my adult years. Often she assumed that her financial help earned her the right to intrude into my personal life. With the purchase of this house, I knew I would have to be vigilant and maintain my boundaries. My husband and I repaid her loan with interest when we resold our house a few years later.

The Lucy Wynne House is one in a block of houses known as Pullen Town, sturdy six- to ten-room brick houses with Victorian porches built in the 1880s by Richard S. Pullen. A lifelong bachelor, Pullen built these houses for his nieces: #404 for Lucy Wynne, #408 for Annie Wynne, a third for another niece, and others for rental income. The Wynne houses mirrored the declining fortune of the Oakwood neighborhood from single-family, middle-class homes in the late 1800s into apartment buildings in the mid-1900s.

Lucy Wynne died in 1907, followed by her husband W. W. in 1913. The Byrum family purchased the house in 1920, keeping

*Lucy Wynne House, 404 Elm Street, Raleigh, 1974.*

the original gas jet lights, but replacing the Victorian posts of the wraparound porch with classical fluted wood columns. The raised basement contained the original kitchen and dining room and an early bathroom; the main floor, parlors and a dining room; and upstairs, four bedrooms. In the early 1940s, Mrs. Byrum moved the kitchen from the basement to the first floor back room, but she got her water from the adjacent back porch bathroom. Like many other neighborhoods ringing the business district, Oakwood experienced white flight after World War II, and houses were broken up into apartments. After Mrs. Byrum's death in the late 1940s, her sons converted the house to four apartments. The next owners, the Lumpkins, purchased it in 1956 as an apartment house, and Gavin and Mabel Dortch acquired it in 1959 as a quadruplex.

When my husband and I set up housekeeping, we combined the two south apartments overlooking Oakwood Avenue as our space and rented out the two north apartments. By that time, the original stuccoed brick walls, with brick red paint scored to imitate brickwork, had been painted white. Oakwood had become a rough neighborhood. A fight in one of the upstairs apartments caused the plaster ceiling downstairs to collapse just before we bought the place. We found a trail of empty Richards Wild Irish Rose bottles tucked by the previous tenant into hiding places throughout the basement.

Of course, the house became a project. Once again, I picked up where Mother left off—instead of just acquiring old houses, I restored them. For two years, my husband and I worked every evening and weekend to restore our Wynne house. He built new screens for the forty wooden sash windows. We cleaned the nearly century-old house with heavy cleaners and breathed a lot of dust and toxic fumes. I cleaned out the ashes and soot from all nine fireplaces and used a caustic acid cleaner to strip the interior basement brick walls when we converted it into our bedroom. We remodeled the four kitchens and four bathrooms located in the enclosed rear two-story porches. We stripped layers of paint off the simple pine mantels with paint remover to reveal their original patina.

Behind the house in the deep loamy soil of the former trash heap, I planted a big garden, inspired by the fertile garden full of vegetables, herbs, and flowers next door at 408 Elm Street, where dear friends Ames Christopher and Bill Caligari lived. My cat Felix rolled on her back in delirious joy in their catnip patch. As I turned the soil to plant carrots and asparagus, intact late-1800s patent medicine bottles emerged to remind me of old times.

Our final touch, painting the wooden double front door a bright cheerful red, was inspired by the welcoming front doors of Episcopal churches. The doors nearly gave our neighbor Vallie Henderson, who lived diagonally across the intersection, a heart attack. Vallie was a formidable garden club matron whose mission was to beautify Raleigh. Some call her Oakwood's founding mother for her attention to the landscape, especially flower gardens, and general appearance. She would practically measure my grass with a ruler to make sure it was mowed properly. It was she who convinced the city to paint the trash trucks pink. She and her husband Archie had fretted over our house as an eyesore for decades. In the 1940s, they petitioned the city to have the old white picket fence torn down. Now the impertinent young couple that bought it had painted their front door fire engine red. Oakwood was changing, but not in the way Vallie had hoped.

We rented to young professionals who made great neighbors, and our lives were full of people and activities. Gary, a professor at NC State's School of Design, fabricated an impressive hanging pot rack in his kitchen. Ellen shared her delicious homemade braided challah bread with us. The "Oakwood Athletic Club" acted as social glue for neighborhood camaraderie. The group held monthly potluck dinners where the athletic part was exercising your elbow when you drank your beer. One night after a dinner at 404 Elm, six of us decided to go "streaking" through Oakwood. We stripped, then ran around the block barefooted and bare-assed in the dark, laughing. I hope Vallie Henderson was asleep! No one reported seeing us, and we saw no one. It felt risqué, but the only harm done was to our feet, bloodied by pebbles and sticks on the pavement.

My husband certainly earned his share of sweat equity during our long effort to rehab the house. The biggest struggle in our marriage was sharing the day-to-day housework. Our deal that I cooked dinner and he washed dishes did not work. Often when I went into the kitchen at the end of my work day to get dinner started, our old-fashioned sink was piled high with dishes. We had no dishwasher and little counter space. I not only put him through school, I had to nag as if I was his mother. He spent much of his home time either out playing his favorite sport of basketball or binge-watching basketball games on TV with his best friend Ivan, who published a handbook on Atlantic Coast Conference basketball. Ivan crashed on our sofa when he visited Raleigh. Sometimes, when I left the house at night or on the weekend for a meeting or event, the two of them hardly saw me leave.

I had been working to save Oakwood during this time, but my young rebellious self chafed under some of the onerous neighborhood traditions designed to make the neighborhood special. At

Christmas, each household had to put an electric candle in every window, and our new house had forty of them! I bought the lights and attempted to plug all of them in, but each room had only one electric outlet, so I bought dozens of extension cords to connect the lights to the single outlet.

Gay men, the advance preservation guard, first recognized Oakwood's potential and became the most important force in the neighborhood's renaissance. A number of gay men bought Oakwood Victorians, often run-down rentals, and beautifully restored them as owner-occupied residences, with new bright colors of paint to replace the monotone white that had become the norm in the early twentieth century. Carriage lamps became the rage—the bigger the better—flanking the front door. The gleaming brass lamps evoked an imagined Victorian past, probably inspired by Charleston or Savannah. The rehabilitations generally followed good preservation practice: repair rather than replace.

At the corner of the Oakwood Historic District, at Oakwood Avenue and North Person Street, the Carey Hunter House was an Oakwood gem of Queen Anne-Colonial Revival style, with splendid Tiffany-style stained glass, a wraparound porch, and a turret. The new owners, a male couple, decided it needed even more style and added a pair of circular rose windows, a balcony, and large out-of-scale brackets salvaged from older Victorian houses demolished by state government. Some wag christened the new look "Homo-Baroque." I wrote a letter to the *News & Observer* decrying these alterations because they detracted from the house's original character and set a bad precedent for Oakwood restoration. The neighborhood became divided between a faction supporting accurate restorations and one that wanted freedom to be able to alter the houses anyway they wanted.

Today, Oakwood has mellowed into a neighborhood that no longer frets unduly about its continued survival as one of the largest collections of nineteenth-century houses in North Carolina. After I moved to Charlotte in 1976, Oakwood became a local historic district with an architectural review board that policed exterior alterations to ensure that houses retained their original character. But there has always been tension between the strict preservationists of Oakwood's architectural character and those who desired more relaxed rules about house rehabilitation.[13]

In 1973, I grew restless working for state government and neglecting my art, and resented paying the bills to put my husband through law school. I spent a year working half-time while I took art and education classes at Meredith College in Raleigh and earned an art teaching certificate. My husband obtained a loan to pay for his remaining law courses.

The right half of my brain reawakened in drawing, photography, and printmaking classes. I made charcoal studies of old leather boots, a frayed shirt, still lifes of baskets and folded towels. I made pencil sketches of Victorian houses and my beloved violin. I inked a still life of a bunch of celery. I painted watercolors of potted plants and boys at a baseball game. In printmaking class, I created etchings of the vendors at City Market at Moore Square in downtown Raleigh and surreal forest trees and roadside grasses. In photography, I learned darkroom techniques and set up a home darkroom.

The final stage of certification, student teaching at Broughton High School under veteran teacher and artist Alice Ehrlich, provided a sobering lesson on what to expect as a high school art teacher. I earned the certificate but realized that high school art classes were a dumping ground for troubled students. Mrs. Ehrlich spent most of her time disciplining sullen teenagers, marking time until age sixteen when they could drop out of school. Retooling my art skills had been a valuable endeavor, but I was happy to return to my historic preservation career for state government on a full-time basis.

By then, I was in my late twenties, and the twin goals of motherhood and a doctorate degree remained distant. I first heard my biological clock ticking around 1974 as I continued to establish myself as an architectural historian in state government and supported my husband's education. When I brought up the topic of parenting a child, my husband wasn't interested. By that point our marriage already was strained because I was the working spouse. We had an understanding that it was my turn to go back to school for my doctorate when he received his law degree. As his graduation from law school in 1976 approached, our Oakwood years were drawing to a close, and my choice of how to achieve an academic career and motherhood loomed.

### The North Carolina Porch

*Before I moved to Charlotte, one of my final projects was writing an article, "The North Carolina Porch: A Climatic and Cultural Buffer" for* Carolina Dwelling, *the 1978 yearbook of the NC State University School of Design. A group of staffers in the State Historic Preservation Office wrote most of the articles—Michael Southern, Catherine Bishir, Brent Glass, McKelden Smith, Davyd Foard Hood, and me. Design student Doug Swaim edited the book. My article was a manifesto that the porch originated in the eighteenth century as an architectural expression of the South's climate and culture. My source material was my fieldwork in the "soft underbelly" region of southeastern North Carolina, where I gained a lifelong passion for porches. A review in the* Pioneer America Journal *in 1980 called my article a unique essay that introduced the porch as a topic that cries for further scholarly treatment.*

On July 4, 1976, we hosted our last soiree before leaving Raleigh, a Bicentennial ball with guests in costume. The party took place in our living room. Our two sets of French doors overlooked the wraparound porch, high on the corner of Oakwood Avenue, and created an elegant space for entertaining. It was great fun to see the guests in their various costumes, and I had a wonderful time sipping wine and laughing through the evening. My life had reached a peak of involvement in Raleigh's urban culture, but I had a premonition of loneliness to come. I knew I would miss Oakwood and was about to leave my friends and causes behind to follow my husband to Charlotte, where he had roots and a new job. I had nothing waiting for me.

# 15
## Charlotte

In 1976, my husband and I sold our Oakwood house and moved to Charlotte, where he joined a law practice and disappeared into his law career and the basketball passion he shared with his best friend. My turn to go back to school was thrown under the bus. We had grown into people who had nothing in common, especially with regard to having children, and within a year we divorced. Finishing law school also ended the marriages of most of our close circle of law students and their working wives. Perhaps, like me, they had waited their turn for completing their education and discovered they had been deceived.

That same year I received my last letter from Pierre, who was writing from Kinshasa, Zaire, where he was a "flying surgeon" for a one-month assignment. He lived in Nancy, France, with Genevieve and their baby girl Frederique. He was thinking of me and how wonderful it would have been if we had stayed together, and then said "enfin la vie passe" (finally life passes).

> *You must be happy, you must have children because they change how you see and understand your life. I need to be sure that we see each other again, if you are in Europe you must let me know. If I am in the US I will let you know so that we can see each other. I keep the period when we were together as an extraordinary souvenir, one of the most beautiful of my life, always imprinted with a certain nostalgia. Often I think that we would have been very happy together and that we would have made a life. You would be afraid to know how my heart beat when I received your*

*last letter telling me about your upcoming marriage. "La vie est parfois mal faite." [Life is sometimes poorly made.]*

*It is your spontaneity and dynamism that is most seductive. You must have kept it and your husband must be very happy. I sometimes am jealous. I'm going to study psychiatry in a few years because now I must move every few years as a flying surgeon. As a psychiatrist I'll have a stable home life and Genevieve can practice as a gynecologist. Don't wait three years to reply—write me every three to six months.*

In 1977, I wrote Pierre to tell him I would be in Italy, leading a group of students on an art history tour, and would like to see him. I don't believe he ever answered, but maybe he never got the letter.

In the meantime, I found my niche and a close circle of friends in Charlotte. I taught art history and art appreciation at Central Piedmont Community College (CPCC), a vibrant institution in downtown Charlotte. The slogan "Learn more, earn more" on CPCC's bumper stickers crystallized the school's mission. While teaching, I also consulted on historic preservation projects in Charlotte to slow down the development boom that threatened historic neighborhoods. Dan Morrill, a history professor at the University of North Carolina at Charlotte, collaborated with me.

In the fall of 1976, I bought a run-down Queen Anne bungalow built by the McCoy family in 1908 on East Kingston Avenue in the Dilworth suburb of Charlotte. I moved in and set to work restoring it. The beautiful house's main asset was a large porch perfect for entertaining artist friends from CPCC. We set up a slide projector and screen for art critiques on the porch. I prepared a National Register listing report for the Dilworth neighborhood, Charlotte's first streetcar suburb, and succeeded in having it listed as a historic district.

My biggest consulting project in Charlotte was the survey of Iredell County, an eight-month job requiring several days of fieldwork each week from 1976 to 1977. Young historian Gary Freeze, a native of the county, assisted me. We learned that German and Scots-Irish immigrants from Pennsylvania moved down the "Great Wagon Road" from Pennsylvania to settle the county in the second half of the eighteenth century. Most surviving houses dated from the first half of the nineteenth century. The untouched treasury of intact back-country farmhouses included log, frame, and brick houses of unusual homogeneity—a rectangular form divided into a large room and two smaller half-sized rooms, with stone and brick chimneys at the ends. The farms often retained huge livestock barns, smokehouses and tobacco barns as well as a few detached kitchens.

Many were abandoned and in ruins, and Gary and I simply walked inside to make notes and take photographs. We found a few log cabins with massive weaving looms in their lofts. These were obviously assembled piece by piece in the loft, as they were too large to fit through the cabin door or up the winding corner stair to the loft. Finding looms in attics reminded me of Sleeping Beauty, the fairy tale princess who pricked her finger on a spindle and fell into a deep sleep waiting for Prince Charming. In some versions, shrubbery grew up to conceal the castle where she slept—much like some of the overgrown properties we visited.

Some hair-raising adventures happened during our joyful discovery of these remarkable abandoned properties. One fall afternoon, Gary and I were surveying an unoccupied large wooden grist mill with a water wheel, built over a creek in the sparsely populated northwest Brushy Mountains of Iredell County. As we walked inside the abandoned old mill, taking photos, we heard a hoarse voice shouting. When we went outside, we saw an old woman in front of a cabin on a knoll above the mill. Her slight frame was clothed in a long cotton dress, and a bonnet shaded her wrinkled face. She pointed a shotgun at us and yelled, "Drop everything and put up your hands!"

I dropped my clipboard and Gary dropped his camera. With hands held high, I started talking loudly. "We're doing a historic building survey of the whole county! We're sorry we scared you! We will get out of here and leave you alone."

*Feimster House, Iredell County, 1979. Photo by Gary Freeze, courtesy of the North Carolina State Historic Preservation Office.*

She kept the gun trained on us as we ran to the car and drove off. Later, county folks told us that we had been on the wrong end of the gun of Granny Shook, whose relatives were in federal prison for selling moonshine. Heck, Granny probably operated a whisky still herself. Granny saw our vehicle, a North Carolina government-issued Buick with an official state license plate, and figured we had come to bust her. Nobody said that trespassing on private land in remote rural areas of North Carolina didn't have its dangers.

The final product for the Iredell County survey was a book that I wrote carefully, including our best photographs. Unfortunately, as with the Greensboro book, *An Inventory of Historic Architecture, Iredell County, North Carolina*, was printed cheaply in 1978, with underexposed black-and-white photographs in spiral-bound report format, by the North Carolina Department of Cultural Resources. These early county survey publications didn't receive the hardcover bindings and high-quality paper treatment of later county surveys, which was disappointing after all the hard work involved.

While living in Charlotte, I wrote the first county architecture catalogue published by the North Carolina Department of Cultural Resources. *An Inventory of Historic Architecture, Caswell County, North Carolina: The Built Environment of a Burley and Bright-leaf Tobacco*

*Economy* contains the inventory data collected by Tony Wrenn and me in 1972. The beautiful hardcover book, published in 1979, was the first of my three early North Carolina guidebooks with a budget sufficient to create a work of art. The brown binding evokes the county's defining tobacco crop, the dust jacket is visually striking, and each chapter has an introductory full-page photo by Tony Wrenn.

This book was an example of a new genre documenting vernacular architecture across the country in the 1970s preservation movement. The vernacular is the language spoken by ordinary people in a particular region; vernacular design refers to the buildings erected by those people. In a 1980 review in the *Journal of the Society of Architectural Historians*, Professor Dell Upton, a pioneering architectural historian, describes my analysis of the vernacular design process in the county as one of the most successful yet attempted in the genre.

Now it was my turn to go back to school, but as fate would have it, not the one of my choosing. One Sunday in mid-November 1977, I spent the afternoon in the library of UNC-Charlotte researching graduate schools with top-quality architecture history programs. The nearest programs where I could major in architectural history were far away, perhaps the University of Delaware, University of Pennsylvania, or my alma mater Brown University.

I returned home, preoccupied with my dilemma about schools. When I opened my front door and walked in, the phone was ringing in my bedroom. I picked it up absently, but came to full attention when I heard the voice of my estranged husband on the other end. When my brother could not reach me by telephone, he had called my ex to convey urgent news. My beloved dad had dropped dead of a heart attack on the Highland Country Club golf course in Fayetteville that afternoon. He was sixty-three years old.

I felt my entire body convulse as if the floor had fallen beneath my feet. I thought of my last visit with my father a few weeks earlier. He and Mother spent the night with me to see my new old house for the first time. As they left, he hugged me and handed me a fifty-dollar bill, a lot of money at that time. I also wished with all my heart that I had not heard the news from my nemesis. I had lost the man whom I most loved in the world and had to deal with the man I most disliked.

As I recall, I managed to drive myself back to Fayetteville the next morning to be with my family. A panic attack hovered over me, but in my grief I was beyond paying attention to it.

In addition to the grief that overwhelmed me, I was faced with a new situation. My father had managed my mother's anxiety and now it became my responsibility. Mother was not doing well. She had become more out of control and a hoarder of the extreme type seen on TV, where narrow pathways threaded through piles of junk in each room. After Dad's death, she camped out on my doorstep and demanded constant attention.

On the heels of losing one parent and having to provide care for the other parent, I no longer felt mentally strong enough to move somewhere far away for graduate school. My brother received Dad's life insurance policy. Dad had expected me to marry and be supported by a husband, so he thought I wouldn't need to be a beneficiary. My brother generously split the proceeds with me. The timing of this windfall was fortuitous as it provided a financial cushion that allowed me to go back to school.

Rather than apply to a school with a strong focus on architectural history, I found myself once again back at the University of North Carolina in Chapel Hill, which offered a graduate program heavy in ancient and European art history. My 1978 admission interview for the PhD program with the male dean of the art history department felt like a repeat of my treatment as an undergrad in the 1960s, when I'd been bullied and diminished because I was female. The dean told me that I was accepted but cautioned that earning a PhD might not help me to teach at the university level because women weren't welcomed in academia.

Undeterred, I made the best of my time at UNC. I created an interdisciplinary course load in the art, anthropology, and folklore departments with a specialty in North Carolina vernacular material culture—ordinary, local architecture and art rather than the elite tradition of national and international design. This didn't feel ideal at the time, but in retrospect, I see that this inclusive education served me well.

## 16
### My Turn to Go Back to School

Once established in Chapel Hill, I found a psychologist to help me repair the emotional damage of losing my marriage and my father in the previous year, and also help in managing my mother. I did my best to be a loving daughter. To her face, I called her "Mother" but in my head and in my journal I called her "Moth," the name she used to sign her 1960s letters, to reduce her to a fragile insect and negate her psychic power.

My therapist lived in an elegant mid-century home in a wooded Chapel Hill suburb. She was given to quoting evocative French phrases, such as "Reculer pour mieux sauter" (jump back in order to jump further ahead), to teach me, a type-A achiever, that it was okay to slow down. My stories of Mother's behavior prompted her to say that Mother was "edging into senility." She said to give Mother a calendar and mark the dates on which we would be together to help structure and calm her mind so that she didn't need to see me so often.

Sitting in the therapist's beautiful den, I finally talked about what I had kept to myself for years. I told her I suffered ongoing panic attacks, usually when I traveled alone. This had not stopped me from taking road trips when necessary, but the panic consistently plagued me. I would feel cramped and trapped inside my head, afraid that I would dissolve or black out and lose control, afraid that I wasn't real—that I didn't exist.

Yann Martel's lyrical description in his book *Life of Pi* best describes panic:

> *For fear, real fear, such as shakes you to your foundation, such as you feel when you are brought face to face with your mortal end, nestles in your memory like a gangrene: it seeks to rot everything, even the words with which to speak of it. So you must fight hard to express it. You must fight hard to shine the light of words upon it. Because if you don't, if your fear becomes a wordless darkness that you avoid, perhaps even manage to forget, you open yourself to further attacks of fear because you never truly fought the opponent who defeated you.*

I explained to my therapist that I was driven to be constantly productive and had trouble relaxing and doing nothing. One anxiety trigger is feeling stupid, unable to remember a fact or a name. For example, when I read in Lewis Thomas's *The Lives of a Cell* that mental disease is untreatable, I began to panic out of fear that my panic couldn't be cured.

I told my therapist about the worst panic attack that I had experienced. It happened during graduate school in October 1979 while I was driving to Charleston, South Carolina, to research porches as a possible dissertation topic. After battling panic for four hours, I abandoned hope of reaching Charleston and stopped for the night at an Econo-Travel Motor Hotel outside the city. Once there, curled up in a fetal position on the bed, I called a cab and checked myself into the emergency room.

The doctor must have given me something to calm me down, but what helped the most was the sweet little old lady on the gurney next to me. She was having a heart attack and kept up a running commentary on her pain in such a charming, sad way that I felt ashamed of myself for being there with no "real" illness. About midnight I took another cab back to my Econo-Travel room, waited out the rest of the night, then drove straight back to Chapel Hill. My trip had been a wild goose chase that accomplished nothing, but at least I was alive.

The therapist suggested that I keep an "anxiety notebook" so I could understand the triggers for the attacks. She said panic wasn't inherently life threatening, but was rather something rising in me that I hadn't acknowledged, so I really was "unreal" in that sense. At the end of my therapy, she concluded that the source of my anxiety is "separation anxiety," being unable to separate in a healthy manner from my over-protective mother who had convinced me that I could not live independently. The dependence/independence conflict is the source of much adolescent anxiety.

I accepted that diagnosis and came to a better understanding of my panic attacks, but they continued to hobble me in some important ways. The dissertation topic, old Southern piazzas, that I had intended to pursue in Charleston was not a casual interest. I had been obsessed with this type of dwelling since the early 1970s when I found many of them in the southeastern counties of North Carolina while working for the State Historic Preservation Office, and perhaps since my childhood when I first visited Beaufort in 1958. As a result of the panic attacks and academic hurdles, I abandoned the whole topic. Instead, I wrote about gravemarkers.

~

I earned my doctorate by teaching at three schools in Durham. From 1978 to 1979, I taught three semesters at Durham Technical Institute in East Durham in the new Preservation Technology program. I worked with two different groups of students for three consecutive courses: architectural history, fieldwork methodology, and a team project to compile an inventory catalogue. Our laboratory became East Durham, a large collection of textile mill villages in a low-income area that was severely blighted after most of the mills closed.

Most of my students were adults retraining to be restoration contractors and preservation consultants, and each group had a strong esprit-de-corps. We produced two catalogues, the first for Edgemont and East Durham Textile Mill Villages (1980) and the second for the Cleveland Avenue-Holloway Street neighborhood (1981). These spiral-bound reports, printed by Durham Technical Institute, testified to the students' quick absorption of the new specialty of historic preservation. Student Patricia Dickinson wrote in the forward to the first catalogue that the course was "taught with enthusiasm, patience and a sense of humor by Ruth Little-Stokes." Pat Dickinson edited the second group's catalogue and learned her way to a distinguished career as a historic preservation consultant. My students had learned so much that both catalogues reached the professional level of my 1976 Greensboro catalogue.

In 1980, while finishing up my doctorate, I lived with dear friends Michael and Kathleen Southern in East Durham. This area of Durham, full of aging turn-of-the-century blue collar houses, had been left behind in the late twentieth century by white flight. Ordinary middle-class amenities such as a supermarket, a bank with an ATM, and a gas station, were missing. Durham was full of artistic inspiration. I spent happy hours at the Durham Arts Council downtown making clay sculpture. I rolled and handworked slabs of clay to create "pop art" copies of my flip flops, quirky clay boxes and bowls, and my tour-de-force giant clay "quilt" that hung at the Durham Arts Council exhibition of clay artists in 1980.

In 1981, I taught art appreciation at North Carolina Central University in Durham for one semester, then was hired by the North Carolina School of Science and Math (NCSSM), housed on the rambling campus of Watts Hospital in Durham. Founded in 1980, the boarding school offered two years of free high school education to precocious students from throughout North Carolina. Unusual for a high school, many of its faculty had doctorates. I was hired to set up a pottery studio and teach students to "throw" pots on a wheel.

I had misrepresented myself as a pot turner but prepared by taking a summer crash course at Penland, the venerable crafts school in the North Carolina mountains. For three weeks, I turned bowls and was ready to "turn and burn" when the Science and Math school started in the fall. I purchased bags of porcelain and stoneware clay, powdered glazes and other chemicals, acquired a bisque kiln and a clay roller, and presided over the pottery studio for three semesters. One memorable project was a large ceramic unicorn mural, created as each student carved a portion of the unicorn's body with the help of local muralist Alice Procter. I also team-taught a humanities course with Professor Jim Lyttle.

NCSSM stimulated me on many levels. The first personal computers that I'd ever seen were in used in the classrooms. The kids loved video games, of course, and a Pac-Man arcade game chattered constantly out in the hall. It was during this time that I completed much of the work on my dissertation on old North Carolina gravemarkers. Art teacher Joe Liles helped me create a colorful screen print of one of the folk German gravestones I was writing about in graduate school. Most significantly, my contact with these bright, charming teenagers made me daydream about having a child who would grow up and attend this wonderful high school.

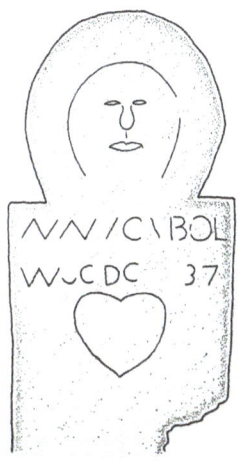

### The North Carolina Gravestone Survey

*My dissertation topic on old gravemarkers was one reason I was motivated to pursue a doctorate. This study honored the vow I made in 1974, when I encountered the rare, mysterious eighteenth-century brownstone monument in southeast North Carolina. Because the Buies Creek stone disappeared between the first sighting and my return visit to it a*

Vanished headstone, estimated to be from the eighteenth century, for an unknown person, Johnson family graveyard, Buies Creek vicinity, Harnett County. Drawing by Daniel Pezzoni, 1996 from a ca. 1971 photo by Buddy Brown.

> short time later, I was shocked into an emotional understanding of the perishability of old gravestones and a hint of their significance as artifacts of material culture. I vowed to record the state's early burying places before the ravages of time, vandalism, and theft destroyed them.

I wrote a grant application to the National Endowment for the Humanities, which funneled a grant through UNC to fund my two-year North Carolina Gravemarker Survey. In 1980 and 1981, I drove thousands of miles to document 1,200 gravemarkers with photography, field notes, transcriptions, drawings, and mapping. These markers stood in 550 graveyards in thirty-four of the state's one hundred counties. The panic was present but overshadowed by the joy of discovery. My collection, documenting the jigsaw puzzle pieces of the state's coastal, piedmont, and mountain ethnic and racial heritages in graveyards and cemeteries, resides in the Southern Folklife Collection at UNC.

The forms and symbolism of homemade gravemarkers express British, Scots-Irish, Highland Scots, and German cultures and beliefs in the eighteenth and nineteenth centuries and of African Americans in the nineteenth and twentieth centuries. I found no eighteenth-century Black gravemarkers. I recorded folk or traditional monuments and the entire spectrum of vernacular, imported, and local professionally made memorials, whether wooden sticks, brick or stone vaults, or stone or cast concrete monuments. To achieve high-quality photographs, I used black-and-white Ilford film from England, purchased at Ritz Camera shop in Raleigh.

While I worked on the grave marker study, so close to finishing my doctorate, another rescue of an endangered antiquity jumped in my path. Through a twist of fate, the bewitching Joseph Lane House that I first saw in the early 1970s was for sale, for the price of one dollar, through the revolving fund of Preservation North

Carolina Inc., a statewide nonprofit. The underlying acreage had been sold; the house had to be moved within a few months to a suitable location and, in accordance with deed covenants, restored to its historic appearance. I viewed the project as a way to fulfill two dreams at once—to rescue an important old house and to create a home.

# 17
## A Two-Hundred-Year-Old Nest

The Joseph Lane House was one of an ancient Southern type, small but with a porch (known in the upper South as a piazza) integrated into the main roof. I named the type the Carolina cottage, but it is usually called a "coastal cottage" because it was built in eastern North Carolina in the second half of the eighteenth and antebellum nineteenth century as a sophisticated elite farmhouse with one or two main rooms, rear and attic bedchambers, and a piazza that adapted it to the hot, humid climate. In South Carolina, the type was built as a retreat where plantation families

*Joseph Lane House, 7408 Ebenezer Church Road, Raleigh.*
*Photo by* News & Observer, *1983.*

lived during summer months to escape malaria and yellow fever.

I'd been fascinated with the house type since my survey days of the early 1970s and was thrilled to save the Lane House, the second oldest house in the county. As Richard Parsons had told me when I first saw the house, the *first* oldest house was the Joel Lane House, built by Joseph Lane's younger brother about 1760. Joel's house was known as the birthplace of Raleigh, because he sold his plantation to the state of North Carolina to establish Raleigh as the state capital.

The house could be mine *if* I could find an appropriate place to relocate it. It needed a rural setting in Wake County to preserve its farmhouse character. I drove western Wake County for many weekends. One afternoon I found a tumbledown early-twentieth-century cabin in a grove of large oak trees on Ebenezer Church Road, off US Highway 70 between Raleigh and Durham. Carolantic Realty was developing a subdivision named Landfall on the surrounding property.

I went to the property and met Carlton Midyette, one of the developers, and told him what I wanted to do. He shook his head. "I don't think our homeowners would be happy seeing a dilapidated little old house moved in among their large new homes."

"But Carlton," I answered, "this is the second oldest house in Wake County! It will be beautiful when I finish fixing it up."

I told him where the house stood and he agreed to drive by and have a look. Luckily, Carlton appreciated history and convinced his partner and Landfall's residents to agree to the sale.

I found a mover, Eugene Chance of Chance Moving Company, who was game for my project. The house would have to move fifteen miles, so its whole roof, including the recessed piazza, had to be dismantled to slip beneath the electrical power lines and to fit on narrow roads and squeeze between bridge railings. The two enormous chimneys of handmade brick had to be removed as well. This significant deconstruction didn't faze me. One of my long-term dreams was to move a house, and this house was my destiny.

As a young woman taking on such a serious project, the least of my worries seemed to be Mother, who couldn't wait to see the house that I had bought for this princely sum. She had dedicated her life to finding bargains and was sure that I had scored a big one. Mother drove from her home in Fayetteville up to Raleigh, and I took her out for her first look at my treasure box. She walked all around it, picked her way through the interior rubble, and finally emerged through the front door. She sat on the edge of the porch and started to cry. "Oh Ruth, I thought you had gotten a real deal, but you've just gotten yourself into a mess." Mother didn't understand that the Lane House was, for me, a salvage born out of her own hobby rescuing old furniture. The house was just a large piece of furniture—no big deal, I thought.

Unlike Mother, colleagues and friends were excited by the project and offered to help. I was teaching a class in a new building restoration program at Durham Technical Community College—a serendipitous coincidence. A group of my students, including Todd Dickinson and Wayne Hall, used the Lane House as a laboratory to learn to carefully dismantle the roof and porch and number the timbers so they could be reconstructed on the new site. While they worked, other students and friends made weekend pilgrimages out to the old house to pry the exterior layer of bricks out of the chimneys, slide them down a wooden trough, and stack them on the ground. As soon as possible, I wrapped the precious 1775 date-brick in a towel and carried it home for safekeeping. Although I kept it in a shoe box, I joked that I kept it under my pillow.

The morning of June 11, 1980, I rode with Eugene Chance in his pickup truck behind the house, which was set on steel beams with wheels attached and pulled by a heavy truck. Friends and family joined the four-hour cavalcade. When the Lane House arrived at its new site, my new neighbors' worst fears were realized. An article in the *Raleigh Times* the next day quoted my assessment of the house's appearance as it arrived: "Right now, it looks like an 18th-century double-wide." At that time, manufactured homes, called "double-wides," were transported on two separate tractor trailers, one half on each.

The labor of love of putting the house back together and finishing the interior as my home took nearly a year. Master carpenter David Patterson reproduced the missing interior woodwork to match the originals and installed the first wiring, plumbing, and heating that the house had ever known. I spent as much time on the project as I could spare from my graduate studies and teaching.

While renovating the house, we also made discoveries. Inside the walls, we found traces of two centuries of families. The original carpenters scribbled their mathematical ciphers in white chalk on the framework. The front door casing was protected from evil spirits by a hex sign: a six-pointed star incised with a compass into the heavy timber beam. Another of these was scratched into the soft brick of the 1775 chimney stack facing into the attic room.

*Compass star*

Another discovery was more personal. I discovered discarded children's leather shoes of many different sizes. The soles were attached by neat rows of tiny wooden pegs. The faded leather sides were squashed open and filled with straw to make nests for mice. As I brought them into the light of day, most collapsed into fragments.

Who were the children who wore out these shoes? The shoes may have belonged to Octavia, Mary, Dexter, Joseph, and Lavena Bennett, who grew up there in the late 1800s, or to Gladys, Alma, Lula, Robert, Anna, Ruby, Troy, and Raymond Wilson, who called this home in the early 1900s. Maybe mice dragged the shoes behind the walls, or perhaps the shoes were shoved behind the baseboards as good luck charms. In early New England, shoes were concealed in walls to trap an evil spirit as it entered the house, explained Robert St. George, a colleague of mine, in his book *Conversing by Signs*. Shoes were seen as a firm foundation and "steadied the body of the house against evil spirits."

Archives and History researcher Jerry Cross revealed the house's history in the 1977 National Register of Historic Places listing report. Combing through colonial records, family papers, censuses, deeds, wills, and court records, Jerry pinpointed Joseph Lane as the original owner. Joseph built the house in his old age, after his son Joseph Lane Jr. had grown and married Ferebee Hunter, daughter of Isaac Hunter. Hunter's tavern became the political center of Wake County in 1788 when a convention gathered there to select the new capital of North Carolina within a ten-mile radius. As previously mentioned, Joseph's younger brother Joel Lane sold his land in 1792 to the state of North Carolina to create the state capital of Raleigh. The Joel Lane House is now a museum in downtown Raleigh. Joseph built his 1775 house in the last decades of his life, dying in 1798 after bequeathing the plantation to his grandson Joseph Lane, the son of Joseph and Ferebee.

In 1819, Joseph Gales of Raleigh rode out to the Lane plantation with his son-in-law Major Thomas L. West of Bertie County. Gales, a prominent English journalist, had moved to Raleigh in 1799 to escape political persecution. He founded the *Raleigh Register*, one of the state's most important newspapers for a half-century. Major West and his wife Caroline had just lost their first child and wanted to move to a healthier part of North Carolina. Joseph Lane III sold it to the Wests, who named it West Hill. It proved to be a healthy seat, and they raised at least seven children in the house. In 1822, Gales and his daughter, who lived in Raleigh, caught malaria. Joseph recuperated for several weeks at West Hill and returned to health; his daughter stayed at the town house and died.

Phares Yates, owner of Yates Mill, one of the county's largest grist mills, acquired the plantation from the West family about 1852. His daughter Eugenia and her husband Joe Bennett lived at West Hill from 1863 to 1906. Their daughter Lavena raised eight children in the house. Her niece Mary bought the old homeplace and lived there until 1932, then rented it to tenants until the 1960s. Lane's fine residence slipped down the economic ladder in those decades and was eventually left to rot. In 1969, Jefferson and Eva Sugg purchased the property as a land investment and sold the house to me in 1980.

In 1981, I moved into the completed Lane House. Like the house, I felt that I had a new lease on life. Early that year, with sheetrock walls and a new roof, windows, and doors, I curled up in a sleeping bag in the attic to spend my first night in the old place. The attic, reached by the little winding staircase, was the children's bedroom. Upon awakening, I recalled dream after dream of children playing around me. It was as if the spirits of children who grew up there visited me in my sleep. I felt their visits as a blessing for my own future in the house when I would become a mother with a child.

By this time, I was teaching bright, enthusiastic teenagers at the North Carolina School of Science and Math in Durham. Soon after, I dreamed that I had a baby who carried on a fluent conversation with me. "How can you talk? You're a baby!" I asked the dream child. Matter-of-factly she explained, "I'm from Brooklyn."

The Lane House's huge fireplace and the porch swing I hung on the piazza proved to be attractive spots for socializing with a new man, a tall handsome Raleigh resident. We met through a matchmaking dinner hosted by mutual friends, and we courted in Durham, where he worked as a financial advisor. His bon vivant love of the symphony, restaurants, and words attracted me. In the garden behind my new house, I grew giant zinnias and gave him bouquets for his office.

Part III

# The Middle Years
## Balancing Family & Career

*Glen Eden, 24 x 30 inch acrylic on canvas, 2017.*

## 18
### Marriage No. 2 and Family

In 1982, I sat on my porch swing to rock in the breeze and ponder my future. I was engaged to the tall, handsome Raleigh man, and I was pregnant. I was also about to earn my PhD and embark on an academic teaching career. Getting a job in my field of American architectural history meant finding a teaching position somewhere else, as there were no preservation or art history programs with architectural studies in our area of North Carolina. My fiancé refused to move away from the Raleigh area because he feared he would lose his brokerage clients. I had to choose between having a unified family or being a single mom with an academic teaching job in a new city. For the second time in six years, I faced the same dire decision between marriage or the career of my choice. In my first marriage, my husband's job prevented me from getting a degree; now if I remarried, my husband's job would prevent me from using my degree.

The feminism born in the 1960s had seemed to promise I could have it all—marriage, a family, and a career. The "Women's Liberation" movement was in full swing by the time I attended college. Betty Friedan's *The Feminine Mystique* of 1963 includes a "Forfeited Self" chapter about psychologist A. H. Maslow's comparison of fulfilled and unfulfilled women. Women are fulfilled by realizing their creative potential. Fulfilled women are independent, have passions and goals, and value their own self-worth. They are free to break rules, do important work, and express anger. They value sex and love, but it does not determine their happiness. Their main goal is the good of mankind, a purpose larger than themselves. Maslow found very few fulfilled women.

Friedan believed that women suffered from identity crises after America's pioneer era ended because their important work was taken from them. During World War II, Rosie the Riveter reclaimed women's creative potential by working in the factories. In America's post-war era, women were once again relegated to the home. They forfeited themselves by falling under the spell of the sexual mystique of perfectly applied lipstick and waxed floors and sought sexual fulfillment and motherhood as their highest goals.

Simone de Beauvoir, Jean-Paul Sartre's life companion and author in 1949 of *The Second Sex*, one of the first feminist manifestos, wrote that when a woman had a child she forfeited her integrity. She must have felt the same way about marriage. She and Sartre were a famous twentieth-century literary couple together for fifty years, but they never married nor had children.

The woman artist who is as passionate and driven as great male geniuses such as Picasso is the rarest of exceptions because "an explanation is required of whether, or how, she dispensed with her femininity and its limitations, with her female biological destiny; of where—so to speak—she buried the body."[14] Many feminists believe that any mother who is passionate about her work is likely to compromise both her career and the truth of herself in order to care for her children.

I didn't read de Beauvoir, Friedan, or Steinem's feminist works in the 1960s because I assumed that my strong sense of self-determination would exempt me from the culture's negative effects on women. I thought I was free to fulfill my potential *and* have a career *and* a husband and children. Anna Quindlen's afterword to the 2001 edition of *The Feminine Mystique* described my generation of women, the post-Mystique generation who came after 1963, as smug overachievers. If I had read the pioneering feminists, I would have learned that I wasn't free—society had molded my subconscious to expect to compromise in order to "have it all."

During my first marriage, I had brought home the bacon and kept the house as well, because the husband I was putting through graduate school lacked the empathy and sense of fairness to share housework. I couldn't imagine how I would add the role of mother to my life, especially if my second husband wouldn't be a full partner in raising a child. Many women I worked with in the 1970s had chosen a career over motherhood. For women to be truly equal, we must have economic independence, and housework and child rearing must be equally shared with a husband or partner.

I didn't compromise; I capitulated. My marriage was all about family, especially my desire for children, and I ignored my career. As with the first marriage, I made a small stab at retaining integrity with my new name. In 1972, I had hyphenated my surname to Little-Stokes; this time I dropped the hyphen and reclaimed my original surname of Little.

A large crowd gathered to celebrate our marriage at the Lane House, mingling on the piazza and the rear deck built by family and friends. All through the afternoon, my friend Kathleen Southern worked in the kitchen to create a triple-decker wedding cake. During the joyous party, I felt the spirits of the Lane House were happy as well. In my new old cottage, with my new husband, I waited for the child I had dreamed about.

～

Thwarted in finding an academic job in Raleigh, my fallback was to take part-time historic preservation consulting projects and to embark on a full-time real estate career that *might* specialize in old buildings. In 1982, I acquired a real estate broker license and became a Realtor. In 1983, waiting for the baby, I was a whirling dervish of selling houses and historical consulting. I assisted Paul Touart with fieldwork on historic buildings in Davidson County, which sometimes involved balancing on the heavy timbers of nineteenth-century barns to take photographs. Before the baby arrived, I finished part of my dissertation on an IBM Selectric typewriter, rented for $75 a month, with a "correcting" key that used white tape.

My new husband and I consolidated our households by selling my Joseph Lane House, selling his house, and buying a new house for the two of us. It was time for a new adventure. My heart stayed in the Lane House, but marriage and motherhood required compromise.

At our new home, I strung up my Pawley's Island hammock between two trees in the side yard and lay in it with my big belly, reading books about how to be a new mother. As I raced to finish up a book manuscript on the historic architecture of Davidson County, I had to sit further and further back from the typewriter. The June 30 due date came and went, and one day it dawned on me that I might be willing the baby not to be born until I met the deadline. I packed away my box of survey files and photographs, unplugged the typewriter, and waited.

On July 9, 1983, my daughter Virginia "Gia" was born. During her first year, she was such a good baby that she napped dependably from about ten to noon and also from about two to four each afternoon, allowing me to complete my dissertation. On Mother's Day, May 13, 1984, baby in tow, I received a PhD from UNC-Chapel Hill, then went right back to selling real estate.

I entered real estate with the blithe goals of being my own boss in order to juggle motherly duties and use my historic preservation skills to help families find and save old houses. My 1984 and 1985 planners are full of real estate activities: answering the phone on the "duty desk" at the real estate office and hoping for a new client; weekly stints at the real estate desk at the Marriott Hotel; taking out-of-town clients house-hunting on weekends; endless phone calls; and monthly meetings of the Raleigh Board of Realtors. Many clients were local first-time buyers with a low budget who spent months of my time looking for the perfect house.

The house I put on the market on April Fool's Day—a 1,000-square-foot, two-bedroom rental house at 1019 Culpepper Drive, a blue-collar neighborhood in East Raleigh, epitomizes the reality of selling real estate. The house had four rooms, each with a different bright-colored wall-to-wall shag carpet that met in the small middle hallway. The owner called me constantly, often came to my office, took the house off the market, then put it back on market. This house that chained itself to me on April Fool's Day finally got an offer to purchase on October 31, Halloween, a date fitting the cruel joke. After I scheduled a plumber to repair the bathroom, the house closed on November 30. The sale price of $43,500 netted a commission of $748 for seven months of torment from the seller. It was one of six houses I sold in November for a total of $387,600 in sale prices. My total income for the month, $6,113.72, seemed decent before understanding that I was working seven days a week and hadn't yet paid my income taxes.

I worked hard to balance career and motherhood. In 1984 and again in 1985, I earned the local Realtor association's "Million Dollar Realtor" award for selling a million dollars' worth of houses. The competitive hustle to attract new clients and close the deals was exhausting. This was not why I earned a doctorate. Real estate demanded the latest communication technology: I acquired a car phone so that I could call ahead to schedule an appointment to show a home and a beeper so that I could be reached to schedule house showings. Somehow, I found the time to write a book—*A Tale of Three Cities: A Pictorial Survey of Leaksville, Spray & Draper*, based on a survey by Claudia Roberts Brown in Rockingham County, North Carolina. It was published in 1986.

In the fall of 1985, Virginia needed a real bed to free up her crib for a new baby on the way. Because my husband and I shared our expenses equally, I asked him if we could buy a new bed and an answerphone (a phone answering machine) to take messages while the baby was feeding and napping. I worked full-time in addition to being Gia's main caretaker because my husband commuted to Durham for work. He resisted both purchases, but eventually gave in. My husband shared expenses but not household and child responsibilities. He used the new answerphone to play an April Fool's Day prank, announcing excitedly "You got a voicemail about listing a house!" When I called the number, thrilled at getting a new listing, it was nothing of the kind. "April Fools," he called gleefully.

New Realtors were encouraged to specialize in a specific neighborhood, known as a "farm," in order to cultivate a clientele. I chose Raleigh's Five Points area, which was full of historic homes. To promote my services, for a year I mailed homeowners the Howard Perry & Walston corporate monthly newsletter along with a two-page brochure I wrote called the "Porch Post." I summarized local mortgage rates, remodeling tips to improve home resale, and seasonal gardening advice customized for old neighborhoods inside the I-440 beltline. Sometimes I included a photograph of a "Porch of the Month" with a story about the owners. I wrote that new home construction in Raleigh was changing from the "Williamsburg Colonial" style to transitional "California modern" interiors with open floor plans and cathedral ceilings. In my last "Porch Post," December 1985, I described a recent real estate education class I had taken and included a photo of Gia dressed as Raggedy Ann. I summarized a newspaper article saying that what Americans really want in a home is a Ranch or Split-Level house with three bedrooms, one and one-half baths, and a front door with carriage lamps.

At our son Britton's birth in February 1986, I retired from real estate because most of the work happened in the evenings and on weekends when daycare wasn't available, and I hated it anyway. The trigger to leave the business was reading Stephen Covey's *Seven Habits of Highly Effective People*. His introduction invited me to imagine myself on my deathbed, telling my family what my life had accomplished. If I continued with a realty career, would I be proud of helping thousands of people buy or sell their recently built homes? It seemed clear that my greatest contribution would come from research and writing and preserving American material culture. I felt confident that this "death-bed exercise" had shown me the true path.

So began the worst year of my life. Following Britton's birth, I suffered a classic postpartum depression that caused insomnia and panic attacks. His infancy was as rocky as Gia's had been smooth. After a quiet first two weeks, he screamed with colic from morning to night, twelve hours a day, for two and a half months. At night when he stopped crying, I was exhausted but couldn't sleep. After about six weeks, the crying became so acute that I began to wonder if this was more than digestive problems. Dr. Turpin, my pediatrician, sent me to the hospital to get Britton's skull x–rayed to make sure his skull plate had not closed up prematurely. Watching my baby on the x-ray table, I promised God that I would never complain about the colic again if his skull turned out to be normal. Thank God all was okay, and in another month, the colic eased off. I wrote in my journal, "Britton's birth overloaded my circuits. I absorb responsibility like a sponge and he is the responsibility that broke the camel's back."

Eventually, I found a psychiatrist who tried various antidepressants and even hypnosis to no avail. The postpartum depression was so debilitating that I fantasized about ending it all, but never would have left my children behind. The drug cocktail that finally worked was Xanax and Adapin for anxiety and suicidal urges and Amitriptylene as an antidepressant in order to sleep. Through the year, my husband continued his daily schedule of commuting to Durham for work and did not help feed Britton at night. By the following year, I started sleeping again, and life became easier.

Until Britton turned four, he would not go to sleep unless I stayed in his room. Even after an hour of reading and singing to him in the rocker, he screamed when I put him in the crib. Dr. Turpin gave me two choices: spend the time with him at night now or deal with a juvenile delinquent when he became an adolescent. I spent the time, and Britton was a loving child who repaid my effort. One night when he was four, I was sitting resignedly in a rocker in the dark nursery, and he called out in his tiny voice from the crib: "Remember ... I love you."

## A New Beach Cottage

One bright spot in 1986 was building a new family beach house in Morehead City. That year, a moving company loaded our old cottage, the still-sturdy military house, on a truck and took it to another site to be repurposed for another use. I designed a two-story "Beaufort-type" cottage, with a separate unit on each floor with doors and big windows that opened into an integral two-story front porch. Morehead City architect James Willis drew up a set of blueprints and the Garner family, experienced builders, erected the large airy cottage with a heavy wooden frame that would provide a "little leisure" for another generation or two. This was unimaginable luxury, with four bedrooms and three baths, compared to the cramped two-bedroom, one-bath Marine house.

*Little Leisure 2, Patterson Street, Morehead City, 1986. Demolished 2015.*

## 19
### Longleaf Historic Resources

In the fall of 1986, I returned to the State Historic Preservation Office as the National Register coordinator, working three-quarter time, six hours a day, while the children were at daycare. I was back where I belonged, saving historic architecture.

When I started the position, the National Park Service in DC had placed our National Register program on probation because an unacceptable number of our nominations had been rejected in the last few years. To get the program on track, I wrote a new state manual on how to prepare nominations, held a two-day workshop for nomination consultants, and edited draft nominations with a fine-toothed comb to ensure that they met federal standards. By 1989, most of our nominations were approved, and it was time for a new challenge. I became the survey coordinator, wrote a manual for survey standards and methodology, and consulted with property owners, developers, survey consultants, and the general public.

In 1990, I decided it was time to leave state government, and I established a historic preservation consulting firm from my home. My children had attended high-quality day care programs, but when they started public school, they needed someone at home in the afternoons and during summer vacations. I named my new business Longleaf Historic Resources after the longleaf pine tree landscape of the Sandhills region where I grew up.

The 1990s decade was my perfect storm of overwhelming responsibility. In those years, I managed the peak of my historic preservation career, the prime years of child care as my children went through public schools and grew into adolescence, a husband who commuted daily to Durham and shared little childcare and housework, and a mentally ill mother who required care. As I lived out my anxieties about balancing motherhood and career, I always felt like I shortchanged each of them.

During the school year, I coped with childcare by hiring a series of afternoon babysitters, students from NC State University, to drive the kids to drum and piano lessons, soccer practice, and play dates with friends. The kids had strong attachments to each: Liz, a sweet young woman with a charming Southern accent; Brandon, an upbeat young Morman man; and Taka, a Japanese tennis player who had a side gig as a DJ. Sometimes Taka's ready-to-eat dinner was waiting when I got home from a long day in the field. During the school year, their assistance was a win-win for all of us. In the summer months, I rearranged consulting work so that I could stay at home with the kids.

From one perspective, the decision to work on my own may have been one of the worst decisions of my life. I left the financial benefits of a salaried position and the camaraderie of my colleagues and set myself up for loneliness and anxiety, which plagued me terribly at times. Perhaps I should have remained in the Historic Preservation Office and continued to pay for afternoon and summer childcare, even though it cost one-half of my salary.

Still, with all the challenges and obstacles I faced at that time, I am forever grateful for the key projects that came my way. For the first time in my life, being a female was an advantage. To give women and minorities a fairer share of public works money, governments set up a Minority Business Enterprises status with the "MBE" acronym. I registered with the federal government and the NC Department of Transportation as a woman-owned business and got contracts to do historic resource surveys for federally funded highway and airport projects to fulfill diversity quotas. North Carolina is a tribal state where connections run deep, and my work often bumped into my maternal or paternal ancestors or a previous area of study. Many projects involved Mother's coastal roots, my home of Raleigh, and the concentric towns of Chapel Hill, Durham, Apex, and Wake Forest. I bid on nearly every historic preservation project I came across, whether State Historic Preservation Office grant projects or those financed by local governments or private individuals.

## Ocracoke

*In 1990, my first consulting project as proprietor of Longleaf Historic Resources took me to an island off the North Carolina coast. It was the first of many consulting jobs on the coast, perhaps inevitable because I've always said that I have saltwater in my veins, given that my grandmother Ruth Rouse White grew up in the 1880s and 1890s only about seventy-five miles from the Atlantic Ocean.*

*Ocracoke, a two-hour ferry ride from the North Carolina coast, is the only barrier island in the state with a surviving and active*

Howard Street, Ocracoke. Photo by Ann Ehringhaus, 1988.

*Ivey and Eliza O'Neal House, Ocracoke. Photo by Ann Ehringhaus, 1990.*

historic settlement. In 1990, the village hired me to create the Ocracoke National Register Historic District to protect it from intrusive new development. Known as "Pilot Town" in the late eighteenth century, boat pilots lived there who piloted small vessels through the shallow treacherous waters inside the Outer Banks to the mainland. The village was a unique collection of 230 historic houses, mostly small frame dwellings, a number created from timber salvaged from shipwrecks.

The "Bankers" (Outer Bankers), following generations of tradition, built low dwellings with small front porches sheltered within dense walls of native vegetation—scrub oaks, cedars, pines, and myrtles. The houses were grouped by kinship rather than any planned design, with sandy paths connecting them bearing names such as "Lossie's Ridge" and "Aunt Sarah Ellen's Lane." Almost everyone made a living from the sea, and the way of life continued unchanged until 1959, when the state ferries connected the island to the mainland.

This rare Outer Banks community needed the protection of a National Register Historic District to preserve the goose that laid the golden egg. Tourists treasured it for its history, vernacular design, and cultural landscape, while developers sought financial gain by building new tourist accommodations. To strike a balance between preservation and growth, National Register designation ensured that the State Preservation Office would review any new building project that needed a federal or state permit to protect the village's historic character. I was fortunate to be the consultant blessed with this important project just as modern resort pressures threatened the village. I felt like John Muir must have when he explored the pristine mountain wilderness of California with his camera in the late 1800s, except that I photographed and studied little wooden houses hidden in the maritime forest. Three or four times in 1990, I made the two-hour Pamlico Sound crossing, sometimes seasick, in a state ferry boat.

Al and Linda Scarborough hosted me in their bed and breakfast, a small traditional house known as a "story and a jump" or "Banker house" because its low upper bedroom level was a "jump" above the main floor. Early houses on North Carolina's Outer Banks islands tended to be small due to a scarcity of building materials, as well as the necessity of moving them as fishing grounds changed. Al was a genuine O'Coker (Ocracoker), descended from eight generations on the island. He met Linda when they served together in the Peace Corps; then she joined his island world.

The first time I got off the boat at the Silver Lake dock, Linda met me and drove me to the B & B. Immediately I could see that, like all island men, Al was a jack-of-all-trades. In the front yard of the house, he operated a combo ice cream stand/bike rental. The house itself was charming. The two small downstairs rooms consisted of the main family room, the "hall," and the smaller parents' bedroom and private sitting room, the "parlor." The "hall-and-parlor plan" was the most common room arrangement in early North Carolina houses larger than a one-room cabin.

Linda led me up a steep narrow staircase in the hall and showed me to one of the two attic bedrooms, then excused herself to get back to chores. While Al operated the front-yard businesses, Linda kept the B & B tidy, managed guests, and cooked hearty, healthy meals.

To collect information on Ocracoke Village, I walked with my clipboard of survey forms, a village map, a pencil with eraser in one hand, and a Nikon camera strapped over one shoulder. Digital photography did not exist, so I carried rolls of black-and-white Kodak Tri-X or Plus-X film in thirty-six exposures and some color film. I knocked on every door and talked to every owner that I found, taking notes on their recollections and drawing a floor plan of the dwelling and a sketch map of the property. I analyzed house shapes and materials and made educated guesses about changes over the building's years. Some homes had brick cisterns connected to the roof gutters to collect rainwater, as wells were impractical on the island due to the high salt content of groundwater. Fish cleaning tables made of two-by-four planks stood near a water hose in most yards.

Some homeowners invited me inside to look at the water lines on their wooden walls, labelled with the name of the hurricane and the year of the flood. The main room sometimes had a hole in the floor to drain water during a flood. A good many dwellings were shuttered because they were summer cottages whose owners lived on the mainland. Walking through the village doing the survey was so absorbing that I felt no anxiety. I even found a survey assistant, a talkative crow whom I nicknamed Heckle, who followed me as I moved about the village. I later learned that crows are so smart that they can learn to recognize individuals.

Seven-year-old Gia was able to accompany me on my final work trip to the island. While I prepared my findings, she delighted in renting a bicycle to explore the village and buying ice cream cones at Al's stand. Meanwhile, I was nervous. That evening I was scheduled to make a presentation to the villagers in the schoolhouse. The stakes were high: I had to be clear and persuasive to make the case for pursuing a historical designation and be ready to take skeptical or hostile questions.

That evening, I went to the schoolhouse and found an excited crowd of locals. During my PowerPoint presentation, a thunderstorm plunged us into darkness and abruptly ended my slide show. In the moment, it felt like a disaster, but the outcome was good: Residents wholeheartedly supported their historical designation. I completed the work to get Ocracoke Village on the National Register, and it was listed in 1990.

### Durham Donut Survey

*The same year I worked on Ocracoke, I also had a project closer to home, in Durham. Since I lived and taught in Durham in the late 1970s and early 1980s, I was familiar with this rough-and-tumble tobacco and textile town, with Duke University on its west side and textile mill villages on its east side. In 1990, I conducted the Durham "donut survey," an inventory of historic properties in the extra-territorial jurisdiction to enable city planners to preserve potential National Register landmarks as the metropolis expanded. Of the 150 historic properties I recorded, one-third were antebellum houses of log and frame construction. Others were late 1800s and early 1900s farms, country stores, schools, and mills. One of the newest landmarks I discovered, a large 1930s Adirondack-style log house, the Stevenson House, was built for the granddaughter of Washington Duke on Bahama Road overlooking Lake Michie. Duke founded the American Tobacco Company in Durham; his son founded Duke University.*

## 20
## Black History Through White Eyes

A third project came my way in 1990: That year, Raleigh's city planning department hired me to select and organize the interviews collected during Raleigh's African American Oral History Project. This is part of Raleigh's long history of dedicating resources to identify, recognize, and protect the city's historic resources, both white and Black. My work became part of *Culture Town: Life in Raleigh's African American Neighborhoods*, a beautiful hardcover book written by Linda Simmons-Henry and Linda Harris Edmisten, published in 1993.

My commitment to document and preserve African American history and culture stemmed from my pride in North Carolina, early on one of the most progressive Southern states in education and civil rights. Regarding education, it was no accident that the first state university in the country was established in Chapel Hill in 1792. (Although, of course, it would be more than 150 years before Black students and women were admitted.) No accident that General William T. Sherman instructed his troops to spare North Carolina the destruction wreaked on South Carolina and Georgia in the last year of the Civil War because, as Sherman put it, "They didn't start the war but have borne the largest number of casualties because of it."

Compared to other Southern states, North Carolina enjoyed a relatively enlightened atmosphere in the early 1960s under progressive governor Terry Sanford and within pockets of liberalism in its larger cities.[15] It was no accident that the civil rights sit-ins to integrate restaurants and businesses started at the Woolworth store in Greensboro, in 1960. After students from Shaw University conducted sit-ins at the lunch counters of the F.W. Woolworth and McCrory's 5 & 10 Cent stores on Fayetteville Street in Raleigh, Shaw University hosted a conference that attracted activists from around the country, and the result was the founding in 1960 of the Southern Nonviolent Coordinating Committee (SNCC), one of the most important civil rights organizations in the South. Founding strategists included the late John Lewis, who of course went on to become one of the greatest and most inspiring legislators and civil rights leaders in America.

While working on the *Culture Town* book, I had the pleasure of reviewing dramatic interviews that described how some African Americans managed to thrive in Raleigh despite Jim Crow segregation. I organized the interviews by neighborhoods and selected photographs to convey the historic character of each area. I found the name of the book in an interview with Clarence A. Toole, who recalled, "We used to call Raleigh 'Culture Town' because of its wealth of culture and education." Shaw University and St. Augustine's College, historically Black colleges established at the end of the Civil War, were twin pillars of strong African American neighborhoods with Black public and private elementary and secondary schools.

My work on *Culture Town* was informed by my first professional brush with African American history when I worked on the North Carolina Gravestone Survey in 1980-1981. In that project I examined the physical objects, resources, and spaces that people use to define their culture. Looking at African American church graveyards in Cumberland County, Davidson County, and New Hanover County, the high number of homemade cast concrete gravemarkers made by local artisans and the use of found objects such as seashells as grave decoration piqued my interest. The dramatically different aesthetic of African American artisans arose from their culture as well as the necessity of creating inexpensive monuments. I deeply empathize with this race that has labored as the oppressed shadow side of white existence for over two centuries. Black material

*Emma Verdell headstone, died 1937, Buncombe Baptist Churchyard, Petersville, Davidson County. This grave monument uses mirror shards to symbolize a moon and stars, symbolic of eternity. Black grave monuments are sometimes startlingly original and repurpose found objects and ephemeral materials such as shells; commercial metal and plastic items intended for functional household use; concrete; or used perishable materials such as sculpted earth and wood. Some monuments incorporate children's playing marbles or a deceased person's possessions, such as a pocket watch to symbolize the end of time. Anyone who loves the African American style of jazz improvisation would see the same individualistic and asymmetrical aesthetic at work in African American material culture. Photo taken in 1997.*

culture—historic buildings, artifacts, and landscapes—became one of my professional specialties.

While working for the State Preservation Office in 1989, I presented a paper on gravestones to the annual conference of the Association of Gravestone Studies. Most members were New England gravestone researchers and their conference was in Lyme, Connecticut. My paper, "Afro-American Gravemarkers in North Carolina," could not have been more different from New England culture. I explained to the Yankees that African American graveyards had given me a deep appreciation for the distinctive Black aesthetic in burial monuments.

The printed conference schedule mistakenly listed my name on a Charleston, South Carolina, researcher's paper and her name on mine, but we Southerners were warmly received. The organization published my paper in *Markers VI: The Journal of The Association for Gravestone Studies*, 1989.

## New Bern

Later in the 1990s, I had the opportunity to do other projects focusing on Black history. In 1994, I partnered with colleague and friend Tom Hanchett to undertake the first inventory of Black historic properties and neighborhoods in New Bern. A historic port town on the Neuse and Trent Rivers on the North Carolina coast, New Bern had the largest free Black population of any town in North Carolina before the Civil War. In fact, during the war, New Bern was the Union army headquarters for eastern North Carolina.

Tom and I produced a meaty report, "The History and Architecture of Long Wharf and Greater Duffyfield: African American Neighborhoods in New Bern, North Carolina." A few years later, I wrote and designed the "New Bern African American Historic Heritage" brochure for the city. The landmarks range from an early

Detail of "New Bern African American Historic Heritage" brochure, produced by me in 1997.

1800s home built by a prosperous free Black man, John C. Stanly, to a 1920s Black hotel, a 1950s Black movie theater, and the Kress dime store and Clark's drug store, where Black high school students held sit-ins in 1960 to integrate lunch counters.

In 1997, I went back to New Bern to document the five oldest Black churches in New Bern for the National Register. Four of them stand in Dryborough, New Bern's historic Black neighborhood. The project provided an insider's view of the myriad indignities and losses Blacks have suffered from the actions and inactions of whites. The church histories illuminate dramatic stories of Black missionaries who pioneered new congregations at the end of the Civil War.

For example, Black missionaries of the African Methodist Episcopal and the African Methodist Episcopal Zion denominations managed to get to New Bern in 1864, along with white Methodist missionaries, each attempting to convince members of an existing Black church, Andrew Chapel, to join their denomination. James Walker Hood won the epic struggle and the church became St. Peters African Methodist Episcopal Zion Church at 615 Queen Street.[16]

## Somerset Place

In 1999, the North Carolina Historic Sites agency asked me to create reconstruction plans for two destroyed buildings that had housed enslaved people at Somerset Place, a state park on the plantation of Josiah Collins III in northeast North Carolina. The agency wished to erect facsimiles of two rare, destroyed buildings—a two-story slave quarters and a two-story hospital that had served enslaved people—to allow visitors to gain a better understanding of the slave experience. The lost slave quarters were unusually large, with four rooms housing four families. The lost two-story hospital was also unusual because few were built by slave masters.

To complete this project, I worked with Dorothy Redford, the site manager of Somerset Place and a descendant of Somerset

Margaret Ruth Little

*Cover of Somerset Report with reconstruction drawing of the Lake Hospital and Large Slave Quarter for North Carolina Historic Sites, 1999.*

slaves. Dorothy made national history when she orchestrated a homecoming of the descendants of the enslaved community that drew over 2,000 descendants to the plantation. Her 1988 book, *Somerset Homecoming*, details her research.

Using archaeological reports, documentary photos, and extant slave buildings in eastern North Carolina, I created conjectural reconstruction drawings for the multi-family slave building and the hospital. Working with Dot Redford was difficult, as my white approach to African American history didn't accommodate the spiritual artifacts, such as chicken bones and voodoo dolls found by the archaeologists in excavation of the building sites. My white eyes were challenged to see and convey what she saw with her African American outlook. The slave quarters and hospital have been reconstructed on their original sites and provide a fuller experience of the life of enslaved people on the Collins plantation.

I developed a respectful and sincere appreciation for African American history and culture through preservation projects and direct experience. Even as a child, I could plainly see how Black people were treated as second-class citizens. As mentioned previously, I was sometimes embarrassed by my mother's racism. I recall her disparaging remarks about Black people in private, and also witnessing her treatment of the Black maids she hired to iron clothes, often accusing them of stealing food.

When I was young, my passion for Black music and dancing led me to say, "I wish I'd been born Black," because my impression then was that Blacks had more fun. Now I know that clearly was not the case. My eyes have been opened to the pervasive white privilege I didn't see then. My hope is that my appreciation for Black history and culture as seen through my white eyes in Raleigh, New Bern, Wake Forest, and other locations can play at least a small part in helping to open others' eyes to the African American experience in North Carolina.

## 21
### Projects in Mother's Counties

I first worked in Mother's home county in the 1970s when I listed the Kennedy Home, a Baptist orphanage, on the National Register. Working in Lenoir County allowed me to satisfy curiosity built up over a lifetime about the county where Mother grew up. Even though she was my biggest threat, her stories filled my imagination as a child. In her book *Women Who Run with the Wolves*, Clarissa Pinkola Estes writes that our scars, our old stories, are doors to understanding ourselves, and that working with our life's stories is the work—the only work.

Sometime around 1993, I was hired by an engineering company as principal architectural historian for the Global Transpark project, a commercial truck and airport transportation hub in Lenoir County—where I had spent so much time as a child with Mother and her sisters. The owners of large historic farms near Kinston who stood to lose farmland they had owned for generations reviled the new hub. The company warned that, in conducting a survey of the historic environment to fulfill federal environmental review requirements, I would be the first consultant to knock on the doors and that several homeowners had made threats. They suggested that I needed a bodyguard for the fieldwork, so architectural historian Betsy Baten became my man Friday.

On our first day, we stopped for gas at a country store and told the proprietor about our project. He said that his neighbor had just caught a big fish in the Neuse River and invited us for fish stew at the neighbor's "party house." We nervously accepted.

The real heart of Lenoir County resides in the "party house," a small detached kitchen out behind the main house. Eastern North Carolina men fish and hunt. Their "man caves" are rustic frame backyard structures with a big eat-in kitchen and sitting area where they can cook and serve their game, free of the hygiene and niceties of their wives' house kitchens.

We walked into the kitchen where six middle-aged and elderly people were already sitting around a wooden table. Our host stood at the stove stirring a big stew pot. As we sat down, the store owner asked where we were from. North Carolina is a network of tribes; his question was Carolina-speak for "Who are your people?" He sought not our professional credentials, but whether we had an experiential, emotional bond with his world.

"My mother's family—the Whites—grew up in LaGrange. My aunt, Appless Lassiter, lived in Snow Hill," I replied.

An elderly white-haired man with blue eyes looked at me and teared up. "Mizz Lassiter taught me fourth grade. She was the best teacher I ever had."

At that, the men and women around the table relaxed. They realized that we weren't unfeeling bureaucrats from Raleigh, but homefolks they could trust. Even if we had no leverage in how the project would affect their property, they could count on us to represent them honestly.

Betsy and I relaxed, too, and enjoyed a memorable meal. That was the best (and only) fish stew we had ever eaten. It was boiled with potatoes and onions in a big pot, served with Merita white bread from the wrapper, and swilled down with Coke and Mountain Dew.

Word spread after we passed the fish stew initiation, and we were graciously received at every old farm in the project survey area. Thanks to Betsy Baten's help, I had only one close call during this high-profile, controversial project. We drove to the county one hot summer day with hundred-degree temperatures and no air conditioning in my car. Sun sickness had become a problem for me. As we walked through a tall cornfield to reach a family graveyard, I began to feel nauseated and dizzy. It wasn't yet lunch time, but in order to prevent heat stroke, we drove to a restaurant to cool off. By the time we arrived, I had turned beet red, so Betsy called an ambulance. The medical personnel applied ice and monitored me until my vital signs returned to normal, and we headed back outdoors for more fieldwork.

Soon after this, I had the opportunity to do more work in my mother's home territory. In 1994-1995, colleague Penne Smith and I surveyed the Lenoir County seat of Kinston. I then authored the county architectural publication, another in the series overseen by the State Historic Preservation Office. The result was a hardcover book that assembled existing documentation, written by many historians over the decades, including a comprehensive survey conducted by historian Robbie D. Jones. I wrote a meaty essay on the county, separate town essays, compiled maps, and selected illustrations. *Coastal Plain and Fancy: The Historic Architecture of Lenoir County and Kinston, North Carolina* was published in 1998 by the Lenoir County Historical Association Inc.

There were many Carolina cottages in Lenoir County, and people still alive who had known my kinfolk. Writing *Coastal Plain and Fancy* achieved a longtime goal to research the places and buildings where Mother's and my aunties' stories took place.

~

Working from home as a consultant in the 1990s made it important to network with professional colleagues whenever possible, but traveling and attending out-of-state conferences sometimes stretched my wings uncomfortably. In 1980, I had been a founding member of the Vernacular Architecture Forum, a national group to support the study and preservation of vernacular architecture and landscapes. We studied ordinary local buildings and their man-made environments that spoke in the local vernacular rather than the elite language created by architects and trained designers. After my first child was born in 1983, I had been unable to attend the yearly conferences, but began to participate regularly again after 1990.

During the 1993 Vernacular Architecture Forum conference in Santa Fe, New Mexico, organized by my architectural historian friend Chris Wilson, I had a panic attack even though I was with friends. While we were on a bus tour of rural New Mexico, the bus slowed down and our guide pointed out the window. "This is one of New Mexico's Civil War battlefields."

I looked out at the unremarkable scrubby landscape. The guide was still talking, but I was no longer hearing him. This couldn't be, I thought. A Civil War battlefield outside the South?

But I realized it must be true. As the tour proceeded, an anxiety attack crept over me—mental numbness, distance from people around me, unreality, erasure. Panic attacks mostly happened when I was traveling alone and felt insecure. This one happened because my basic ego felt threatened. Knowing stuff—having a command of facts—makes me feel in control; when I don't know stuff, I feel out of control.

My work and its travels produced anxiety, which exacerbated and magnified the other stresses I was already carrying. Mother had disrupted my life since my father's death in 1977. During her frequent visits, she spread negativity, applying an "ugly" or "attractive" filter to the world. She judged people by their surface appearance, as if that was all that mattered. She involved me in lawsuits against Dad's business partner and also contractors and architects who worked on her rental properties and her beach cottage, demanding that I handle her legal correspondence with lawyers and go to court with her. In 1991 when an architect subpoenaed me to the trial over the beach cottage because Mother refused to pay him, I agreed to testify. Mother's lawyer knew my testimony would sink her case and convinced her to settle out of court.

My marriage also continued to be a source of stress and conflict. Every few years, I sought help from a different therapist to decide whether to stay or pursue a divorce. My husband and I didn't have a true partnership, and there was virtually no affection between us. He slept in on Saturday mornings and during Sunday church services. Our only joint family activity was the kids' weekend soccer games. Being a single mom wouldn't be any harder, but I worried about how a divorce would affect the children. I heard them talk about their friends who shuttled weekly between divorced parents' houses. At the time, therapists advised that even a bad marriage is better for children than a divorce, a theory now debunked.

These challenges added to the stress of work projects, which often took place outside Raleigh. As a consultant, traveling alone and sometimes lost, my old bugaboo of panic attacks came with the territory. I projected an outward veneer of strength and self-control to protect my dignity, but throughout my consulting career, the anxiety was a hidden liability. As an independent consultant, it often wasn't possible to work with a companion. On consulting trips in the '90s, I had no cell phone or GPS software to guide me to my destination. It helped to set up a meeting with someone, but then I became anxious about being late for the appointment.

Leaving home alone without any contacts waiting for me set me up for sure stress. A few days before a trip, I would start to dread it. I tamped down the anxiety by obsessively setting out my equipment—clipboard, survey sheets, maps, camera, film, a picnic lunch. I would pack several valium pills in case an attack hit. When I was on the road, taking one eased the anxiety enough to continue driving. When the time to leave finally arrived, the attack would often hit. It began with intense anxiety and a tightening in my chest. As the fear gripped me tighter and tighter, I hunched my shoulders to cradle my chest, fighting a desire to curl up in a fetal position. I felt helpless, as if my spine wasn't strong enough to support my body.

In my wallet, I kept a small set of mantras, taped to one of my business cards, to recite out loud if I felt a panic attack coming on.

LIVING WITH PANIC
*I am not ashamed. What can I learn as a student of panic?*
*I will face the symptoms to gain skills. It's OK to be anxious here.*
*I won't guard myself against anxiety. This is practice.*
*I can tolerate uncertainty. It's OK if the anxiety continues.*

Since the 1970s, when my Chapel Hill therapist diagnosed me with separation anxiety, I've learned that panic attacks can be caused by insecure attachment. Attachment theory is one of the most important constructs in child psychology. Children attach to their caregivers securely if the child believes he is loved and will be safe. A securely attached child can separate calmly because she has developed independence. If the caregiver is anxious, inconsistent, and overprotective, the child may have separation anxiety away from the caregiver. The brain responds to separation anxiety by instantly releasing adrenalin and cortisol hormones that can cause panic attacks.[17]

I kept a dream journal to understand my attacks. During these years, I dreamed endless variations on being blocked from travel: baggage problems, having too many clothes to fit into a suitcase, losing my suitcase on an ocean liner or at the airport, or suddenly discovering that I had packed or was wearing only one shoe. I interpreted these recurring situations as symbols of my life not moving forward. How can I leave home without my suitcase or with only one shoe? Through these dreams, my subconscious was attempting to resolve the existential conflict between my passion for travel and fear of leaving home. Everyone carries around some kind of baggage. As my dreams indicated, my baggage was separation anxiety.

## 22
### Fayetteville: You Can Go Home Again

In the mid-1990s I followed in my father's footsteps with several projects at Fort Bragg. I grew up in Fayetteville because my father worked at the nearby Fort Bragg Army Base in the early 1950s during the US Army's Cold War expansion. He surveyed land parcels and laid out housing complexes for the 82nd Airborne paratroopers. The work lasted for so long that Mother finally relocated the whole family from Lexington to Fayetteville. She finished out her teaching career as a first-grade teacher at Bowley School at Fort Bragg.

So when the Public Works Directorate of Fort Bragg and the National Park Service contacted me about doing work in Fayetteville, it created a homecoming of sorts for me. They hired me to survey the buildings in the same areas that my father had surveyed in order to construct them. Never did I expect to become an expert in military base architecture.

Growing up with a negative view of Fort Bragg because I opposed the Vietnam War, I discovered the main post to be a beautiful ensemble of historic buildings and landscapes. I learned about the vagaries of Congress's appropriations for military readiness and struggled with bureaucratic military maps and numerology. Each of the 285 historic buildings, including garages, on the base is identified only by a block number and a five-digit unique number, creating a nightmare when I prepared the inventory list spreadsheet.

The main post, built from 1927 to 1940,[18] is one of the best examples of the army's design philosophy of Beaux Arts campus layout for permanent masonry bases, as opposed to temporary wood construction bases. The principals of design incorporated generous open spaces with axial views, monumental architectural groupings, and landscape design.

The Quartermaster Corps and early city planner George B. Ford selected the Spanish-Colonial Revival style of hollow tile construction covered with stucco for residential buildings and load-bearing brick Georgian Revival style for non-residential buildings. The lushly landscaped winding streets of Spanish-Colonial Revival officers' housing, picturesque Spanish-Colonial Revival officers' club, imposing blocks of three-story brick barracks, ornate Georgian Revival hospital, and headquarters buildings create an impressive ensemble. The golf course, parade ground, and polo field complete the main post.

Fort Bragg's mature trees and shrubbery present a verdant oasis in the barren scrub oak and pine landscape of the Sandhills region. In 1941, Fort Bragg's 67,000-man army post made it the largest base in the United States. Ironically, my study was never officially listed in the National Register because the army refused to tie its hands from being able to alter or destroy these historic resources. Instead, the base used my documentation as a guide to properly maintain the resources as long as they were left standing.

The next year, the National Park Service and Fort Bragg hired me to survey the entire Fort Bragg Reservation, covering a portion of five counties in the Sandhills. Ellen Turco helped as my field assistant. I grouped the resources into property types and analyzed each type for its eligibility for the National Register in a bureaucratic report known as a "Multiple Property Documentation Form." Included in the survey were the one thousand remaining "temporary" buildings—frame barracks, warehouses, etc., that were left of some three thousand built in 1940–1941 to ramp up for World War II, as well as the non-military churches, hunting lodges, and farmhouses built prior to the base's establishment. North Carolina had a compliance agreement with the army that none of the temporary buildings would be eligible for the National Register because

Market House, Fayetteville. The black protective fencing was installed after several arsonists set the building afire during an otherwise peaceful demonstration on May 30, 2020, during the George Floyd protests of the Black Lives Matter movement across the United States. Photo by Terry Eason, 2021.

the army reserves the right to "burn" these as the need arises. I haven't been back since the 1990s and wonder if any of them are still standing.

~

In 1999, Fayetteville's preservation planner, Bruce Dawes, hired me to list Fayetteville's commercial core, containing 113 historic buildings as the Fayetteville Downtown Historic District. The city's original 1783 English-style "Lancaster Square" street plan features a central square containing the town hall and four principal radiating streets of Hay, Green, Person, and Gillespie. After the Great Fire of 1831 destroyed the town, a new town hall modeled after an eighteenth-century English town hall was built— today's Market House. As the uppermost section navigable by boat on the Cape Fear River, Fayetteville was the state's second largest antebellum city after Wilmington, which is located at the river's mouth to the ocean. When the earliest railroads bypassed Fayetteville in the 1840s, it was isolated until railroads arrived in the 1880s, and its mid-nineteenth-century infrastructure remained intact.

On the four corners of Market Square stand landmarks: the Second Empire-style Sedberry Drugstore building of the 1880s and its neighbor the five-story Lawyers Building of 1916; the Knights of Pythias Building of the 1890s; the first skyscraper, a ten-story National Bank of Fayetteville, built in 1926; and the diminutive 1850s Fleishman Store. Green Street holds a Greek Revival-style Presbyterian church and a Gothic Revival-style Episcopal church.

The town cemetery, Cross Creek Cemetery No. 1, was established downtown in 1785. Here lies the largest collection of handsome mid-1800s marble monuments carved by famed stonecutter George Lauder, prominently mentioned in my *Sticks and Stones* book, discussed in the next chapter. He emigrated from Scotland to Raleigh to erect the state capitol in the 1830s and then set up shop in Fayetteville. Nearby stands the oldest building, Cool Spring Tavern, a 1788 wooden two-story house with a double engaged front porch.

At the edges of the district are the 1890 Cape Fear and Yadkin Valley Railroad Depot of red brick Romanesque Revival form and the 1922 Atlantic Coast Line Station, a Dutch Colonial Revival building. The latter station is where my father arrived home from World War II in 1945 on the train.

## 23
### Sticks and Stones

In addition to doing my Longleaf consulting work, another big project during the 1990s involved ongoing research and writing on gravemarkers. I was determined to turn my unpublished 1983 gravemarker dissertation into a book, but it was difficult to find the time. Finally, in 1992, I began making field trips to cemeteries in the North Carolina mountains to expand my research for the book.

On one trip to Boone, I took my son Britton along for company. At six, Britton had three secret powers: X-ray vision, an extra pair of eyes above his regular eyes, and a brain that was, in his own words, "almost as smart as God." Whenever my Volvo's radiator overheated trying to climb the steep Blue Ridge mountain ridges, he activated his secret powers and helped forestall my panic attack.

Britton's powers used up a lot of calories: the first night of our trip when we had dinner at the Daniel Boone Inn in Boone, where food was served "country style" in platters on long tables, Britton ate more than any adult. The inn was a fitting venue for him. At seven, he read his father's boyhood book on Davy Crockett and learned to play the "Ballad of Davy Crockett" on the piano. He wanted to be Davy, or at least Fess Parker's Davy in the 1950s Disney movie.

Becoming Davy became a joint project for us. Britton and I dyed unbleached muslin cloth with brown Rit dye in the bathtub. I sewed pants and a shirt, adding fringe from an old fake leather jacket I found at Good Will. We were missing a real coonskin cap, not available in local shops. On a family vacation, we found the cap at a general store in Durango, Colorado. It had been made in

*Book of Ruth ~ Taming Ghosts, Saving History*

*Sticks and Stones: Three Centuries of North Carolina Gravemarkers was published in 1998. It was the first systematic, analytical study of a Southern state's grave monuments as cultural artifacts.*

Cherokee, in the North Carolina mountains, but we had to go to the Wild West to find it.

I was glad to mix book research with family time, especially since getting the book completed and published was a long process. In an upsetting dream of this period, my children came to visit my grave, where I lay beneath a beautiful old gravestone. The graveyard was the only place where I could talk to them, an apt dream for spending so much time on the gravestone manuscript that it had metaphorically buried me. I shepherded it through an arduous review until 1996, when the University of North Carolina Press accepted it for publication.

The title is taken from the old children's rhyme "Sticks and stones may break my bones but words can never hurt me." I liked the associations among sticks and stones and bones and words, the four elements of my book. I found an epitaph for my own gravestone, which has yet to be created. "She hath done what she could…" appeared on a number of gravestones of women who died in the late nineteenth century. Often selected by the women's husbands, these words seem to damn the women with faint praise. Actually, the phrase has a deeper meaning. It is taken from the Bible, Mark 14:8, and refers to the woman who anointed Jesus's body with costly ointment before his burial. This epitaph expresses my life attitude of throwing myself wholeheartedly into worthwhile projects, such as the study of vanishing grave markers.

Holding the first copy of the book in my hands, I knew it was one of my life's major accomplishments. That year, the Association of Gravestone Studies awarded me the Harriet Merrifield Forbes Award for the best gravestone book of the year.

## 24
### Cape Lookout

The second island project of my career, listing the historic district of the village at Cape Lookout, happened in 1998. Cape Lookout, the tip of the island of Shackleford Banks, is a treacherous promontory created by the tidal action of Bogue Sound, where many ships were wrecked in the days of sailing vessels. The cape is accessible only by water, a forty-five-minute boat trip from the coastal town of Beaufort.

A tiny village of eighteen historic buildings, primarily fishermen's dwellings, nestles in the sand dunes near the Cape Lookout Lighthouse that guided boats from running aground on the "Graveyard of the Atlantic." The lighthouse's distinctive black diamond pattern on the white tower, visible on clear days from the mainland, serves as the most famous landmark of this section of the North Carolina coast.

The village is one of the last surviving historic settlements on North Carolina's Outer Banks. In the 1970s, the National Park Service acquired all of the land to form the Cape Lookout National Seashore, a national park. The agency purchased the private houses by eminent domain and then leased them to the former owners for twenty-five years. As the leases would begin expiring in 2000, tenants contributed to a fund to hire me to nominate the village for the National Register of Historic Places. The motivation of these families, many of whom had owned their houses for many years before creation of the park, was not to extend their leases but to prevent the National Park Service from destroying the village. They wanted the cape's heritage as a life-saving settlement and fishing village to be preserved along with the natural beauty of the seashore.

*Barden Cottage, Cape Lookout, NC. Photo by Ruth Little, 1998. Courtesy of the North Carolina State Historic Preservation Office.*

My first visit to the island on a Fourth of July weekend, arriving in a motorboat with one of the village tenants, was traumatic. Unlike the larger village of Ocracoke, which had a tree canopy, Cape Lookout village lay in open sand dunes, with no trees to shade the brutal sun. I adore the ocean environment and islands in particular, but Cape Lookout not only fatigued and overheated me but triggered a half-day panic attack as I hiked around the village to acquaint myself with the buildings. The settlement had no commercial district like Ocracoke and I felt marooned on a desert island.

In the fall, I returned to the island with Michelle Kullen, my assistant for the fieldwork, a much more enjoyable experience in cooler weather. Michelle was a talented and agreeable architectural historian who worked for me for several years in the late 1990s. Dr. Graham Barden and his wife Mary of New Bern graciously hosted us for two nights in their island cottage while we completed our fieldwork. The Bardens bought one of the lighthouse keeper's quarters as surplus property from the Coast Guard in 1958, moved it to another site, and had occupied it as a summer cottage since then.

*Cape Lookout Lighthouse and Keeper's Quarters, Cape Lookout, NC. Courtesy of the North Carolina State Historic Preservation Office, 1998.*

Our time on the cape cast me as the hero in one of the island adventure books I read as a child. Michelle and I each slept in our own upstairs bedroom of the lighthouse quarters, me with a view of the lighthouse outside my window. Every room of the quarters had wooden beaded wallboards that Mary Barden had painted a different shade of clear blue or green, like a North Carolina coastal romance novel by Nicholas Sparks. Every seven minutes, all night long, I saw the bright light pass my window. With no curtain and no way to block the light, I lay awake for hours anticipating the light's next transit of my eyelids.

Meeting David Yeomans, the keeper of the island's old ways and old stories, was the highlight of the Cape Lookout experience. The wiry fisherman, wearing a pair of khaki shorts, his bare chest tanned nut brown from the sun, told us stories in his thick Old English "Banker" brogue.[19] In his late seventies, he was still at the top of his fishing and storytelling abilities.

David, the youngest son of Eugene Yeomans, told me about his father's life as a cape fisherman during the heyday of fishing clans in the late 1800s and early 1900s. These family crews followed the shifting fisheries between the mainland and the Outer Banks and moved their small portable houses from one location to another by whaleboats. Eugene built a house on Harkers Island, near the mainland, in 1870. In 1875, he strapped two twenty-four-foot whaleboats underneath the house, as pontoons, and floated the house over to Diamond City, on the island of Shackleford Banks. When the Hurricane of 1899 destroyed the settlement, Yeomans moved his house back to Harkers Island. David lived in a newer house on Harkers Island but spent most of his time in his cottage at Cape Lookout.

The Cape Lookout Village nomination was an unusual project, not just because of its island location, but also for the irony of the project itself. If the nomination proved that the district met the eligibility criteria for listing in the National Register, the National Park Service would be forced to list their own property and to preserve the buildings against their will. I finished the nomination in 1998, and the park service stonewalled for a year, delaying a judgment because the agency preferred to focus on nature rather than spending time and money on manmade features. The park service finally listed the Cape Lookout Village Historic District in 2000.

Thanks to the village's status as a National Register Historic District, a number of the sturdier buildings have been repaired and are being interpreted as historic sites. My career has been full of projects like this that preserved the cultural landscapes—nature plus mankind—of North Carolina.

～

The year of the Cape Lookout project, 1998, was also memorable because of personal stresses. My workload, marital issues, and child-care challenges continued to be stressors, and panic attacks happened whenever I traveled out of town alone. I recall one incident in particular when I was driving home to Raleigh after working at Cape Lookout and I started to fight an attack around the halfway point, Goldsboro. A voice inside said, "You're not going to make it. You are going to have an attack and will have to pull over and stop. Then there will be no way for you to get home. You're too weak to make it the rest of the way."

I took half a valium, which helped me enough to talk back to the voice. "How *dare* you tell me that I don't have enough stamina to drive myself home! I'm a strong person and can do whatever it takes to take care of myself." When I got mad, my spine straightened up, my shoulders unhunched, and the road wasn't a scary place anymore. But the panic came in waves and returned after fifteen minutes. "You can't stand to be trapped in the car, and panic will descend."

Who was this voice? Even then I knew it was Mother's—I had internalized her message that I am a weak woman and the world is a scary place. That left me with a despairing question: how could Mother continue to cripple my psyche after all these years?

## 25
## Projects Close to Home—1990s

Raleigh was a sweet, simple city in the 1990s. The boom in new construction that peaked in the 2000s had just begun. Thanks to enlightened citizens and governmental officials, some of Raleigh's iconic landmarks and neighborhoods were protected by historic designations in this decade. I was privileged to work on a number of these preservation projects, which continue to need defending. In recent years, the renaissance of downtown Raleigh has prompted battles between the adaptive reuse of the historic industrial buildings and new high-rise construction.

An area that became a focal point in my personal and professional life was Raleigh's Glenwood Avenue between Hillsborough and Peace Streets, now known as Glenwood South. I ran many errands and went on many outings in this old commercial corridor

*Askew-Taylor Paints, 110 Glenwood Avenue, Raleigh, 18 x 24 inch acrylic on canvas, 1999.*

that was developing a distinctly artsy vibe. I often ate lunch at Sunflowers,[20] a pioneering vegetarian restaurant, and browsed at Sam Tarlton's antique shop, Marita Gilliam's art gallery, the Frame Shop, and National Art Interiors. I bought my house paint at Askew-Taylor's Paint Store, 110 Glenwood Avenue.[21]

Much of my preservation work was for landmarks and historic neighborhoods in older sections of Raleigh and nearby Chapel Hill and Durham. With young children and the risk of panic attacks, I was glad to get interesting local projects without the stress of travel. Every few weeks I went to Raleigh Blue Printers on West Martin Street and bought US Geological Service maps required for the National Register nominations that I wrote by the dozens. Some of the most notable included these:

### Dorothea Dix Hospital

At the south end of downtown Raleigh, Western Boulevard was becoming a four-lane divided highway. The Friends of Dorothea Dix Hospital hired me to list the campus to protect portions from being taken by eminent domain. The Dorothea Dix Hospital Historic District that I listed in 1990 includes the dense core of the campus containing fourteen pre-1939 buildings and "the Grove," a thirty-acre wooded hill and grassy swale at the front.

In the State Library of North Carolina, I combed through the biennial reports of the hospital from 1880 to 1942 for mentions of "the Grove," with its large oak tree canopy and early twentieth-century gazebos, as the most significant element of campus design because the tranquility of nature was considered an important component in the healing process. Hospital buildings were deliberately constructed to preserve the Grove, overlooking a magnificent view of downtown Raleigh.

## Chapel Hill Log Cabins

My first consulting work in Chapel Hill occurred in 1992, when colleague and friend Kelly Lally and I surveyed the township containing Chapel Hill, one-seventh of Orange County. During sixteen field days, we drove nearly two thousand miles to inspect every older building outside the city limits of Chapel Hill and Carrboro. Scotch-Irish and German settlers moved into the county in the 1700s and established small farms, most operated without slaves.

Our most important discovery was the network of nineteenth-century log cabins that still existed in the beautiful, unspoiled piedmont woodland. Of the 160 historic properties that we recorded, some fifty were one-room log cabins from the 1800s. Surprisingly, most of them were still principal residences in the 1990s, although enlarged with wooden wings or a front frame addition. Orange County citizens appreciated their heritage and craftsmanship, either because these were ancestral homesteads or because of the educational level of this university area. Often the descendants of the builders lived in newer houses on the same land parcel and rented the cabins to university students.

These log cabins followed the same form for generations because

*The Sam and Laura Nunn House, Chapel Hill vicinity. Photo by Ruth Little, 1992. Courtesy of the North Carolina State Historic Preservation Office.*

the community built them according to ancestral tradition. A local African American woman named Annabel Lloyd, who lived in one of the cabins, told us a story that illustrated the collaboration that made the cabin possible. Her parents, Sam and Laura Nunn, moved into the cabin about 1905. Sam and three local men built the two-story log house themselves, with one man standing at each corner to fit the logs into place.

On Smith Level Road at the Smith-Cole House, a rare large frame farmhouse built in 1845, we talked to the son of the former farm manager who bought the house in 1904. Smoking a cigarette whose ash always threatened to fall to the floor, the old man regaled us with his father's stories of his childhood before the Civil War. But in the twentieth century, it was the history of the farm's slave descendants that resonated most. Famous African American civil rights activist, author, and Episcopal priest Pauli Murray's maternal grandmother was enslaved on this farm.

### Pine State Creamery

The old Pine State Creamery, 414 Glenwood Avenue, a 1920s milk factory of Art Moderne design with a distinctive milk bottle sculpture above its corner entrance, still bottled milk in the '90s. In 1996, the milk plant, a Raleigh fixture since the early 1900s, was forced into bankruptcy by a school milk price-fixing scandal. I was hired to write the National Register nomination that listed the plant in 1997, enabling the new owner to use federal historic tax credits for an innovative adaptive reuse into restaurants and night clubs, designed by architects Steve Schuster and Thomas Sayre, Raleigh's pioneering architects of adaptive reuse.

### Roscoe Tilley House

Often in my career, a synchronicity—a new consulting project connected to a family or a subject I had previously studied—clicked into place and made for joyful work. In 1999, I was hired to list the Roscoe Tilley House in Durham County on the National Register to protect it from further incursion from Lake Michie. The reservoir had taken part of the tobacco farm in earlier years. The ca. 1880 two-story frame farmhouse, built around an earlier log house by the Tilley family, retained most of its original architectural character but had a replacement front porch and a large 1950s rear den addition.

I had qualms about the likelihood for success of this project. This was a typical house type built throughout North Carolina during the era, so unless it was a pristine example, it would not meet the threshold of architectural integrity necessary for the National Register. When I interviewed the current owners and discovered that it was the home of one of my favorite historians, Nannie May Tilley, my fear disappeared.

Tilley, granddaughter of the original owners, was born in the house and lived there until 1947. One of the first female North Carolina historians, she earned a doctorate at nearby Duke University. UNC Press published her dissertation, *The Bright-Tobacco Industry: 1860–1929*, in 1948. I had used her definitive book to understand tobacco warehouses and factories in Durham, as well as the thousands of tobacco barns scattered across North Carolina. Tilley's family innovated the culture of bright-leaf tobacco in the 1860s, and she grew up steeped in the history of this important crop. Tilley's significance to North Carolina history meant that the farmhouse qualified for the National Register as the residence where she spent her formative years, as well as her most productive years. How often do we have the chance to experience the early life of a writer we admire?

### Taking Time to Teach

*Teaching summer school from 2001 to 2004 at the University of North Carolina-Greensboro was one of the most rewarding periods of my career. Each June, I introduced students to the history of American architecture and taught them to survey buildings in the old residential neighborhood around the university. As a final project, each student wrote a National Register nomination for a building. I worked closely with Jo Leimenstoll and Lisa Tolbert in the departments of interior design and history. I mentored dozens of talented students, some beginning their careers, some switching careers. A number of them, including Sara Lachenman, Carrie Erfurth, and Heather Wagner Slane, are now successful historic preservation professionals.*

## 26
## Liberation

In 2001, after raising the kids in a nurturing environment with both parents for many years, it was time to save my own soul: I divorced my husband. For me, the new century has been a time of simplifying for greater happiness. As my grad-school therapist always said, "Reculer pour mieux sauter." (Jump back in order to make a better jump.) Our children adjusted well to the divorce because, for their sakes, their father and I have maintained a cordial relationship and celebrated holidays with each others' families.

Gia grew into a bright young woman with the same curiosity about the world and knack for science and math as the students I was teaching when I dreamed about her. She became one of those kids herself when she attended the North Carolina School of Science and Math for her last two years of high school. Britton, equally talented, could have gone to the same school, but stayed in his Raleigh high school because of its terrific jazz program. They've maintained a loving relationship with each of us individually.

Life moved fitfully forward, and panic attacks continued, but they didn't always prevent my travels. During the early years of the new millennium, I globetrotted to Spain, France, Mexico, India, and China to celebrate my post-divorce freedom, dragging my panic-attack baggage with me. Sometimes I traveled alone but usually studied at a school or took a tour. The structure of a language school, with new friends, and lodging with a family kept anxiety at a minimum, although the inevitable travel fiascos take a bigger psychic toll on a sufferer of panic attacks. And I had some fiascos. For example, traveling to San Miguel, Mexico, in 2004 involved a plane delayed by a volcanic eruption, a midnight arrival in Mexico at my hotel to find my reservation cancelled, and a midnight taxi ride across town to another hotel. The next day, I arrived at my landlady's house in San Miguel to find that the language school never notified her about my visit.

There were other smaller incidents that were intensely stressful for me. In 2000, I studied Spanish for two weeks in Seville in southern Spain, then met my children in Paris for their first trip abroad. I still vividly recall dragging my suitcase behind me, filled with panic, as I tried to find my hotel without a map. In 2007, a boyfriend and I visited Paris, where I amused myself while he attended daytime meetings. Because I habitually become anxious on subways, I walked from one tourist landmark to another rather than taking the metro. In 2010 during three weeks in India, my girlfriend and I got lost walking to our yoga ashram in Rishikesh and got lost again on a night walk trying to get back to the hotel in Jaipur.

I still dreamed of baggage, sometimes having too much, sometimes not enough. In one dream, I board the plane with an empty suitcase, telling everyone that it's okay, I'm taking the trip anyway. In another, I arrive in Cuba and realize I forgot my money and presents for Cuban children but decide I will be fine. In another, I travel to France to attend school but get lost trying to find my landlady. Apparently, I left my clothes behind, because I'm standing naked in a library looking at a map, then the police help me find my apartment. Baggage problems also hindered my search for true love. I dreamed that I had a chance to take a trip with a new man but can't get my bag packed in time, and he leaves without me.

～

Getting a divorce allowed me the psychic freedom to dedicate part of my time to art. I said, "I'm not going to do that anymore, I'm going to do this." After my fifteen-year sabbatical of child-raising, I started pursuing art again in 1998 as I realized that the divorce was coming. Julia Cameron's artistic unblocking book, *The Artist's Way*, became my bible. My first art class with Toni Capel at Raleigh's Sertoma Art Center opened the art door that had been locked while my children grew up. In 1999, I looked for a new art series to work on when I helped Toni out by tending her studio a few afternoons a week at Artspace in downtown Raleigh.

We had just moved Mother into Manor House, an assisted living facility in Raleigh where she could get needed medical care. She had refused to let anyone into her house in Fayetteville out of shame that a half-century of hoarding had stuffed it from floor to ceiling. I gained access to her house for the first time in many years and photographed each room as a portrait of madness. A phantasmagoria of layered thrift shop finds and trash bags collected on the street concealed her furniture. Resettling Mother in a safe group home near us in Raleigh and beginning the long process of sifting through each room to separate valuables to keep, reusable items to recycle, and trash to throw away resulted in the end of her hoarder house.

Breaking through Mother's hoarder block also released my artist block. Incorporating old rags and clothing as collage elements, I began to paint large canvases of each room in her house. The urge to create something beautiful out of the horror of a trash dump provided a catharsis to me and visitors to Toni's studio. People's jaws dropped when they saw paintings of a living room, a kitchen, a hallway, and bedrooms with a tsunami of old clothing draped over the furniture. Almost everyone commented, "This reminds me of my great-aunt's (cousin's, etc.) house." With each room that I painted, I healed another scar on my homeplace and opened another door to my art.

In 2000, I hung "Keeping House," my first art show—six large acrylic collage paintings—at the Cameron Village Public Library in Raleigh. The wall text described the show's name as a play between Mother's hoarder lifestyle that imprisoned her and prevented visitors and Grandma Ruth's nonchalance about keeping a perfect house. My grandmother said, "Come in if you can get in." Mother wouldn't open the door, but with these paintings, I opened the door to let life in.

> *"Keeping House" is an artistic exploration of a domestic twilight zone. The collaged clothing piles create almost abstract patterns of color and shape. The rooms bring to mind my grandmother's favorite saying. Instead of calling out the usual apology about the house not being tidy, Grandma Ruth would say to visitors knocking at her door: "Come in if you can get in. I don't keep house, the house keeps me."*

The "Keeping House" paintings supplied the psychic energy to spend the next four years cleaning out my mother's hoarder house.[22] The cuckoo clock I sent her in 1967 from Switzerland was one of a million items that we sorted during our years of weekly trips

*Mother's Bedroom, 24 x 30-inch acrylic on canvas, 1999.*

to Fayetteville. Some items we donated to thrift shops, some we trashed in a dumpster, and I collected old aprons and embroidered linens to give to friends. The most precious memorabilia—old photos and letters—I kept. One such treasure was a small photo album of Mother's cousin Gee from the 1920s. The photos of a vacation at the Carolina coast have inspired me for years.

One Saturday in November 2000, I made a list of the items that I cleaned out that day:

- bags and bags and bags of toilet paper and paper towels
- bags of pastel-colored slips with store tags (she hadn't worn slips in many years)
- letters written to her friends as long ago as 1971 and never mailed
- boxes of stationery never opened
- cute greeting cards
- bags of bath towels and hand towels
- packages of window curtains and shower curtains, all still in the store bags with receipts
- dented rusty soldier's helmet (WWI?)
- boxes and bags of other people's trash containing old clothes, shoes, kitchen utensils, shoe shine kits, and toiletries.

Finally we opened the doors, cleaned up the floors, and discovered that mildew in the crawl space had rotted out the floor beams. We sold it to a new owner who bulldozed it and replaced it with three new townhouses.

~

My art journey since 2000 has included classes with many talented and generous art teachers who helped me loosen up the art scar tissue that blocked my creativity. I progressed in scale from small to large paintings and from tight representation to looser, semi-abstract imagery. I took watercolor classes with Jane Harrison and Julie Eastman in the Raleigh arts program and a watercolor

*Boone Breakthrough, 12 x 18 inch watercolor, 2004.*

workshop with Charles Sharpe in Durham. A five-day workshop with Skip Lawrence at Cheap Joe's Art Store in Boone became a repeat of the harsh critique I received at the university in the 1960s. I aspired to paint large semi-abstract watercolors with abandon, like those Skip created in class demos. During the first critique of our work, he challenged me to explain why I couldn't loosen up my painting style and I was tongue-tied. After a week's struggle to abandon control and risk making an image that looked "ugly" to me, the loose and lovely watercolor I painted on the last day hangs in my house.

## 27
### Projects Close to Home — Early 2000s

As my personal life changed and blossomed, I continued to be immersed in my work. In the early 2000s I worked almost exclusively nominating early twentieth-century neighborhoods in Durham as National Register Historic Districts. In 2000, Jim Goodmon, CEO of Capitol Broadcasting Company, purchased the American Tobacco Company's fifteen-acre plant and hired me to nominate it as a National Register Historic District.

At the heart of this complex was the 1874 Bull Durham Tobacco Factory, the city's oldest tobacco factory, that I had listed on the National Register in 1974. As the most important landmark of tobacco processing, Durham's raison d'etre, it was later designated a National Historic Landmark by the National Park Service. After the US Surgeon General labelled smoking as a serious health hazard, the industry declined, and the plant closed in 1987.

I had learned my craft roaming through Rhode Island's textile mills. It was an architectural historian's delight to examine the dense warren of brick and metal buildings where tobacco leaves were stored and smoking tobacco and cigarettes were manufactured. The complex included Romanesque Revival warehouses, a coal shed, a power plant, a 1950s lunchroom, and the Lucky Strike cigarette factory. Goodmon hired Durham metal sculptor Al Frega to collect the plumbing, electricity, and machinery for repurposing as furniture and sculpture in the future entertainment destination and office development. Goodmon also contracted with me to create reference scrapbooks of all published information and advertising materials on the plant for use in interpretive signage around the complex.

*American Tobacco Historic District, Durham, NC. The now fully revived complex of restaurants and a public outdoor concert venue is the largest commercial development in downtown Durham in many years, serves as the gateway to the central business district, and has breathed new life into the city of Durham. Photo by Ruth Little, 2000, courtesy of the North Carolina State Historic Preservation Office.*

### School of Science and Math and Durham Neighborhoods

In 2001, my daughter Gia graduated from the North Carolina School of Science and Math, a high school in Durham operated by the state of North Carolina. That year, I listed her school campus, along with the surrounding neighborhood of Watts-Hillandale, as a National Register historic district. The campus is an adaptive reuse of the early twentieth-century Watts Hospital buildings, located in a beautiful wooded grove. Local historian and resident Tom Miller introduced me to neighbors and provided crucial history for my work. One of the hundreds of stylish bungalows in the district was the home and studio of scrap recycling artist Bryant Holsenbeck, who taught paper- and bookmaking to the Science and Math students, including my daughter. She gave me an inspiring tour of her studio.

In the next few years, I listed four more of Durham's historic neighborhoods as National Register districts. The streetcar suburb of Lakewood Park, built in the early 1900s around the Lakewood Amusement Park, has sixty-some buildings that include early 1900s working-class Queen Anne cottages, 1920s and 1930s bungalows, and a small commercial district with three historic groceries. I doubled the size of the Trinity Park Historic District,[23] a turn-of-the twentieth-century streetcar suburb around the original Duke University campus near the business district. I added 269 additional buildings, predominantly small- and medium-sized Queen Annes, bungalows, Tudor cottages, and Colonial Revivals built from the 1920s to the 1940s and some early architect-designed 1950s Modernist Ranches.

I also listed Durham's first golf-course suburb, built in the 1920s around the Forest Hills Park course. Forest Hills, along University Drive in south Durham, became an exclusive haven for Durham's upper-class tobacco executives and other businessmen. Atlanta landscape architect Earle Sumner Draper designed it with a picturesque curvilinear street plan including circular streets that crown two of the hills.

Local architect George Watts Carr designed many of the houses and is the only architect I've studied who learned architecture through a mail-order correspondence course. The name of the institution offering the course is lost to time. In the 1950s, his son Robert W. Carr designed a number of Modernist houses, including his own residence. I had a memorable interview with son Robert and grandson Robert W. Carr Jr. in their office of many years on the top floor of the Hill Building, an Art Deco 1930s bank tower with similarity to the Empire State Building. One of my favorite downtown Durham buildings, it has been rehabbed as a 21C Hotel, with exhibitions and installations reflecting global contemporary culture.

### North Carolina Agricultural Experiment Station Cottage, Raleigh

Right in my own University Park neighborhood, in 2001, I listed the North Carolina Agricultural Experiment Station Cottage in the National Register. The state agricultural agency built the research station in 1886, the second such facility in the United States.

The land-grant college, North Carolina College of Agriculture and Mechanic Arts (now North Carolina State University) was founded on adjacent land in 1887. The experiment station conducted research in tobacco, cotton, rice, and fertilizer. The "model middle-class farmhouse" functioned as the superintendent's residence and office. The simple up-to-date Queen Anne design includes a front wraparound piazza with floor-length windows into the parlor. A separate piazza door opens into the office. The cottage, whose address is now 2714 Vanderbilt Avenue, is the oldest building associated with NCSU. Agricultural research for North Carolina farmers continued on the grounds until 1926, when it was sold for residential use.

### Raleigh Warehouse District

No-frills industrial buildings always excite me more than the fancy residences of a city's elite families. In 2002, I listed Raleigh's Warehouse District in the National Register as the "Depot District," named for its collection of three railroad depots. As the state capital, Raleigh served as a distribution hub for central North Carolina in the late 1800s and early 1900s. In the Warehouse District, the behind-the-scenes industrial southwest quadrant of downtown, wholesale distributorships built functional warehouses with front offices along the four gridded blocks around Union Station beginning in the 1880s.[24] The Warehouse District lost its raison d'etre after World War II, when long-haul trucks operating on highways replaced railroad freight hauling, and suburban warehouses took over from the downtown warehouse district. Yet the area was still in industrial mode in the early 2000s.

### Wake Forest

The town of Wake Forest has provided stimulating consulting projects throughout my career. Wake Forest, where in the 1830s enlightened Baptists founded the state's second oldest college, Wake Forest University, is located fifteen miles north of Raleigh. The college taught a liberal arts curriculum similar to that at the University of North Carolina. The town combined an enlightened academic atmosphere on a small, beautifully landscaped campus surrounded by avenues of stylish houses, college buildings, churches, and commercial buildings. (Mother attended college there in the mid-1930s and often reminisced about dancing off-campus in that Baptist town, where dancing was forbidden inside the town limits.) In 2003, I listed the campus and town core as the Wake Forest National Register Historic District.

Wake Forest was the site of one of my luckiest and most memorable discoveries.

In 1989, historian Kelly Lally and I were walking in dense woods of town-owned property and suddenly stumbled upon an old house. It sat like a fairy tale ruin in a haunted wood so overgrown with trees and shrubbery that the town had no idea it existed. I pulled out my Wake Forest topographic map, drew a circle around the location, and wrote "slave?" I suspected that it was an antebellum slave dwelling, but I was preoccupied with other assignments and did not document it.

I forgot all about the discovery of this house until 2008, when assistant Heather Wagner Slane and I conducted a survey update in Wake Forest, and we rediscovered the mysterious building off North White Street in a wooded grove at the edge of the East End neighborhood. The partly burned one-and-a-half-story frame structure is a "saddlebag," two dwelling units flanked by a central chimney. After doing some research, I realized that it was the oldest African American building in town, but it was not a slave dwelling. This two-family duplex was built for African American farm laborers about 1875, one of four built by William G. Simmons, a chemistry professor at Wake Forest College. This dwelling has a fascinating history that is being preserved in Wake Forest. It is the childhood home of Allen Young, principal of the town's first Black school from 1905 to 1957. The Young School educated hundreds, perhaps thousands, of Black children in northern Wake County. While so many of the East End's early buildings are gone, this small two-unit workers' quarters survived against all odds by being hidden.

I wrote a National Register nomination for the duplex and succeeded in convincing the town of Wake Forest to preserve the building. Historic preservation planner Michelle Michael adopted the challenge wholeheartedly. She obtained grants to stabilize the building and manages an ongoing fundraiser for its full restoration. Allen Young's great-grandson, Ricardo Young, has joined the preservation project. Ricardo says, "I want my children and grandchildren to appreciate his legacy. We hope that many who learn about the Ailey Young House and about my great-grandfather will be inspired to better their world and strive for success just like he did."

## Old Ugly

*Back in the 1960s, my parents purchased a rental house in Morehead City at 1407 Shackleford Street, directly behind their cottage. An unknown contractor erected dozens of these modest one-story Victorian dwellings in town at the turn of the twentieth century. My father hilariously nicknamed it "Old Ugly" because its World War II-era asbestos wall shingles were a faded, unattractive shade of blue-green. In 1993, the city condemned it, and I decided to rehabilitate it to use for my family. One of my first actions was to paint the old wall shingles salmon pink, so the neighbors call it the "Pink House."*

*In 2003, after Hurricane Floyd devastated Carteret County, I converted it back into a rental. I hauled its furniture to the Salvation Army Thrift Store, which they were overjoyed to receive, even the mattresses that normally weren't accepted, because*

*Old Ugly (Pink House), 1407 Shackleford Street, Morehead City, 2020.*

so many families desperately needed new beds. I hired a contractor to install replacement windows and a new HVAC and to reattach drooping ceiling boards. Since then, I have rented Old Ugly as a cozy rental home for a high school teacher, a chef, a military family, and a high school secretary.

## 28
### Preserving the Recent Past

In the early twenty-first century, preservationists began fighting to preserve "the recent past," buildings and landscapes of the mid-twentieth century that had become old enough to be historic. If modern architecture signifies a progressive outlook, Raleigh qualifies. The city is said to contain the third largest concentration of Modernist design in the United States, after New York City and Los Angeles. In 1948, NC State University (in its first incarnation as a land-grant college) created a school of design and hired Henry Kamphoefner, a professor at the University of Oklahoma, as the dean. He brought to campus a team of pioneering modern architects, including George Matsumoto, Eduardo Catalano, Milton Small, Edward "Terry" Waugh, and John Latimer as design professors.[25]

Avant-garde families hired university professors and architects trained at the university to design bold modern suburban houses carefully integrated into their sites through split-level floors with patios and porches, open floor plans, innovative roof shapes, and large windows. The west Raleigh suburbs around the NC State University campus, including Cameron Village and Country Club Hills, contain the majority of these 1950s and 1960s Modernist homes.

Many of the mid-century landmarks built by these pioneering architects have been destroyed in recent years. On the university campus, the student union, the student bookstore, and the round classroom building Harrelson Hall have been bulldozed or enlarged beyond recognition by the university. Architect Milton

*Minimal Ranch at 2604 Crestline Drive, Fairway Acres, Raleigh. Photo by Ruth Little, 2006, courtesy of the North Carolina State Historic Preservation Office.*

Small's elegant International Style architectural office on Brooks Avenue stands, but his downtown Wake County Office Building and suburban Northwestern Insurance Office, 3515 Glenwood Avenue, are gone.

In 2004-2005, Raleigh's planning department hired me to conduct the first comprehensive survey of the post-World War II buildings of Raleigh, and also the first post-war survey for a city in North Carolina. What an unlikely choice I was to take on this work. I grew up in a Ranch house that I considered ugly in comparison with older, stylish houses. I always vowed to retire from historic preservation before Ranches reached fifty years of age, the minimum age to be considered potentially architecturally significant. With this Raleigh project, I was forced to research the ubiquitous Ranch house, built from the late 1940s to the mid-1970s, that dominated Raleigh's suburbs. In 2005, architectural historians had not yet published critical literature on the house type, so there were no academic sources to consult.

My yearlong survey[26] evaluated over 18,000 buildings, primarily dwellings, many in new suburban subdivisions. Modern architecture became mainstream as the city area tripled, population doubled, and developers built around the city limits to meet housing demands. Leading developers Willie York, Ed Richards, and Seby

Jones transformed Raleigh's outlying farmland into suburbs. (York's Cameron Village of the late 1940s included retail, office, and residential components, the first mixed-use suburban development south of Washington, DC.)

Raleigh's Ranches revealed a social, attitudinal, and economic divide. In order to evaluate the design and historical importance of the Ranch house, I invented a typology of two forms: minimal (small) and rambler (large), and three styles: archetypal, Colonial, and contemporary.

Colonial Ranches dominated in affluent conservative neighborhoods where families preferred the Colonial Revival style for its nostalgic nod to styles of the antebellum South, when variations of classical revival architecture were popular for dwellings. Minimal Ranches of archetypal (typical) character, with a side-gable roof, front picture window, small high bedroom windows, brick and wood walls, and sometimes a carport, were built by developers as speculative housing in tract subdivisions such as Raleigh's Brentwood and Ridgewood. These archetypal Ranches reflected the typical Ranch house built across the United States.

The Contemporary (mid-century) Ranch, usually custom-designed by an architect, incorporates large windows; clerestory windows just below the roofline; post-and-beam frameworks; and terraces, porches and carports that integrate the house into its typically hilly site.

Split-Level and Split-Foyer houses are post-war speculative variants of the Ranch. They were favored by IBM employees who moved into North Raleigh subdivisions as they relocated to Raleigh in 1965 to work at the first local IBM plant. Developer J.Y. Creech is credited with the earliest Split Foyers, a raised basement house with the front entrance set between the two levels that was larger than the standard Ranches and Split Levels. The type became known as an "IBM Split Foyer."

Based on my survey and report, I identified a number of 1950s and 1960s subdivisions in Raleigh as significant examples of post-World War II architecture and urban planning. Some were listed on the National Register, some remained potentially eligible but not listed. I drew attention to these mid-century houses just before they had become common targets for teardowns. During the real estate boom that followed the Great Recession of the late 2010s, many of Raleigh's older subdivisions were gradually destroyed by new, large residences.

Ten years after my first post-World War II survey of Raleigh, the State Historic Preservation Office hired me to update my earlier survey by surveying the 1965–1975 decade and surveying non-residential properties only. "Post-World War II and Modern Non-Residential Architecture in Raleigh, 1945-1975" was a year-long project in 2017-2018 that evaluated 2,500 buildings in the city limits. Able assistant Jenny Harper and I took a critical look at the rest of the post-war built environment that I hadn't concentrated on a decade earlier.

The hundreds of utilitarian tire shops and hundreds of churches of vanilla (Colonial Revival) flavor or chocolate (Gothic Revival)

*Among Modernist non-residential establishments, the iconic 1960 Char-Grill hamburger hut on Hillsborough Street wins the prize for a crazy roof. Photo by Ruth Little, 2018. Courtesy of the North Carolina State Historic Preservation Office.*

flavor did not excite us, but we loved the three-dozen bold and lyrical Modernist churches. I gained a new appreciation for the small concrete or brick branch banks with funky roofs and large windows that I remember from my childhood. I considered them ordinary then, but now understand them as symbols of the modern "get-up-and-go" energy of the business community after World War II. These little jewels are almost extinct—we found only three survivors in Raleigh, and all are threatened.

The biggest surprise was the disconnect between the business community's embrace of Modernism for commercial buildings and their allegiance to conservative Colonial Revival design for their homes. In fact, mid-century Raleigh's default commercial style is Modernist. Raleigh had more architects per capita than most cities because NC State's School of Design trained so many architects who stayed in Raleigh. As North Carolina's capital, Raleigh hosts a number of state offices for various organizations, such as the Parent Teacher Association and the Masons. Such headquarters consistently used Modernist design to symbolize a progressive attitude.[27]

## The Black Middle Class and Mid-Century Modernism

In 2012, I published an article on segregated Black subdivisions in Raleigh—"Getting the American Dream for Themselves: Postwar Modern Subdivisions for African Americans in Raleigh, North Carolina"—in the journal of the Vernacular Architecture Forum, *Buildings & Landscapes*.[28] Of the seventy-five suburban housing developments I documented, only three were built for Blacks. While white developers were busy after World War II building neighborhoods for young white families such as Hi-Mount, Cameron Village, Country Club Hills, and North Hills, middle-class Black families were trapped in sub-standard housing in southeast Raleigh. Would-be Black developers lacked the capital and political clout to acquire acreage and get financial backing.

Rochester Heights in South Raleigh, the earliest African American subdivision, was platted in 1957 by a white developer, Harry Phillips, around the 1950 Fuller Elementary School for African Americans. Teachers, attorneys, doctors, and other middle-class Blacks, who lived in the early 1900s neighborhood around Washington High School at the south end of Fayetteville Street, were thrilled to build custom Ranches and Split Levels in Rochester Heights.

Black developer John Winters platted Madonna Acres in 1960 on land behind St. Augustine's College, the historically Black school on Oakwood Avenue in east Raleigh. Middle-class families, many public school teachers or faculty and staff at St. Augustine's, designed their Ranches and Split Levels with the help of Winters, and his building company erected the houses. Battery Heights, platted in the 1930s east of the business district, saw construction of custom homes of this type in the late 1950s and early 1960s for Black doctors, teachers, and other professionals.

Anecdotal evidence in the South tends to confirm a correlation between the Black middle class and mid-century modernism. Madonna Acres and Battery Heights houses display the progressive upscale character missing from most of the white subdivisions of Raleigh, where homeowners favored the same revivals of Colonial and English Tudor houses that were popular before the war.

Educated, upwardly mobile African American World War II veterans, their wives, and their children, the early boomer generation, have built enduring suburban cultural landscapes by choosing modern design. When they could afford it, African Americans in the 1950s wanted their homes to project the American dream rather than nostalgia for the Old South or imitation of British styles. As a Madonna Acres resident said, "We'd been shotgunned. We weren't part of the American dream. We wanted the dream—big and new. Come on, let's go get it ourselves." Modernism was in the air. A neighbor in Battery Heights noted dryly, "We weren't into columns."

Harold Webb House, 1509 Tierney Circle, Madonna Acres, Raleigh. Rendering by architect Jerry Miller, 1962. Collection of Jerry Miller.

The houses in Raleigh's Black subdivisions include clean lines, Roman brick, stone veneer, large picture windows, carports, and open floor plans with cathedral-ceiling living rooms and tall masonry fireplaces—the types of features often found in popular magazines such as *Better Homes and Gardens* and *Good Housekeeping*. All three subdivisions—Rochester Heights, Battery Heights, and Madonna Acres are listed in the National Register of Historic Places.

Black families came to Jerry Miller, an NC State School of Design dropout who went on to design thousands of Raleigh houses in the sixties. Miller remembers, "They didn't say, 'I don't want what the white people have.' They said, 'I want my house to look different from everybody else.' They did not want Colonial; they preferred contemporary."

Miller designed Harold Webb's home in Madonna Acres in 1962. Webb, a Tuskegee airman in the US Air Force during World War II, graduated from NC Agricultural and Technical College, the state's African American land-grant college, and had a career as a teacher, principal, and state education department administrator. His two-story frame Modernist house features common areas on the second story, above a large recreation room that opens into a carport. My work to preserve Black neighborhoods continues to this day.

## 29
## Circling Back and Revisiting

One of the wonderful parts about my work is that often I have a chance to return to an area or topic I have investigated earlier, and so get an opportunity to study it from a different angle. One especially memorable return revisit occurred in 2000, when I last worked in the eastern North Carolina counties where my maternal relatives lived. That year, I listed the twenty-block center of Snow Hill on the National Register, creating a Snow Hill Historic District. That area included my Aunt Appless's house—the same one where I had enjoyed so many Thanksgiving meals and forbidden slides down her banister.

The town of Snow Hill, an agricultural seat, was a time capsule of the early 1900s. It had no connection to railroad lines and major highways and was one of the least changed towns in the state's coastal plain. One of the oldest houses in town, 112 West Greene Street, is a Gothic cottage built about 1860 from an A. J. Downing[29] pattern book and now the home of local historian Francis Sugg Jr. In the 1800s, most of the heads of household were gentleman farmers who owned extensive farmland but lived on Greene Street near schools, churches, stores, and society. Walking around town for the fieldwork, I chatted with people who recalled my Aunt Appless, including one former neighbor who used to zip App's dress in the morning before she went off to teach school.

### Revisiting Durham

In 1980, when I lived in East Durham with Michael and Kathleen Southern on North Driver Street, the old neighborhood was waiting for a rebirth. In 2004, when I created the East Durham National Register Historic District there, it was still waiting. Doing fieldwork in the neighborhood was a trip down memory lane. The largest historic neighborhood in Durham, the 563 buildings, primarily historic houses, comprised a high-poverty, high-crime area. Some sections were considered such a high risk for theft or muggings that I conducted the fieldwork with a local preservationist as a field assistant.

The oldest dwellings of late Victorian design date to the 1910s, bungalows were built until the 1940s, and many duplexes were built from the 1920s to the 1960s. A small neighborhood commercial district contains historic grocery stores and a bank; six churches and three public schools are interspersed around the neighborhood. Public and private nonprofit organizations have worked to market the dilapidated houses to economically and racially diverse first-time homeowners and working families. Because of East Durham's convenient location at the edge of the city and the affordability and historic tax credits available thanks to the area's National Register listing, the district now bustles with new families who are sensitively rehabilitating the old houses.

In 2013, the last Durham historic district that I created, the Foster-Geer Streets Historic District, was challenging because its post-war car dealerships, tire dealerships, and service stations surrounded by large parking lots were just on the verge of being historic. The R. J. Reynolds Tobacco Prizery of 1938, where tobacco leaves were pressed and stored prior to delivering them to the tobacco factory, is one of Durham's last and most interesting tobacco buildings. The 1948 Durham County Agricultural Extension Office, an Art Moderne design, originally contained an indoor curb market for produce.

Bold mid-century Modernist landmarks, such as the 1959 Home Savings and Loan building with dramatic metal canopies supported by a curved stone wall, add architectural delight to downtown Durham and would probably have been demolished without the recognition and tax credits available with the historic district status. The Savings and Loan building has been rehabilitated for architect Ellen Cassily's offices.

## Revisiting Fayetteville

In 2005 I prepared a separate National Register listing for The Capitol, a department store on Hay Street, Fayetteville's principal downtown shopping destination in the mid-twentieth century. Built for the Stein merchant family, The Capitol symbolizes the cultural and commercial contribution of the city's early twentieth-century Jewish immigrant citizens. The elegant Modernist white marble and gold mosaic façade with a convex upper display window with flanking balconies was inspired by a Viennese department store. The "Bird Cage" luncheonette on the mezzanine lured Fayetteville's wealthy matrons, wearing their Capitol finery, to lunch with their friends. Eating there was my childhood ideal of retail sophistication. When I cleaned out Mother's hoarder house in the early 2000s, most of the bags of never-used clothing had been purchased at The Capitol.

My last consulting project in Fayetteville, the Haymount Historic District Addition, in 2007, added two blocks to the Haymount Historic District, including the four-story Highsmith Memorial Hospital of 1926, where childhood health crises were treated. At age seven, my broken arm was set there in a plaster cast, later removed with a noisy chain saw. But stronger than my memory of the chainsaw are my memories of the panic attacks I suffered during the fieldwork. Even in 2007, forty years after my first panic attack and now relatively close to home, I continued to battle my demons that flared up so often when I ventured out.

## Revisiting Chapel Hill

Time spent in Chapel Hill earning a bachelor's degree in the late 1960s and a PhD from 1978 to 1983 gave me the deep

Bill and Ida Friday House, 412 Whitehead Circle, Chapel Hill. Photo by Claudia Brown, 2006, courtesy of the North Carolina State Historic Preservation Office.

understanding to write *The Town and Gown Architecture of Chapel Hill, North Carolina, 1795-1975*, published in 2006.[30]

Modesty and modernity became the themes of this first study of the town as a whole. The modern architecture was an outcome of UNC's progressive spirit as the first public university in America. Two centuries of faculty and staff imported fresh ideas from around the world and valued knowledge over material ostentation. The book includes a detailed first look at post-World War II Chapel Hill, when architects Jim and John Webb designed modest Modernist Ranches and Split Levels on sloping wooded lots in the campus suburbs for university families. The Webbs followed a regional northern California style of wood and stone created by William Wurster, a fusion of Frank Lloyd Wright's American modernism with European ideas and Japanese architecture's connection to nature. The early 1950s home for UNC President Bill Friday and his wife Ida on Whitehead Circle, a sleek rectangular frame Ranch with a private façade and a translucent rear wall of windows overlooking the woods, is typical of the Webb brothers' design.

## Russell School, Durham County

In 2009, I was blessed to work with a group of elderly African Americans to list Russell School, one of only two surviving of the eighteen 1920s Rosenwald Schools in Durham County, on the National Register. Chicago philanthropist Julius Rosenwald, the head of Sears, Roebuck, and Company, established the Rosenwald Fund in 1917 to construct Black schools in the South from carefully designed plans with money matching the funds raised locally. Between World Wars I and II when typical public schools for Blacks were small shacks, these modern schools provided substantial, dignified education buildings for several generations of African American children.

Russell School's two large classrooms separated by hinged doors allowed the space to open into an auditorium, with a small industrial/home economics classroom in the front. The school closed in 1945 but remained in use by the adjacent church, which preserved it in nearly mint condition. I was able to locate several people who had attended the school sixty-four years earlier and still lived in the community: Pearl Mack Holman, Russell Mack, Peggy Mack,

*Russell School, 2001 St. Mary's Road, Durham County. Photo by Ruth Little, 2009, courtesy of the North Carolina State Historic Preservation Office.*

David Cooper, and Bessie Pearley. They told me stories about their families of ten to twelve children who worked with their parents on their farms, raising corn, tobacco, cows, and other crops and livestock. The school year started in the fall after the tobacco was harvested and cured and continued until time to plant the spring crop. The humble Russell School harbored their memories of a good education in a building testifying that their education mattered.

## Revisiting Graves

In 2008 and 2009, I also had an opportunity to continue exploring gravemarkers, one of my longstanding passions. A group of Raleigh preservationists established Raleigh City Cemeteries Preservation Inc. in 2006 to preserve and promote Raleigh's neglected public cemeteries. Jane Thurman, Betsy Shaw, Dean Ruedrich, Terry Harper, and others have educated many citizens on these important spaces of memorial and history in our midst. Knowing my interest in historic cemeteries, the RCCP hired me in 2008 to list Raleigh's City Cemetery, 17 South East Street, on the National Register. The park-like cemetery attracted two of Raleigh's homeless men every night, and in the mornings I quietly worked around them to avoid waking them up while doing my survey.

Raleigh's City Cemetery, established in 1798 just outside the city limits on East Street, was four acres laid out in four squares bisected by driveways: the north two for citizens, the southwest one for "strangers," and the southeast one for "Negroes and persons of color." It is one of the earliest public cemeteries in North Carolina and one of the few that provided space for African Americans, albeit carefully separated. City Cemetery served as the principal burying ground for citizens until the late nineteenth century.

Approximately 1,800 monuments crowd the cemetery's grounds, generally arranged in family plots with masonry or iron borders. Persons of eminence in Raleigh's and North Carolina's history interred here include governors, newspaper editors, Confederate military leaders, ministers, doctors, attorneys, farmers, bankers, the British stonecutters that constructed the state capitol in the 1830s, and members of Raleigh's earliest families, including the Lanes. The most famous African American buried in the cemetery is Anna Julia Haywood Cooper, born an enslaved woman in Raleigh in 1858, who became a prominent scholar, author, educator, and Black feminist activist during a long life that ended in 1964.

The cemetery offers one of the finest collections of nineteenth-century funerary sculpture in North Carolina. The monuments include head- and footstones, box-tombs, obelisks, and mausolea cut by professional, out-of-state stonecutters, as well as by a group of Raleigh artisans. Especially evocative are the marble and native granite monuments carved by William Stronach, a Scottish native and one of the stonecutters imported to Raleigh in the 1830s to construct the state capitol with local granite. Stronach remained to serve as Raleigh's principal gravestone carver until his death in the late 1850s.[31]

Another cemetery project came my way in 2009 when the Raleigh City Cemeteries Preservation Inc. hired me to list Mount Hope Cemetery on the National Register. After the African American section of City Cemetery was full in 1872, Raleigh opened the new Mount Hope Cemetery at 120 Prospect Avenue.

The new location was an eleven-acre rural garden cemetery in the predominantly Black southern section of the city. Like many other African American historic landmarks in Raleigh, this is part of Raleigh's history largely hidden to white people. The hilly picturesque garden cemetery contains a significant collection of nineteenth and twentieth-century funerary sculpture, including locally made granite headstones from the 1840s and 1850s that were relocated there after 1872.[32] There are also marble headstones and obelisks of the late 1800s and early 1900s, twentieth-century granite monuments, box tombs, one mausoleum, and family plot enclosures.[33]

## Revisiting Porches

While busy with many other projects, I continued to think about loose ends from my past. After the harrowing trip to Charleston with an intense panic attack, I had dropped my first-choice dissertation topic in graduate school: early Southern piazzas. I had been obsessed with this type of dwelling since the early 1970s when I found many of them in NC's southeastern counties, and perhaps since my childhood when I first visited Beaufort in 1958. I still wanted to explore the coastal or tidewater cottages with piazzas that were built in eastern North Carolina in the 1700s and 1800s. My obsession with this type of dwelling had not diminished.

For years, dear friends had been cheering for me to find the courage to regroup and get the job done—to write about Carolina porches. Twenty-five years later, I picked up the unfinished business again. I published a porch article, "Vernacular Hospitality in the Carolinas: The Tidewater Cottage and the Preacher Room," in *Arris: Journal of the Southeast Chapter of The Society of Architectural Historians* in 2004.

One porched cottage from the article appeared on the journal cover. The cottage included a "preacher room," a small, shed room partitioned into the front or rear porch of a cottage that often served as a guest chamber that rural North Carolinians called a preacher room or a "stranger room." The rooms generally served as extra sleeping space, but their placement, often with no direct access into the house, allowed families to host travelers passing through in this era when commercial hotels rarely existed. In my article, I used the preacher room as a symbol of Southern hospitality.[34]

I still didn't feel finished writing about the Carolina porch house, but my chance came. The Great Recession of 2008 left me with little paid consulting work, so I decided it was time to get up and get the whole job done. The previously published article became the "Stranger Rooms" chapter of a full book, *Carolina Cottage: A Personal History of the Piazza House*. To create a popular history that my children might find readable, I folded the architectural history into a memoir of saving the Joseph Lane House, an example of a piazza house and of porch fieldwork throughout my career.

This was the first time I had the luxury of writing in the first person rather than in history's anonymous passive voice. The book jacket explains that "Margaret Ruth Little's new book is a celebration and a history of one of the most recognizable vernacular house types in the Upper South, the Carolina cottage. The one-and-one-half-story side-gabled cottage—with its most distinctive feature, the piazza—offers not only beauty and hospitality, but a rich history. Intertwined with this history is the author's own account of rescuing and living in a 1775 cottage near Raleigh, an experience that inspired and helps shape this charming book."

## 30
## Notable Projects After 2010

After 2010, I took on fewer, larger preservation projects that represented opportunities to take on unfinished business in my summer county of Carteret, in my favorite historic Raleigh neighborhood of Cameron Park, and in the old coastal town of New Bern.

### Carteret County

My penultimate work on my summertime county was the Carteret County Survey, my fourth comprehensive county inventory in North Carolina. I said goodbye to our Morehead City waterfront family cottage by staying there during the survey. We sold it in 2014 because my scattered family didn't spend much time there.

From 2011 to 2012, I spent three days a week in the county to drive every road and investigate every building. My inventory documented 600 individual historic properties, 95 percent of them houses. The east half of the county, known as "Down East," from Beaufort east, is a great pocosin (a swamp on a hill), sheltered from the ocean by a chain of sandy islands with only a few inlets to the ocean. In this archipelago of islands separated by marshes and open water, people traveled by boat until the 1920s and 1930s, when the government constructed highways and bridges. With sea level rise, it may again become an archipelago.

In volume one of *A New Geography of North Carolina*, author Bill Sharpe described Carteret County's people as "old, old families, but there is little outward pretension to aristocracy." The population was characterized by an egalitarianism of social structure and housing. Communities intermarried and carried the same surnames—especially Bell, Piver, Piner, and Guthrie. The geographic isolation preserved a regional British dialect that still exists. "High tide" is pronounced "hoi toide;" thus, Down Easterners are known as "Hoi Toiders." Most of the small homogenous rectangular, side-gable frame houses stand on the water or on the highways. They are a story and a jump or a full two stories, with a hall-and-parlor plan and an enclosed winder stair to the upper bedrooms. They feature a full porch along the long front side and waste no expense on decorative details.

I hold lifelong memories of the mosaic of Carteret County—by far the most beautiful landscape that I ever was blessed to investigate. Carteret is sandy lanes sheltered by ancient live oak trees in the historic district of the town of Atlantic, sturdy two-story houses built by carpenter Curtis Davis of Marshallberg,[35] and cemeteries filled with cedar grave markers in groves of live oak trees. The buildings stand out to me, too—the stark beauty of the 1805 Carraway House overlooking the water in Merrimon and the 1960s California modern Atlantis Lodge behind the sand dunes on Emerald Isle, to name just a couple of the county's glories. My motivation for completing this survey was strong: I wanted the humble man-made landscape of Carteret, built for function and comfort—not for show—to be preserved.

At the end of the Carteret County survey, I placed twenty-six houses and churches, one school, one harbor, several cemeteries, several motels, and an ocean fishing pier (one of the only two in the county that survive) on the eligibility list for the National Register. I identified two eligible historic districts—the core of the towns of Atlantic and Newport.

My final project in Carteret County was to bring scholars from Colonial Williamsburg to Beaufort to research the oldest houses, known locally as the "Beaufort type." These are the same one- and two-story frame houses with integral front porches that I called the "piazza house" in my book.

I organized summer field schools of students from the College of William and Mary in Williamsburg, Virginia, to investigate Beaufort in 2011 and 2012. The goal of the field schools was to systematically study as many as possible of the so-called "eighteenth-century houses" with historic plaques displaying construction dates in the 1700s issued by the Beaufort Restoration Association. The dates often reflect the date the original owner acquired the property rather than the dwelling construction date, because often the current house replaced the original one.

The oldest porch on a "Beaufort-type" house is at the Josiah Bell House, original to the 1825 construction. The most surprising feature discovered by the field schools is at the Piver House, 125 Ann Street, built in the early 1800s. Most porch rafters are concealed by a ceiling, but the Piver front porch was open to the rafters, allowing the breeze to ventilate the attic bedroom through a wooden vent in the bedroom wall. Such porch wall vents into attic bedrooms are common in the Deep South, but this may be the only one known in North Carolina.

I coordinated the field schools, selected the houses, and worked with generous townspeople, the Beaufort Garden Club, and the

*Piver House, 125 Ann Street, Beaufort, NC. Photo by Carl Lounsbury, 2011.*

Carl Lounsbury and me on a Front Street porch in Beaufort, 2011, by an unknown photographer.

Beaufort Women's Club to provide food and housing for the participants. Most homeowners enthusiastically welcomed the field school into their basements and attics, where experts and students looked at wooden beam saw marks, nail manufacture, and the assemblage of floor, wall, and attic beams.

Carl Lounsbury, Willie Graham, and Jeff Klee, the visiting scholars who supervised the study, have worked for many years for Colonial Williamsburg in Virginia. These building detectives do forensic research on building materials, design, and evolution in order to determine construction history. The field schools accomplished the major goal of firmly documenting the North Carolina piazza house to the period between 1800 and the 1830s, thus stripping Beaufort of actual eighteenth-century houses. The research also took some of my *Carolina Cottage* house dates out of the eighteenth century, but the truth is always a historian's goal.

The 2011 field school findings were published in a beautiful report containing field notes, house plans, and high-quality digital photographs: *Early Domestic Architecture in Beaufort, North Carolina, and Tidewater Virginia* (College of William and Mary and Colonial Williamsburg Foundation, Summer, 2011 Field School in Architectural History). Although we provided a great service to the town of Beaufort, the homeowners clung to their 1700s plaque dates—the Beaufort myth—instead of Beaufort fact. But these houses don't need 1700s dates to be precious.

### Duncan House

*The building detectives traced the evolution of the Duncan House, a Carolina cottage that I had fixated on as a twelve-year-old in 1958 that helped determine my future as an architectural historian. The dates and functions of the house's various parts had never been firmly documented; hence it remained a mystery until our Colonial Williamsburg detectives studied it. Carteret County is a maritime place, connected with the sea and seafaring activity, and the house epitomizes the "Beaufort-type" house of two stories with a full-length double integral porch. Well-known Beaufort builder J. Davis constructed the house on a foundation of ballast stones from ships' holds. The east four bays with its center-hall plan was built about 1815; the west half, a ships commissary and office, was added about 1832. Ship masts serve as support columns in the big open commissary room on the first floor for the second-story bedrooms above. One of the only brick rainwater cisterns left in Beaufort stands beside the back porch.*

### Cameron Park and the Chancellor's House

In 2013, Preservation North Carolina president Myrick Howard asked me to write a book about the Cameron Park neighborhood to commemorate its centennial as a planned early twentieth-century suburb located across Hillsborough Street from North Carolina State University. I knew Cameron Park well because many of my colleagues and friends have lived there for decades. The book, *Cameron Park, Raleigh, North Carolina: A Remote Retreat on Hillsboro Street, 1910–2010*, published in 2014, with lovely photographs by resident photographer David Strevel and a beautiful cover painted by resident artist Abie Harris, is more about the residents who have acted on the Raleigh stage for a century than it is about the architecture of the houses.

The old streetcar suburb contains houses of neighborly design, social homogeneity, and flexible floor plans that often allowed more than one family to share the large houses. "Discreet Duplexes" are one of its most interesting house types. The narrative tells the story of a neighborhood's birth, decline after World War II, and its revival against all odds in the 1970s. Writing this book taught me that often the most meaningful aspect of a neighborhood is its people rather than the buildings themselves.

Around this same time, my artist friend Susan Woodson, the wife of NC State University chancellor Randy Woodson, asked me to write a book to celebrate the role of the old chancellor's residence as it was replaced by a new residence on the university's new Centennial Campus. Writing a "house book" did not interest me, but researching the vision and family life of each of the nine university leaders who occupied the house with their families taught me the gripping story of the university, a land-grant institution founded in 1887 as the North Carolina College of Agriculture and Mechanic Arts. Corresponding with and meeting descendants of the early leaders, and interviewing recent chancellors, convinced me, a lifelong "Tar Heel" fan of the University of North Carolina, to make room in my heart for the "Wolfpack" of North Carolina State University. I named the book *Through the Crystal Ball of the Chancellor's Residence: North Carolina State University 1928–2012*.[36]

## Dryborough Community, New Bern

In 2015, I returned to New Bern to add the Black community of Dryborough to the New Bern Historic District, which already contained the historic white sections of the coastal town. Ethel Staten, a charming and distinguished Dryborough resident who lives in a Craftsman Foursquare house at 828 Bern Street built by her grandparents in 1924, provided much of the oral history of the neighborhood for the report.

Dryborough's story of exclusion and devaluation is a case study of African American history in North Carolina. Since the 1850s, the community has been the center of Black life in New Bern and the location of the oldest Black churches. The oldest public Black cemetery in North Carolina, Greenwood Cemetery, was established there in 1860. As I discussed in my 1997 project with New Bern's historic Black churches, the white part of town was saved by city firemen during the Great Fire of 1922, which destroyed the entire Dryborough neighborhood. Middle-class Black families rebuilt two-story Craftsman-style houses on their property by 1924, and the next generation of educated Blacks built substantial brick homes in the neighborhood during the mid-twentieth century.

As part of the current Black Lives Matter movement in 2020, one urgent trend in historic preservation is to preserve places for people of color that have been neglected. Any freedmen's villages, historic Black churches and schools, Black business buildings, and cemeteries that still exist in North Carolina should be high priority on the list of landmarks that should be preserved.

## Part IV

# Mama Cool Exorcizes Her Ghosts

*Dancin' on the Porch, 36 x 36 inch acrylic on canvas, 2018.*

# 31
## Roundabout

In 2011, I co-founded an artists' association in Raleigh named the Roundabout Art Collective with Susan Woodson, a friend and artist mentioned previously. Thanks to Susan's connections and a lot of hard work, our collective of twenty artist members—painters, jewelers, photographers, craftspeople, and sculptors—was able to rent gallery space, first a former pawn shop on Hillsborough Street across from NC State University, later an old house on Oberlin Road. The gallery displayed our art for sale, and as part of downtown Raleigh's "First Friday" event of each month, we hosted an art opening for a guest artist or special promotion of one of our members. First Friday was always a gala party with many family and friends who loved art.

I continued to take art classes at Pullen Art Center in Raleigh and painting workshops. These classes and the Roundabout Art Collective gave me a professional structure, a congenial competitiveness to produce new art each month. Compared to history, my art had felt frivolous since the putdown in college. Now I had a community that inspired me to carve out time from my consulting career to make paintings.

During the 2010s, I painted new art in Longleaf Studio, shared with my Longleaf Historic Resources office, every month to exhibit at the Roundabout Art Collective gallery. My creativity has been primed by painting classes with Mary Ann K. Jenkins, Leslie Pruneau, Kirk Adam, Brandon Cordrey, Lori Jones, and Peter Marin in the city of Raleigh's arts program. Cheryl Weisz, a fellow Roundabout artist, taught a creativity workshop that chipped away at my art scars (the door!). Incomparable Roundabout jeweler Mary Ann Scherr provided constant helpful critiques. I painted old buildings, landscapes, fish houses, disappearing frogs, people dancing on porches, and tobacco barns in watercolor, acrylic, oil, and collage and mixed media. Each painting is like a child that I send out into the world to be adopted by friends and strangers.

The "real" career of historic preservation always tries to upstage my creation of art. A puzzling dream symbolizes this hierarchy of importance. When I (in reality) published the book on NC State's chancellor's residence in 2013, which my friend Susan Woodson had lived in, I stood on the house's main stair for a book event. In the dream, I opened a door below the stair and found a spring with deep, clear, beautiful water with green plants and goldfish bubbling up from the basement. The force of the crystal-clear water, the greenery, and flashes of gold mesmerized me. Susan and I knew it was a miraculous phenomenon that University Facilities would want to destroy so that it wouldn't flood the house. I looked out the window and saw suited men walking into the house and woke up.

The dream represented the systematic stuffing of my creative impulses. I had a childhood of repression by authority figures. Mother thought I wasn't ladylike. My college professor disparaged my artistic talent, so I decided to be an art historian. In the dream, I opened the door of my basement scar and found a deep spring of creativity hiding from the authority figures.

Our Roundabout Art Collective gallery stood at 305 Oberlin Road, across from the Cameron Park Fire Station, until 2017. The charming house had been built by an African American family in the Oberlin Village neighborhood in the early 1900s. We used the four rooms downstairs as our gallery, the little kitchen in the back as our sales office, and the attic bedrooms as studios. The gingerbread front porch made a great bar space for parties. An out-of-state developer (another authority figure) bought most of the block for a mixed-use project, cancelled our lease, and destroyed our collective. That was the end of the Roundabout, but our website www.

roundaboutartcollective.com lives on, and we artists have found new venues to share our art.

My Longleaf Studio artist statement:

*People could say of me, "Her habit of moving quickly keeps her ahead of old age and worry." I paint like I move—really fast. Since I'm not afraid of mistakes, I let it rip. I sometimes fail, then start over on the same unfinished canvas. I look for "happy accidents" when my new layers interact with older layers. I love painterly paintings that celebrate thick paint, color, brushstrokes, and texture that create form but never look like reality. I want to convey a passion for spontaneity: I don't like tight, careful paintings.*

Working in my Longleaf Studio.
Photo by Warren Davis, 2014.

*My paintings usually depict landscapes and cityscapes. They celebrate the heartbreaking beauty of nature and people wandering around old buildings. I often incorporate paper and cardboard in order to add depth or whimsy. Sometimes I paint from my own black and white photographs, which I recreate in fantastic combinations of complementary colors—especially orange and blue, with no relationship to reality. I'm learning to let myself go. Sometimes I leave my brain out of the painting by looking out the window and letting the land and trees jump into my canvas without thinking.*

## Art Side Trips

*Bryant Park, 24 x 24 inch oil on canvas, 2012, captures my discovery of the park in Manhattan on a spring morning, with the blue shadows of people merging with tree shadows. At the time, my son worked in a nearby office building, and I wandered the surrounding blocks to soak up the New York City vibe.*

*View from Dix Hill, 24 x 24 inch oil on canvas, 2012, features an abstracted view of the Raleigh skyline seen from Dorothea Dix Hospital.*

**At right:** *Frances, 11 x 11 inch watercolor, 2013. Ccreated for a "Disappearing Frogs" art exhibit to raise money for research to protect amphibian habitat.*

**Below:** *Fertile Ground, 24 x 30 inch oil on canvas, 2016, is a memory of my Caswell County architecture survey. I collaged crimped newspaper to simulate a freshly plowed field. The name is a pun for my habit of reading the newspaper, fertile ground for my imagination.*

*Glen Eden 1, 24 x 30 inch acrylic on canvas, 2017. In painting from nature (plein air), I just look at the shapes and let my brush respond.*

~

Mother passed in 2005. At age ninety-one, her dancing days were long gone. In an old African American proverb, when an old person dies, a library burns down. In her last years, she suffered from Alzheimer's disease and believed her children were her parents, which in many ways was true. During my frequent visits to her assisted living home, I brought old family photos saved from emptying her house. Like me, Mother treasured photos and had collected them from her own family and Dad's family; unfortunately, they were not only disorganized, they were sifted one by one or a few here and there in the junk in her hoarder house.

Until a few years before her death, Mother's memory of the long-ago was as sharp as her short-term memory was non-existent. She provided names and stories for photos of her family and friends from her youth and long life, which I wrote on the back of each photo. She had labelled many of them years ago in the neat print that she had taught her first-grade students during her career as a teacher. I wrote in her obituary that "Virginia was a unique individual who will be remembered for her great energy, love of practical jokes, and her gifts for storytelling and writing poetry. She was a gregarious person who loved being out visiting friends. Her vivacious teaching style brought the world of reading to hundreds of youngsters."

My life simplified greatly after I was no longer Mother's caretaker, and my dreams reflected the change. The baggage symbol in my night stories was joined and then eventually replaced by shoes, a symbol of a new path and future plans, and Mother was replaced by my children. In one dream, my kids made me give up all my baggage except what I could carry, but while cleaning out my bag I accidently sabotaged myself by giving away my comfortable sneakers.

I dream I'm at a Vernacular Architecture Forum conference, where I keep losing a shoe, so I make an amusing fashion statement by wearing one stylish shoe and one clunky shoe. I dream that I forget my backpack and tell my daughter that the only thing I cannot do without are sleeping pills. She says I'll be okay because she has a whole pharmacy—I trust her and we travel on. In another dream I check out of a motel and go to my daughter's room, where the drawers and closets are stuffed with clothes Mother gave her. My daughter leaves them behind, so I do too. In another, I organize a family reunion and fifteen young cousins carry my belongings to a new dormitory room.

In a dream of sabotaging new love, I get on a train and sit beside a handsome, flirty man. At the next stop, I get off to go to the bathroom and the train leaves without me. Why didn't I fly to meet the train like my grandmother Ruth did in her dream? Finally, in another dream, I'm staying in a rundown boarding house in a foreign country. I find a baby in the sofa and take it outside so her feet can touch the ground. A baby is a symbol of new life—I'm the baby and I'm getting off the couch.

Although I had escaped from my marriage and Mother, panic attacks continued to happen regardless of whether I was traveling for work or pleasure. In 2005, the Degraffenried Park Historic District in New Bern required three separate field trips from Raleigh to New Bern. Traveling alone on the first two trips, I had crippling attacks. For the third trip to attend the evening public meeting at the courthouse, I took along an assistant yet still suffered attacks on the way, during the meeting, and returning home. In 2007, a consulting project required multiple trips to Smithville, a historic village on the upper Cape Fear River near my hometown of Fayetteville, and triggered a panic attack each trip. I commuted to Sanford to spend weekends with a boyfriend in 2007. The next year, I commuted to Oxford to spend time with another boyfriend. Making these drives often brought on panic attacks, so it was important to drive during daylight hours when there was less risk of getting lost.

～

After Hurricane Katrina nearly destroyed the Gulf Coast in 2005, I volunteered as a preservation consultant in Mississippi, a career highlight because its Creole culture and architecture have always beckoned me. I worked with a colleague, Jennifer Baughn of the Mississippi State Historic Preservation Office, for a week in October. We conducted emergency field surveys of flooded historic neighborhoods in Gulfport to identify eligible National Register historic districts to prevent wholesale demolition of damaged historic houses.

It is hard to describe the destruction I witnessed as I walked through a neighborhood of beautiful late 1800s and early 1900s houses. These houses were pushed off their foundations, with trash mountains of furniture, carpets, and household goods awaiting FEMA dump trucks. I wrote architectural descriptions and sketched boundaries on a field map on my trusty clipboard and took photographs. In the African American early twentieth-century

*Me with my clipboard documenting the destruction in Gulfport, Mississippi, after Hurricane Katrina, 2005.*

community of Turkey Creek at the back edge of Gulfport, the creek had flooded every house. I created an inventory of the entire community, interviewed a number of people, and wrote a historic district report that led to its listing on the National Register.

During spring break of 2009, I chaperoned a UNC-Chapel Hill jazz band trip to New Orleans, where the students volunteered with Habitat for Humanity. The students, including my son Britton, worked in the Lower Ninth Ward during the day to erect new houses on the sites of the dwellings destroyed by Hurricane Katrina. We slept in classrooms at Camp Hope, a formerly flooded middle school repurposed as a Habitat dormitory, in wall-to-wall bunk beds and ate in the school cafeteria. Most of us succumbed to the "Camp Hope crud" because of the close quarters, but everyone kept working and danced to jazz in the cafeteria some evenings after supper. Other evenings, the band played jazz concerts around Louisiana.

Being a part of thousands of college students who spent their spring break rebuilding houses in the Lower Ninth Ward after Hurricane Katrina instead of partying at a beach resort filled my heart with hope for the future. The millennial generation to which my son and daughter belong will surely help to solve the big problems of racial justice and the environmental crisis in the world. I had seen my daughter and her friends' commitments to make the world a better place. In New Orleans, I saw my son and his friends' dedication not just to music but also to social activism. One night I watched the jazz band play at the famed Snug Harbor jazz club in the French Quarter. Britton played swing drums with his hero Jason Marsalis, the youngest son of New Orleans's Marsalis family—the current first family of jazz. On our last night, everyone received an award; mine was a piece of a 2 x 4 plank declaring me to be "Mama Cool."

# 32
## Oberlin

In 2006, I sold the middle-class brick Colonial home where my husband and I had raised our children. It was a museum of their childhoods but also haunted by my marriage and too big for one person. I bought a house that combined my interest in mid-century modern style with the adventure of living in Oberlin Village, a nearby historic African American community. The living and dining room with a soaring cathedral ceiling became my own art gallery, where I hung my paintings of New York City street scenes and also large paintings by friends Bob Irwin, Ellen Gamble, and Gayle Lowry. Many of my heirloom plants moved with me into the new garden. Getting rid of one-half of my possessions, then painting and decorating the new house to suit my own colorful taste liberated me.

My new neighborhood has an interesting history. Formerly enslaved people who had been freed settled the area after the Civil War and named it "Oberlin" in honor of James Henry Harris, an African American who attended Oberlin College in Ohio and became a Raleigh leader and settlement promoter. The village remained independent until annexed by Raleigh in 1920. Families lived in humble frame houses during most of the segregated Jim Crow era, then after World War II erected brick Ranches and Split Levels like those in East Raleigh Black neighborhoods. By the 2000s, Oberlin's proximity to NC State University and the migration of families to suburbs resulted in many of the weathered bungalows being converted into white student rentals. The neighborhood contained three uneasy constituencies—older Black families who owned their homes, student rentals, and white gentrifiers like me.

Since moving to Oberlin, I've worked to preserve the village's character and history. In 2007, a developer tried to demolish a fourplex on Chamberlain Street and rezone it for overly narrow lots, so we neighbors organized a neighborhood association to fight the action. In 2011, we founded the Friends of Oberlin Village, a coalition of village descendants, white residents, and concerned citizens. Among the notable Black leaders of this group are Joseph Holt, Cheryl Williams, Sabrina Goode, and Karen Throckmorton. I researched Oberlin Cemetery in the heart of the village and designated it a Raleigh Historic Landmark in 2012, then listed it on the National Register in 2018.[37]

Oberlin Cemetery, established in 1873, is a literal and symbolic repository of the African American pioneers, many born into slavery, who established the freedmen's village of Oberlin during the Reconstruction Era. As a segregated Black cemetery from Reconstruction through the Jim Crow era, it embodies African American traditions and socioeconomic circumstances. Many early gravestones are cast concrete monuments made by local masons that reflect African American vernacular artisanry outside the white commercial mainstream. The cemetery was neglected because its ownership was ambiguous. Since then, we have worked to assume legal responsibility for it and to restore the monuments and landscape to their original appearance.

Historic Black neighborhoods in Raleigh will be gentrified out of existence without the protection of historic districts and landmark designations. As downtowns revitalize and people seek walkability, old Black-owned dwellings, often rentals, are razed to build expensive new houses for affluent whites. Until our neighborhood association was formed, the wishes of Oberlin's residents were ignored. There were almost no people at the table who desired preservation of existing buildings, and investors and developers

*John and Roberta Parham House, 2312 Bedford Avenue, Oberlin Village Historic District, Raleigh, 2017.*

had acquired a number of land parcels in anticipation of wholesale demolition and infill construction.

An ever-growing group, the Friends of Oberlin Village, coalesced to preserve some physical fabric, but I was one of only a few members who actually *lived* in the proposed historic district. In 2018, when the Graves-Fields House, one of Oberlin's most significant landmarks, was purchased by a developer and slated for demolition, the city hired me to survey and designate the Oberlin Historic Overlay District. Although Oberlin Village is being redeveloped, many of the properties—Wilson Temple United Methodist Church, Oberlin Baptist Church, the Community Deli corner store, the village cemetery, and rows of African American nineteenth and early twentieth-century homes—are protected by historic district zoning. Exterior changes to buildings must undergo review; any demolition requires a one-year delay. Preservation North Carolina, a statewide historic preservation nonprofit, purchased the Graves-Fields House and moved it next door to the Plummer T. Hall House to become their new state headquarters. These stylish 1880s houses with shiny new paint announce to thousands of passing cars that Oberlin Village will survive.

My sweet house, the John and Roberta Parham House on 2312 Bedford Avenue, stands in the historic district. Parham, an administrator at Shaw University, and Roberta, a schoolteacher, had it built in 1966 for their family. The mid-century modern Split Level is one of the African American houses that I surveyed in 2005 before buying it in 2006. In 2018, I obtained the first certificate of appropriateness in the Oberlin Historic District to replace my four original flimsy plywood doors with new energy-conserving fiberglass and wood doors of compatible design. Now I sit at my writing desk beside the patio door without freezing. If I sell, my middle-class African American home might not be bulldozed, at least until the year's waiting period is over. As Raleigh erases its past, I want 2312 Bedford Avenue to survive. Raleigh friends are also working to preserve their beloved historic homes. When they sell in order to downsize, they write restrictive covenants into their deeds to prevent demolition by new owners.

## 33
### I Know Who You Are

In 2013, during a two-week tour of China, I made some progress in managing panic attacks. At the end of our tour, I spent a day shopping alone in Kowloon, Hong Kong's densest island. The commercial streets were a high-rise, chaotic assault to the senses: jammed with vehicles, sidewalks gridlocked with pedestrians, signs and digital advertising billboards stacked vertically ten stories high, and names of streets invisible amid the chaos of imagery. I tested a strategy to explore one block—exiting the hotel and taking three left turns at each street brought me back to the hotel. After that accomplishment, having memorized some visual landmarks such as a particular shop or restaurant or bank, I could access an adjacent block, one at the time. I explored Kowloon like Ulysses did the labyrinth, with a ball of twine to show me the way out. I envied fellow travelers who recounted stories of their visits to waterfront museums and other Hong Kong sights with no fear of getting lost.

Visiting my children as they globe-hopped in young adulthood forced me to marshal all my fortitude against anxiety. To visit Britton in Brooklyn, I landed at JFK Airport and took the Long Island Railroad into downtown Brooklyn, then tamped down my fluttering heart while I waited for him at the main train stop. With him, I was unafraid. From his apartment, I'd take the subway into Manhattan with him to his office, then explore his surroundings with the same system I used in Hong Kong, one block at a time to establish landmarks. If I had to travel alone on the subway, I used written directions but would also ask other passengers on the platform and on the trains to help me find my stop.

Traveling with Gia in El Salvador and Guatemala in the early 2010s allowed me to get off the beaten path without anxiety, but there were limits. One day in Antigua, Guatemala, where a magnificent volcano spews plumes of smoke at regular intervals, we visited a jade shop, then agreed to go in separate directions and meet at our hotel. My sole objective was to return to the hotel, but once I started walking, a panic attack blocked my normal navigational skills and even my ability to read the map I carried. Eventually I arrived, shaky with stress, at our room.

One day in El Salvador we hiked in a national park with several other young tourists to a volcano that had recently erupted. We passed the ruins of houses recently destroyed by lava. I had read in our tour book that tourists should have a tour guide for protection from local robbers, so I got increasingly uneasy after pickup trucks carrying local men with machetes passed us. Finally, I could no longer tolerate the fear, probably a rational one rather than a panic attack, and ordered my daughter to turn back with me, which she did reluctantly.

Sometimes panic attacks are dangerous. In 2013, visiting Gia in Boulder, Colorado, where she taught Spanish, I stayed alone at an Airbnb apartment with her car. The next morning, without any breakfast, I left the house to pick her up, ran a stop sign, and totaled her car because of anxiety and unfamiliarity with the route to her house.

~

After two insecurely attached marriages that didn't work, I had a chance to figure out what type of guy I needed. I wanted a man who was smart, athletic, politically moderate, creative, and with whom I had good chemistry and communication. Unfortunately, the narcissistic, domineering type appealed to me because I had grown up with an authority figure like that. I didn't yet understand that I needed a man who loved me enough that I could trust and feel safe with him, a secure home base.

From 2000 to 2014, I blundered around on dating websites looking for my match. Although the overall result was a tragicomedy, I wouldn't take anything for the adventures I've had exploring the entire spectrum of the male gender. Finding Mr. Home Base took a lot of rejections, both by me and of me. One of the saddest aspects of the dating game is that each time you break up is like your house being destroyed. You lose all that time and emotion and have nothing to show for it. But, undeterred, I told my friends, "I'll never give up looking for someone to share life with."

At the end of 2011, a dream offered tips for finding true love. In the dream, I'm sleeping outside on a trip and hear a thunderstorm coming. I seek shelter from a flood in a car, or maybe a boat. The next morning, when people arrive to help me, my violin is nearly ruined. A nice man with a teasing smile reassembles the bow, which looks smashed but has only come unscrewed. He reattaches the bridge and strings and hands it to me, still glistening with floodwater. I take the hem of my long skirt and dry it off slowly to delay the moment of reckoning when he will see that I've forgotten or never knew how to play the fiddle. I enjoy the drying, so feminine and old-fashioned and sensuous. At this pre-resolution point, I wake up. The violin is me. The dream tells me I will find love by taking a risk, sleeping alone on a trip, wearing feminine clothes, and being baptized by a flood.

In early July 2014, still searching for love on Match.com, I had a triumphant dream about finding my way home. In the dream, I was piloting my Boston Whaler boat around Manhattan but didn't know how to get back to Brooklyn where my son lived. A dock worker pointed me in the right direction, and I headed off to my son's apartment, then woke up.

About this time, my art teacher and friend bought a plant from a man in Raleigh who sold plants on the Craigslist website. He confided to her that he was widowed and looking for a new woman. She saw a chance to put two lonely hearts together and recommended her friend, Ruth Little, an artist and an architectural historian. She emailed me his photo to see if I was interested. The Universe sent me a man! But I was getting ready to travel to Alaska for a vacation with my children and didn't take time to reply to my art teacher and answer its knock on my door.

When I returned from Alaska in late July, I opened up my Match profile to continue my search for the right guy. One of the "daily 24" men that appeared on the screen that day jumped out at me—a handsome, late-middle-aged man with a sweet, warm smile. His profile intrigued me as well: a biologist with a graduate degree who lives in North Raleigh and who said, "At this point in my life I am dedicated to finding ways to help people."

Although I almost never emailed guys first because they never emailed me back, I clicked on his profile and messaged that I thought he had a wonderful face. One hour later he replied enthusiastically. I wrote back and told him about my historic preservation career. His next reply shocked me to the core—*I know who you are*. He said he had sold plants to a woman a month earlier who told him about me because she thought he would like me, but he never got her phone number to follow through. Just like that, the universe put Warren Alan Davis in front of me for the second time.

The next day, July 22, we met at Serena's restaurant near his home in North Raleigh and ate dinner. He was a good talker and we marveled at how the universe put us together. He kept on talking and talking, telling me his life story, while I was left out of the conversation. I had met a lot of conversation hogs and thought he was another. On our way out to our cars, I said, "If we ever meet again, maybe you will find out something about me." He emailed an apology the next day, and we agreed to a second meeting the next week. On our second meeting, the conversation and chemistry flowed, and we've never looked at anyone else since then.

We've both had a life of unhappy relationships—his two wives were both troubled and abusive to him. One was unfaithful, the other suffered from one mental illness after another and diverted their joint financial assets to go to her family rather than to him

*Warren and me in Lyon, France, 2019, revisiting where I spent my university year abroad and where Warren traveled many times for business.*

after death. A few years earlier, he had survived a brain tumor that required many months of physical rehabilitation. We recognized in each other strength, resilience, and an optimism and openness to the future that makes each day a new adventure.

Warren is my secure attachment—the safe, snug shelter and "warren" that I've looked for my whole life. The word means a network of interconnecting rabbit burrows or a labyrinthine district, and the English surname meant "guard." He is my last Match.com man, because I will be with him until death do us part. Since we met in 2014, we've rarely been apart. We alternate staying at his house and my house and help each other fix up our abodes. We take fishing expeditions to the mountains and the coast. We walk and bike the greenways. We cook the venison that he hunts, the fish that he catches, and the backyard vegetables that he grows, using recipes that we improvise as we go along. We shop at Mexican groceries and Middle Eastern markets to buy unusual grains and spices to give the food international flavors. We take turns reading the same books. Each year we take a long vacation in Europe. We fret over each other's ailments. We might as well be married, but since each of us had two unhappy marriages, we think we are good just like we are—engaged for life. Every day he asks me, "How did I get so lucky?" and I answer, "How did WE get so lucky?" or I say, "The universe put us together," or sometimes, "This is our karma for all the suffering we've endured—it's our turn to be happy."

The security of Warren, my safe person, apparently slayed the panic attack demons.

A week after meeting Warren, I had a dream that I named the "Graduation from Crawl Space" dream. A friend and I are "tending" stuff in a dirt crawl space underneath a house. Her stuff is more important than mine. I realize my stuff is just old junk and trash that doesn't need tending, so I drag it out and throw it away. The stuff was my useless baggage, my anxiety. Since then, my panic attacks have been practically nonexistent.

## 34
## Losing a Cottage, Revisiting Caswell County and Dad's Roots

As my children grew into adulthood and moved out of state, Little Leisure 2, our fancy waterfront beach cottage, saw less and less use. We finally sold it in 2013 to a Raleigh-area builder who planned to use it as his own cottage, making only minor renovations. In October 2014, Warren and I drove to Old Ugly, my old house behind the fancy cottage, to meet with a painting crew. It was my first trip back to Morehead since we had sold our beautiful former cottage, and I looked forward to showing it to him.

As the car neared Little Leisure 2, I looked for its familiar silhouette on the water, but instead I saw a two-story mountain of debris. I had a moment of disorientation; this couldn't be the site of our former cottage. But then I recognized the front porch posts lying on the ground and knew that it was. A large bucket loader was busily pushing debris toward dump trucks.

When I got out of the car, over the noise of the machinery I heard the cries of the house's floors, walls, and ceilings. The heavy timbers creaked and groaned as the bucket shoveled them into the truck beds. I walked in shock around the demolition site and yelled to the operator that he was destroying my house. He grimaced and said, "This house did not want to come down! It was built to last a hundred years!"

I walked back to Old Ugly, one lot to the rear, with tears streaming down my face, mourning the loss of the cottage with so many memories that we sold, but took solace that Old Ugly was still standing and that I still owned it and could protect it.

Warren, my safe attachment, became my fieldwork assistant when I revisited Caswell County in 2014. Dr. Howard Holderness, great-grandson of William Henry and Sarah Holderness, repurchased his ancestor's house after 150 years and hired me to list it on the National Register. For many years, I had longed to study furniture maker Thomas Day's work more closely; now I could document one of his finest creations, the William Henry and Sarah Holderness House.

Three miles west of the Caswell County seat of Yanceyville, it is one of the most intact Greek Revival-style houses with Thomas Day interior woodwork in North Carolina. Built about 1855 by the Holderness family, the two-story frame house features a low hip roof, a one-story, pedimented entrance portico with Doric columns, and one-story wings, each with a matching portico, that are a rare element of Greek Revival-style houses in North Carolina. To the rear are the ruins of an original log double quarters where enslaved people had lived. As a county commissioner and sub-agent of the Confederacy during the Civil War, William Henry Holderness played an important role in husbanding county foodstuffs during three years of bad weather that caused a local famine.

Thomas Day (1801–1861), a free Black man and master artisan, lived in Milton, in Caswell County, from the 1820s to his death in 1861. He became the state's most successful cabinetmaker at that time, producing furniture and architectural woodwork for the leading white citizens in the Dan River Valley region in North Carolina and Virginia. Working within the dominant antebellum Roman and Grecian styles disseminated by pattern books in New York City and Baltimore, Day created a personal aesthetic whose sinuous, dynamic curves and elaborate openwork expressed an African American sensibility unique in American furniture and architectural woodwork. Day's work reinterprets elite furniture with bolder curves and spirals for a more three-dimensional effect. His success as a cabinetmaker followed the rising fortunes of Caswell County's tobacco planters. In the Holderness House, one of seven surviving houses with the full ensemble of Day woodwork, the central hall contains a staircase with a free-form newel, stair brackets and handrails. Flanking parlors and sitting rooms feature ornate mantels and flanking storage niches.

In 2016, State Historic Preservation Office colleagues, including Michael Southern, Claudia Brown, Marvin Brown, Catherine Bishir, and I hosted the 2016 conference of the Vernacular Architecture Forum. Catherine and I were charter members of this national organization of architectural historians, historians, and other disciplines focused on the local and regional character of the historic American-built environment. Based on my knowledge as author of the Caswell County architecture book, I organized and led a daylong tour, "American Bright Leaf Culture, Thomas Day, and the Built Environment of Caswell County, North Carolina" on June 2. With great difficulty, I persuaded homeowners in Caswell County to open their landmark homes to two buses full of strangers.

The tour included little-known antebellum towns, plantation houses, slave quarters, outsider art, and opportunities to study the remarkable furniture and woodwork of Thomas Day. We explored the once-busy river town of Milton, which is located just across the state line from Virginia. With a town plan and architectural features common to Virginia, Milton is now a remote outpost of 166 inhabitants. Among the eight antebellum buildings rarely open to the public were elegant Federal and Greek Revival-style houses, two churches, and the Milton State Bank. The Thomas Day Museum, built in 1818 as a tavern and later the residence and shop of Day, was a highlight. Milton offered exemplary brickwork, unusual floor plans, stylish woodwork by Day and other artisans, and urban outbuildings, including two likely slave quarters.

After lunch at Millie's Pizza in Milton, we were headed to Yanceyville in the humid ninety-seven-degree heat when my bus revolted. The air conditioner simply stopped. I looked around and could

*Gia, Ruth, Britton, Clair, and Warren in Florence, Italy, 2015.*

see sweat quickly forming on the faces of my passengers. It soon became clear that people were becoming heat stressed. We reached the Holderness House, which I had been excited about showing to my visitors, but the biggest thrill was not Thomas Day's incomparable woodwork but the brand-new central air-conditioning.

The tour included the nearby Yancey-Womack House that also contained Day's bold interiors, as well as a detached antebellum law office and a large antebellum tobacco packing, ordering, and stripping barn—the oldest known in the state. In the county seat of Yanceyville, we explored the eclectic antebellum courthouse where a white carpetbagger was murdered by the Ku Klux Klan during Reconstruction, the 1908 jail, and a main street of large and small houses and an antebellum brick store. In the late afternoon, we toured "White Rock Village"—two-dozen miniature stone buildings that incorporate found objects—created by folk artist Henry Warren in the '60s and '70s. Afterwards, we waited in the shade beside the highway for our replacement bus. We arrived an hour late for the post-tour cocktail party, but the participants' feedback rated Caswell County one of the conference highlights.

⁓

To celebrate my seventieth birthday, Warren and I and my family vacationed in Italy with the goal of living like Italians for ten days. I was forced to quit drinking my daily can of Diet Coke. Upon returning home, I continued the Coke fast. Six weeks after kicking the can, I found myself so sleepy one afternoon that I took my first nap in forty years. I had never been a napper and had a hard time sleeping even at night, much less in the daytime. Eventually, I was able to throw away the sleeping pills as well, because my system had been cleansed of the Diet Coke chemicals that caused insomnia most of my adult life and perhaps aggravated my panic attacks. None of the doctors who had prescribed sleeping pills ever asked me if I drank diet soda. I never imagined that a twelve-ounce Diet Coke at lunchtime could cause insomnia.

Another major diet shift was foretold in 2016 by a frightening dream about nearly losing a calf and nearly losing Warren, too. In the dream, I ride on a black cow swimming across a river. We make it to the other side and the cow births a black calf. I clean out its mouth, and it starts moving. We find an old hardware and feed store where the mama cow gets some grain. I love playing with the calf, but I have lost my purse and cell phone so I'm out of touch with Warren. I expect him to save me, but I have amnesia about how I came to be in the river and wonder if there has been an accident. Then a shopkeeper buckles a metal lock around the belly of my little calf, making me so angry that I wake up.

It seemed obvious to me that the calf was my soul, about to be destroyed by an evil person. Soon afterward, Warren and I read the moving passages in Yuval Noah Harari's *Sapiens* book about the cruelty of industrial meat production to billions of cows, pigs, and chickens in the United States. We stopped buying industrial meat. Instead, we eat the deer that Warren hunts, the fish he catches, and pasture-raised chickens from our farmers' market, which we stockpile in the freezer. We built a deer-proof fence and produce most of our vegetables in the backyard, so our diet is field-and-stream and farm-to-table.

~

In 2017, I dreamed that an important archival document was about to be destroyed because the building was scheduled for demolition. When I woke up, I had a hunch that the dream was reminding me about a letter in my possession, three handwritten pages written by Oscar Hardin in 1909 asking my great-grandfather, Dr. Hannibal McDuffie Little, for his daughter Suma's hand in marriage. I had found the letter in 2006 in the bottom of a hand-carved wooden box, put it away, and lost it. It needed my attention, because this document represented my father's roots that I had neglected all my adult life. After an intense three-week search, I rediscovered the letter, and that inspired me to embark on a quest to find out about my father's Aunt Suma, whom he never talked about. Did she have a long and happy life?

Suma Little Hardin, ca. 1915. Collection of Suma Hardin Bolick.

All my paternal elders have passed away, so I despaired of finding a relative who could tell me anything about Suma. I found the name of her granddaughter, named for her, and her married name in a genealogy book. When I googled her, one of the hits was TruthFinder, a public record search service launched a few years earlier. It contained the North Carolina Resident Database with Suma's phone number! Trembling and expecting the number to be out of service or nonexistent, I dialed up Suma.

A lovely female voice answered. "Is this Suma Bolick?" I asked hesitantly.

"Yes, it is," she replied sweetly.

"My name is Ruth Little, and I believe we are cousins."

"It's so nice to talk to a relative!" she exclaimed.

My father descended from seven generations of Littles in North Carolina. The original North Carolina ancestor, Captain Daniel Little, was born in Germany, immigrated to America, and moved to Salisbury in the mid-1700s, where he operated a tavern. Unlike most German immigrants, he anglicized his name from Klein to Little at that time. He died in 1775 and is buried in the Old English Cemetery in Salisbury. His son Peter Little and grandson Peter Little Jr. moved west to Catawba County, owned farms on the Catawba River, and for a century operated a ferry across the river to Iredell County before a bridge was built. The next generation, Joshua Butler Little, fought for the Confederacy in the Civil War and became county sheriff during the Reconstruction era. His son Hannibal McDuffie Little, a wealthy mountain doctor, left his medical account books to my father, his grandson.

The Little clan is so numerous that it publishes a magazine, "The Family of Captain Daniel Little," for thousands of descendants across the country. On the way to Boone with Warren to visit Cousin Suma, we stopped in Catawba County to find my great-great grandfather, Confederate soldier Joshua Butler Little's gravestone. We arrived at St. Paul's Lutheran Church cemetery, containing thousands of gravestones. "We'll never find it," Warren despaired. At the first gravestone on the edge of the cemetery, he yelled, "Oh, I think I've found it. Here's a Little." I ignored him because I knew how vast Dad's Catawba County tribe was. I walked to the center core of the graveyard with older graves, and there, under a large ornate marble obelisk, lay Joshua, next to a matched monument for his wife Susannah.[38]

Cousin Suma and I were so happy to meet. She gave me this photo of her grandmother Suma, a tall artistic woman with a long neck and long dark hair who loved fashionable clothes. She graduated from Davenport University, a girls' school in Lenoir, North Carolina, in 1906 and married Oscar in 1909. They had two boys and built a graceful Colonial Revival house on North Water Street in Boone in 1927, but Oscar died the same year. Her mother moved in with her and the boys, and Suma rented rooms to three young civil engineers. In 1932, Suma died of a quickly fatal stomach cancer, and the boys were left alone and sent to boarding schools for the rest of their childhoods. Suma had a short but happy life.

When I told my high school friend Carol Stein LaVack that I was tracing my father's ancestors back 250 years in North Carolina, she replied, "You're so lucky to be able to do that!"

"Can't everyone do that type of search?" I asked.

Sadly, Carol said, "My family came from eastern Europe in the early 1900s, and their real names and records are lost. My grandmother was from Lithuania. Her last name was Ellis because that's what they named her when she came through Ellis Island as an immigrant. If I went back to Lithuania now to do family research, I don't even know her real name, and all the records have been destroyed."

As a historian, it's a great piece of luck that the information has been there, waiting for me—I just had to dig.

## 35
### Having It All After All

Researching myself during the past three years for this book has been the hardest historical research I've ever done. The process started out feeling self-indulgent, but less so as, one by one, I took a new look at the dark or faded ghosts from my past and held them up to the light: my mother and her mental illness; my artist's block; a lifetime of nearly debilitating panic attacks; my resentment at forfeiting an academic career for motherhood; and the years of unsuccessful searching for true love. In late middle age, I can look back, acknowledge my abusive childhood, patriarchal university education, date rape, a youthful heartbreak, and a nervous breakdown. I was born to an anxious mother to whom I was insecurely attached, which caused a lifetime of anxiety and panic attacks. I grew up believing in a vengeful God. At age twenty-two, I turned my back on love in France to return to my geography—Mother's counties of eastern North Carolina and its beaches, Dad's counties of western North Carolina and its mountains. For me, all this territory came with much to explore, and much to preserve: houses, porches, factories, cemeteries, towns, cities, islands, and genealogies.

My parents descend from vast tribes that have lived in North Carolina since the eighteenth century. My lifelong attachment to this state comes from three hundred years of roots, from the coast to the mountains.

In the new millennium, I have exorcized my ghosts. I downsized Mother from her hoarder house to assisted living and downsized my household to just me. And I reclaimed the art I had neglected for decades.

Among the gifts of my research is the revelation that I integrated career and motherhood without sacrificing my integrity. In the end, I did have the academic career that I thought I had sacrificed in order to raise my children in a family. I gave up a university career to be a mother, but I didn't forfeit academic pursuits. I've created a fifty-year career doing unprecedented work in North Carolina as an independent scholar. I have a legacy of hundreds of National Register listings and architectural surveys that became the standard reference on buildings of certain geographical areas of North Carolina. I've inspired students to historic preservation careers and trained them in fieldwork and research. I've published a dozen books and a number of journal articles. I donated my time to preservation and cultural organizations such as the Vernacular Architecture Forum, Southeast Society of Architectural Historians, the Roundabout Art Collective, and the Friends of Oberlin Village. I taught a National Register class at the University of North Carolina at Greensboro and volunteered on the Gulf coast to save historic buildings from the ravages of Hurricane Katrina.

I would describe myself as a "quiet worker bee who gives as easily as I breathe." Others have told me that I have a great eye, an infectious passion, tenacious detective skills, and a gift for writing. My hope is that my writings have drawn attention to some of the hardest-to-love or ignored outer edges of historic fabric—industrial buildings, cemeteries, African American neighborhoods, and humble vernacular houses from worker housing to cottages to Ranch houses.

Not everyone who works hard receives notice; I have been extraordinarily fortunate to receive several professional recognitions. In 2002, the Historic Preservation Society of North Carolina, the state's private nonprofit organization, awarded me the Robert E. Stipe Professional Award, its annual recognition of a preservation professional at the peak of their productive career. In 2003, my first academic article, "The North Carolina Porch: A Climatic and Cultural Buffer," published in *Carolina Dwelling* in 1978, received special recognition from NC State's College of Design. It was one of only two articles from *Carolina Dwelling* selected for reprinting in a retrospective of articles in the college of design's yearbooks from 1951 to 1985. In 2010, after *Carolina Cottage* was published, I was named "Tar Heel of the Week" in the Raleigh *News & Observer* for my career as a historic preservationist and author.

My name has exemplified many things: mother, preservationist, professional, historian, artist, educator, and writer. "Mother" comes first because I would not take anything for the experience of raising two children. Looking back, I would not change my decision back in 1983 to choose marriage even though it altered my career. I didn't lose my career—I gained my children—the lights of my life. They are my north stars and have given me strength to jettison my separation anxiety, to keep up with digital technology, and to travel around the world. I juggled most of it with panic attacks, artist's block, and without the security of a true partner. The new century brought me Warren, a secure love and a safe person who has banished my panic attacks.

With a great deal of struggle, I have had it all after all.

# Endnotes

1. The Boll Weevil Panic of the early 1920s caused Hugh to lose the insurance business he operated at that time, and the family lost their home. They moved to LaGrange and rented the Shade Wooten House, a ca. 1860 Gothic Revival cottage, from a relative. The oldest and most distinctive building in town, it still stands at 204 West Railroad Street, facing the Atlantic and North Carolina Railroad tracks laid in the late 1850s.

2. The Italian term "piazza" referred to public squares that were enclosed by buildings with open arcades. The arcades came to be called "piazzas" as well. The term came into common English usage in the 1600s and was in common parlance in North and South Carolina by the mid-1700s.

3. The quote appears in Betty Friedan's *The Feminine Mystique*, 1963.

4. However, the University of Georgia admitted females as full students beginning in 1918, and they outnumbered male students for the first time during World War II when so many men served in the military. (Wikipedia, June 20, 2019)

5. *Daily Tar Heel*, November 18, 1964.

6. Alas, the bulldozer devoured that International Style building during the real estate boom in Raleigh that began in 2011 at the end of the Great Recession.

7. Classmates at UNC who eventually had art careers included gifted abstractionists Frank Faulkner and Herb Jackson.

8. Abortion in North Carolina, Wikipedia, accessed June 13, 2019.

9. J. S. Dorton Arena (Raleigh) 4/11/1973. https://files.nc.gov/ncdcr/nr/WA0012.pdf

10. The school was renamed the College of Design in 2000.

11. Nancy Friday's 1977 book examined the psychological relationship between women and their mothers, and the need for healthy separation.

12. The name "Velvet Cloak" derived from the legend that Sir Walter Raleigh chivalrously laid his cloak on the ground to keep Queen Elizabeth's feet from getting muddy.

13. In the 1980s, the architectural review committee objected to a Cape Hatteras lighthouse lamp post that Mrs. Mary Earp installed in her front yard. Mrs. Earp operated Earp's Seafood, a popular local seafood market on South Saunders Street. The protracted battle, reported in Raleigh newspapers, generated much

support for the widow, and her lighthouse was allowed to stand.

[14] Rachel Cusk, "Where the Body Is Buried," *New York Times Magazine*, Nov. 10, 2019, 41.

[15] For example, in 1963, Raleigh Mayor William Enloe's skillful diplomacy convinced merchants to integrate their stores and restaurants.

[16] This church has experienced tragedies and travesties, but always rises again. The congregation rebuilt the sanctuary in 1914, only to see it burned in the Great Fire of 1922 that destroyed most of Dryborough. New Bern's fire crews saved the core of the town where whites lived, but Black New Bern was destroyed. Using salvaged materials, the disheartened, penniless congregation slowly rebuilt the church, completing it in 1942.

[17] My family doctor used to say I had too much adrenalin. He never knew about my decades of addiction to one small can of diet soda a day. I started drinking Tab in my twenties and switched to Diet Coke when it was introduced in 1982. Aspartame (artificial sugar) contains phenylalanine, which can worsen anxiety if you cannot metabolize this chemical or have an anxiety disorder. The Diet Coke at lunch kept me alert all afternoon, but perhaps aggravated my natural anxiety and caused insomnia at night.

[18] Fort Bragg functioned from the 1920s to the end of World War II as one of the major field artillery training ranges in the United States, a laboratory for the Howitzer field gun, the army's workhorse.

[19] Linguists have studied the survival of Old English expressions and vocalizations on North Carolina's remote Outer Banks for many years.

[20] Sunflowers opened at 311 Glenwood Avenue in the 1980s, a catalyst for change among the tired commercial buildings along South Glenwood Avenue south of Peace Street. The sweet corner brick building with its diagonal corner entrance and big plate-glass windows, full of sunshine and fresh flowers, had a happy, hippie atmosphere.

[21] T.K. Taylor, the owner, had a yellowed sign above the cash register: "Husbands desiring to purchase paint must have note from wife." The commercial storefront was tacked onto an old two-story frame house that backed up to the railroad tracks. Inside a small door of the main floor was a wooden staircase to the second floor, where the bedrooms and hallway of the old house had faded wallpaper and a treasure trove of artist canvases, framing materials, and art paper. T.K. and his son Kirk were famous for their custom paint colors mixed by hand in the back, whose floor and walls were streaked with splatters of all colors of the rainbow.

[22] The trip from Raleigh to Fayetteville became shorter when a new bridge was built to carry I-95 across the Cape Fear River to north Fayetteville in the early 2000s. The first time I took the shortcut, it turned out to be miles of open countryside with no highway signs and no river in sight. I had no cell phone or GPS, felt lost,

and suffered a panic attack. Eventually, I crossed the river and was soon in Fayetteville.

23 Durham's historic preservation history began in Trinity Park in the 1970s, when neighbors downzoned to prevent the subdivision of homes into student rentals. Their efforts were rewarded by preserving the city's largest suburb, chock full of charming, well-maintained dwellings.

24 The Cotton Seed Oil plant nearby on South Harrington Street was Raleigh's largest factory when built in the 1880s. Southern Railway's ca. 1912 freight depot, a striking brick building with granite trim and covered loading platforms, is the district's principal landmark. The 1920s Firestone Tire Company and 1930s Dr. Pepper Bottling Company display Art Moderne design. Other buildings include packing and flour companies, wholesale groceries, and electric supply houses, some connected to the rail lines by spur rails.

25 Raleigh's post-war civic buildings, beginning with the 1953 Dorton Arena at the state fairgrounds and continuing to the 1963 North Carolina Legislative Building in the state government complex downtown, are known throughout the United States. Edward Durell Stone of Washington, DC, designed the legislative building as a version of his 1950s American Embassy in New Delhi, India, based on the Taj Mahal.

26 "Post-World War II and Modern Architecture in Raleigh, NC," 1945–1965, (8/11/2009) https://files.nc.gov/ncdcr/nr/WA7242.pdf

27 Many small Modernist offices survive in west Raleigh near NC State University and Cameron Village, such as the 1962 offices of architect F. Carter Williams on Hillsborough Street and of architect Milton Small of 1966 on Brooks Avenue. Both International Style buildings stand on tall piers to allow parking underneath.

28 This piece received the 2013 Southeast Society of Architectural Historians' prize for the best article on Southern architectural history during the year.

29 A. J. Downing was a New York City designer, landscaper, and author from the 1830s to the early 1850s. His designs for rural houses and gardens of picturesque Gothic and Italianate style, published in journals and pattern books, influenced architecture and landscape architecture throughout the United States.

30 Background sources included the published histories of the University of North Carolina and many guides to Chapel Hill's architecture. Eminent architects and planners for the campus included Alexander Jackson Davis of New York City in the mid-1800s and Frank P. Milburn in the early 1900s. John Nolen of Cambridge, Massachusetts, and McKim, Mead & White of New York City were the urban planners of the 1920s expansion, assisted by architects H. Alan Montgomery, Arthur C. Nash, and H. R. Weeks.

[31] City Cemetery National Register listing, Raleigh: https://files.nc.gov/ncdcr/nr/WA3905.pdf

[32] The headstone for Nelson Lane, who died in 1859, bears the signature of Columbus Stronach. Columbus was likely enslaved by William Stronach, who was Raleigh's principal antebellum monument carver. Raleigh's famous Delany sisters, Sadie and Bessie, who had a relatively privileged childhood as children of the Black Episcopal bishop on the campus of the historically Black St. Augustine's School, are buried here in the family plot; Bessie died in 1995 and Sadie in 2000. The book *Having Our Say: The Delany Sisters' First 100 Years*, by Amy Hill Hearth, published in 1993, is a best-selling oral history of their trials and tribulations as civil rights pioneers during their century of life.

[33] Mount Hope Cemetery: https://www.files.nc.gov/ncdcr/nr/WA3792.pdf

[34] In the 1850s, when Frederick Law Olmsted, a nineteenth-century American landscape architect, journalist, and social critic, traveled through North Carolina and later published *A Journey in the Seaboard Slave States* in 1856, he included an engraving and a description of a coastal cottage that he passed by. It was built of logs, and a small room was partitioned into the front porch. He called it the "better class" of the typical cabins he passed, but unlike plantation houses and poor white cabins, neither of which offered him acceptable hospitality, this housed the middle class of society who were inclined to offer lodging to a stranger. Known as the father of American landscape architecture, his most famous design is New York City's Central Park.

[35] Master carpenter Curtis Davis (ca. 1872-1962) built vernacular Queen Anne-style houses in his home community of Marshallberg and in Harker's Island from the 1890s to the 1920s.

[36] The "crystal ball" is a round glass globe on the main staircase's newel post that reflects a panoramic view of the interior of the house. Pictured on the cover, it symbolizes how the house is a crystal ball of North Carolina State University's history through most of the twentieth century.

[37] https://files.nc.gov/ncdcr/nr/WA6388.pdf

[38] Joshua may have been a white supremacist slaveholder, perhaps even a Ku Klux Klansman after the Civil War, but I haven't done the research, and the Klan affiliation, if any, is probably unknowable. I'm not ashamed of my ancestors who fought for the Confederacy, as they were products of an evil system, but I would be ashamed by a Confederate ancestor who engaged in violent suppression of African Americans after the Civil War.

## Also by Ruth Little

*An Inventory of Historic Architecture, Greensboro, NC.* City of Greensboro, Division of Archives & History, NC Department of Cultural Resources, 1976.

*An Inventory of Historic Architecture, Iredell County, NC.* Division of Archives & History, NC Department of Cultural Resources, 1978.

"The North Carolina Porch: A Climatic and Cultural Buffer," *Carolina Dwelling*, ed. by Doug Swaim. NCSU School of Design, 1978. Reprinted in *The Student Publication: Volume 30 Continuum*. Raleigh: North Carolina State University, 2003.

*Caswell County, North Carolina: The Built Environment of a Burley and Bright-Leaf Tobacco Economy*. The Caswell County Historical Association Inc. and Division of Archives & History, NC Department of Cultural Resources, 1979.

*A Tale of Three Cities: A Pictorial Survey of Leaksville, Spray & Draper*. Written and photographed by Claudia Roberts Brown, edited by M. Ruth Little. The Eden Historic Properties Commission, 1986.

"Afro-American Gravemarkers in North Carolina," *Markers VI: The Journal of the Association for Gravestone Studies*. Lanham, MD, and London: University Press of America, 1989.

"The Other Side of the Tracks: The Middle-Class Neighborhoods that Jim Crow Built in Early-Twentieth-Century North Carolina," *Perspectives in Vernacular Architecture VII*, edited by Annmarie Adams and Sally McMurry. Knoxville: The University of Tennessee Press, 1997.

*Sticks and Stones: Three Centuries of North Carolina Gravemarkers.* Chapel Hill: University of North Carolina Press, 1998.

*Coastal Plain and Fancy: The Historic Architecture of Lenoir County and Kinston.* City of Kinston and Lenoir County Historical Association, 1998.

*The Historic Architecture of Morehead City: North Carolina's First Coastal Railroad Resort.* Downtown Morehead City Revitalization Association, 2001.

"Vernacular Hospitality in the Carolinas: The Tidewater Cottage and the Preacher Room," *ARRIS: Journal of the Southeast Chapter of The Society of Architectural Historians,* Vol. 15, 2004.

*The Town and Gown Architecture of Chapel Hill, North Carolina, 1795–1975.* Chapel Hill: Preservation Society of Chapel Hill, 2006.

*Carolina Cottage: A Personal History of the Piazza House.* Charlottesville: University of Virginia Press, 2010.

"Getting the American Dream for Themselves: Postwar Modern Subdivisions for African Americans in Raleigh, NC," *Buildings & Landscapes: Journal of the Vernacular Architecture Forum,* Spring 2012.

*Through the Crystal Ball of the Chancellor's Residence: North Carolina State University, 1928–2012.* Raleigh: NCSU Libraries, 2013.

*Cameron Park, Raleigh, North Carolina: A Remote Retreat on Hillsboro Street.* Cameron Park Association and Preservation North Carolina, 2014.

"Rooted in Freedom: Raleigh, North Carolina's Freedmen's Village of Oberlin, an Antebellum Free Black Enclave," *North Carolina Historical Review,* October 2020.

## More About the Art

Part I: Coming of Age. *(Page 1.) Fish House, 16 x 20 inch oil on canvas, 2013. In a small scrapbook of black-and-white photos from the 1920s, rescued from Mother's house, a beautifully dressed cousin poses on a fishing dock in the Down East village of Atlantic in Carteret County. Behind her, a small fish house for nets and gear stands on stilts in the water. A common building type along the bays and sounds of the North Carolina coast in the early twentieth century, it has disappeared. Because I am a Pisces, the fish house form has become a favorite motif, often depicted with pieces of coastal geological survey maps collaged to the surface and painted in whimsical blues and oranges. Sometimes the cousin turns into a mermaid.*

Part II: Launching. *(Page 67.) View from Dix Hill, 24 x 24 inch oil on canvas, 2012, features the iconic skyline view of Raleigh, seen from the hilltop grove of Dorothea Dix Hospital. Since I listed this campus on the National Register in 1990, the grove has been one of my favorite destinations. I could have sold this painting a dozen times.*

Part III: The Middle Years: Balancing Family & Career. *(Page 127.) Glen Eden, 24 x 30 inch acrylic on canvas, 2017. In painting from nature (plein air), I look at the shapes and let my brush respond. As I wandered through my middle years, finding a balance in the woods of family and career became harder. The landscape grew tangled and dark.*

Part IV: Mama Cool Exorcises Her Ghosts. *(Page 211.) Dancin' on the Porch, 36 x 36 inch acrylic on canvas, 2018. This large acrylic painting depicts a Depression-era photo I found in the Library of Congress's Lomax Collection of folk music and folklore documentation. I painted the black-and-white photo in my favorite complementary blue and orange colors. The girls in diaphanous turquoise dresses dance around Granny in her rocking chair, wearing a polka-dotted frock. Here is a celebration of African American dance and the freedom of movement and joy of a porch.*

# Index

*All place names located in North Carolina unless otherwise noted.*

62nd Corps of Engineers, 3, 5

Adam, Kirk, 212
Adrenalin, 155, 244 (no. 17)
American Tobacco Company, 142, 180
American Tobacco Historic District, 180–181, *181*
Artspace, Raleigh, 80, 176
Asheville, 91
*Askew-Taylor Paints* (painting), 110 Glenwood Avenue, Raleigh, *168*, 169
Association of Gravestone Studies, 145
Athens, Greece, 43
Atlantic (town of), 205
Atlantis Lodge, Atlantic Beach, 205

Barden Cottage, Cape Lookout, *164*, 165
Barden, Dr. Graham and Mary, 164–165
Baten, Betsy, 150–152
Battery Heights, Raleigh, 192–193
Baughn, Jennifer, 219
Beaufort Restoration Association, 206
Beaufort, NC, 9, 12, 115, 135, 163, 202, 204, 205–206, *206*, *207*, 208
Bell, Josiah, House, Beaufort, 206
Bishir, Catherine, 104, 234, 258
Black Lives Matter, 158, 210
Black middle class, 191–192, 210
Bladen County, 94
Blue Ridge Parkway, Watauga County, 3
Bolick, Suma, 237–238
Boll Weevil Panic, 243 (no. 1)
Boone, 3, 9, 179, 238–239
Briggs Hardware, Raleigh, 86–87
Briggs, Jimmy, 86
Briggs, Thomas, 86
Broughton High School, Raleigh, 103

Brown University, Providence RI, 55, 58, 59–62, 72, 110
Brown, Claudia, 132, 198, 234, 247, 258
Brown, Marvin, 234
*Bryant Park* (painting), *215*
Buies Creek, Harnett County, 96, 117
Bull Durham Tobacco Factory, Durham, 180
Bumgarder, Harvey, 82
Byzantine churches, 42, 54

Café Luna, Raleigh, 80
Caligari, Bill, 100
Cameron Village, Raleigh, 29, 87, 176, 187, 189, 245 (no. 27)
Cameron Village Public Library, Raleigh, 176
Cannon Mills, Kannapolis, 4
Cape Lookout Lighthouse and Keeper's Quarters, 163, *165*
Cape Lookout, NC, 163–167
Capel, Toni, 176
Capital Landmarks Inc., 78–81
Carolina Cottage, ix, xii, *120*, 120, 152, 202–203, 207, 208, 242
Carr, George Watts, 182
Carr, Robert W., 182
Carr, Robert W. Jr., 182
Carteret County, 8, 185, 204–205, 208
Cassily, Ellen, 196–197
Castaneda, Professor, 41
Caswell County, 71–72, 109, 216, 232–236, 247
Central Piedmont Community College, Charlotte, 107
Chance, Eugene, 121–122
Chancellor's Residence, NC State University, ix, 209, 213

250

Chapel Hill, NC, 25, 26–27, 33–38, 39, 50, 55–56, 59, 111, 113–114, 118, 138, 143, 155, 169, *170*, 170, *198*, 197–198, 220, 245 (no. 30), 248
Char Grill, Hillsborough Street, Raleigh, *190*
Charleston, South Carolina, 62, 102, 114, 115, 145, 202
Charlotte, NC, 13, 93, 102, 104–105
Christopher, Ames, 100
City Cemetery, Raleigh, 200–201, 246 (no. 31)
Civil War, 63, 86, 143, 144, 147, 153, 222, 233, 238, 246 (no. 38)
Civilian Conservation Corps (CCC), 3, 68
Cleveland Avenue-Holloway Street, Durham, 116
Cobb, Carolyn, 47–48, 258
College Hill, Providence, 61
College of Design, NC State University (see School of Design)
College of William and Mary, Williamsburg, VA, 24, 206–207
Colonial Ranch, 189
Colonial Revival style, 102, 159, 189, 190, 191, 192
Colonial Williamsburg, VA, 95, 207
Contemporary Ranch, 189
Cooper, Anna Julia Haywood, 201
Cordrey, Brandon, 212
Cotton Seed Oil plant, Raleigh, 245 (no. 24)
Country Club Hills, Raleigh, 187, 191
Crabtree Valley Mall, Raleigh, 87
Craftsman style, 210
Cross Creek Cemetery No. 1, Fayetteville, 159
Cross, Jerry, 123
*Culture Town: Life in Raleigh's African American Neighborhoods*, 143, 144

Davidson County, 130, 131, 144, 145
Davis, Alexander Jackson, 245 (no. 30)
Davis, Curtis, 205
Davis, Warren, 229, *230*, 230–231, 258
Dawes, Bruce, 158

Day, Thomas, xii, 233–235
De Beauvoir, Simone, 129
De Leotoing, Marquise Henri, 40, 47
Degraffenried Park Historic District, New Bern, 219
Delany, Sadie and Bessie, 246 (no. 32)
Dickinson, Patricia, 116, 258
Dickinson, Todd, 122
Diet Coke, 236, 244 (no. 17)
Dilworth, Charlotte, 107
Discreet duplex, 209
District of Columbia, Washington, 4
Dodd-Hinsdale House (Second Empire Restaurant), Raleigh, *79*, 77–79
Doris Day, 39
Dorothea Dix Hospital, Raleigh, 75–76, 169, *215*, 249
Dorton Arena, Raleigh, *73*, 73–74, 243 (no. 9), 245 (no. 25)
Down Easters (see Hoi Toiders), 205
Downing, A. J., 195, 245 (no. 29)
Downing, Antoinette, 59, 62, 69
Dr. Pepper Bottling Company, Raleigh, 245 (no. 24)
Dryborough, New Bern, 147, 209–210, 244 (no. 16)
Duncan House, Beaufort, 9, 208
Durham, 12, 24, 26, 27–28, 77, 115–116, 121, 122, 125, 132, 134, 137, 138, 142, 169, 172, 179, 180, *181*, 181–182, 195–196
Durham County, 172, 196, *199*, 199–200
Durham Technical Institute, 115–116

Earp, Mrs. Mary, 243 (no. 13)
Earp's Seafood, Raleigh, 243 (no. 13)
East Carolina Teachers College, Greenville, 2
East Durham Historic District, Durham, 195–196
East Durham, Durham, 115–116, 195–196
Eastman, Julie, 178
Edgemont, Durham, 115
Edmisten, Linda Harris, 81, 143, 258
Ehringhaus, Ann, 138, 139

251

Ehrlich, Alice, 103
Elizabeth City, 93
Enloe, Mayor William, 29, 244 (no. 15)
Erfurth, Carrie, 173, 258
Erwin, Tom, 78

*Fantasia*, xi, 41–42
Fayetteville, 2, 4, 6–7, 11, 14–17, 18–23, 30, 43, 89, *90*, 90–91
Fearing, Fred, 93
Feimster House, Iredell County, *109*, 109
*Fertile Ground* (painting), *216*
Firestone Tire Company, Raleigh, 245 (no. 24)
Five Points, Raleigh, 29, 133
Food Workers' Strike of 1968–1969, 55
Forest Hills, Durham, 182
Fort Bragg Army Base, Cumberland County, 6, 7, 23, 156–157
Foster-Geer Streets Historic District, Durham, 196
France, xi, 4, 37, 39–42, 46–52, 174, 175, 230, 240
*Frances* (painting), *216*
Freeze, Gary, 107–109
Frega, Al, 180
Friday, Bill and Ida, *198*, 198
Friday, Bill and Ida, House, 412 Whitehead Circle, Chapel Hill, *198*, 198
Friedan, Betty, 22, 128–129
Ft. Blanding, Florida, 3

Galopin, Pierre, 46–52, *47*, 53–54, 56–57, 64, 84–85, 106–107
Gamble, Ellen, 222
Gaston House, Raleigh, 77
Geneva, Switzerland, xi, 2, 41, 48, 50, 177
Gia, Ruth, Britton, Clair and Warren in Florence, Italy, *235*
Gilliam, Marita,169
Glass, Brent, 104
*Glen Eden* (paintings), *127*, *217*, 249
Glenwood Avenue, Raleigh, *168*, 168, 169, 171, 188, 244 (no. 20)
Global Transpark, Kinston, 150

Gloria Steinem, 7, 129
Goode, Sabrina, 223
Goodmon, Jim, 180
Gothic Revival style, 85, 159, 190, 243 (no. 1)
Graham, Willie, 207
Graves-Fields House, Raleigh, 224
Great Depression, 3
Greek Revival style, xii, 159, 233, 234
Greensboro, 25, 93–94, 116, 144, 173, 241, 247
Greenwood Cemetery, New Bern, 210
Grove Park Inn, Asheville, 91
Grove, E. W., 91
Gulfport, Mississippi, *220*, 219–220

Hall-and-parlor plan, 140, 205
Hall, Wayne, 122
Hanchett, Tom, 146
Hardin, Oscar, 237
Hardin, Suma Little, *237*, 237–239
Harkers Island, Carteret County, 166
Harper, Jenny, 190, 258
Harper, Terry, 200
Harris, Abie, 209
Harris, James Henry, 222
Harrison, Jane, 178
Hauck, Alice, 62
Haymount Historic District Addition, Fayetteville, 197
Hege Inn, Lexington, 3
Henderson, Archie and Vallie, 100–101
Highsmith Memorial Hospital, Fayetteville, 197
Hill Building, Durham, 182
Historic American Buildings Survey, 68
Holderness, Dr. Howard, 233
Holderness, William Henry and Sarah, 233, 235
Holsenbeck, Bryant, 181
Holt, Jacob, 77
Holt, Joseph, 223
Hong Kong, 226
Hood, Davyd Foard, 104
Howard Street, Ocracoke, *138*

252

Hudson Belk department store, Raleigh, 85
Hunter, Carey, House, Oakwood, 102
Hurricane Floyd, 185
Hurricane Katrina, 219–221, 241
Huxtable, Ada Louise, 59–60

In-A-Gadda-Da-Vida (song), 57
Iredell County, 107–109, 247
Irwin, Bob, 222
Italianate Revival style, 62, 63, 77, 245 (no. 29)

J. Pierpont Morgan Library, New York City, 61
Jacobs, Jane, 59–60
Jenkins, Mary Ann K., 212
John and Roberta Parham House, 2312 Bedford Avenue, Raleigh, *224*, 224–225
Johnson family graveyard, Buies Creek vic., Harnett County, *117*, 117–118
Johnson, Jan, 78
Jones Brothers Bakery, Greensboro, 94
Jones, Dr. H. G., 71
Jones, Lori, 212
Jones, Robbie D., 152
Jordy, Dr. William F., xii, 59, 61, 62, 69
Joslin, Bill, 78

Kannapolis, Cabarrus County, 4
Kappa Alpha Theta, 54–55
Kennedy Home, Lenoir County, 150
Kinston NC, 9, 10, 150, 152, 248
Klee, Jeff, 207
Ku Klux Klan, 235, 246 (no. 38)
Kullen, Michelle, 164–165, 258

La Grange NC, 2, 9, 10, 151, 243 (no. 1)
Lachenman, Sara, 173, 258
LaFayette Hotel, Fayetteville, 4
Lakewood Park, Durham, 181–182
Lally, Kelly, 170, 184, 258
Lane, Joel House, 95, 121, 124
Lane, Joseph House, 95, 96, 118, *120*, 120–125, 131, 203

Lane, Nelson, 246 (no. 32)
Lassiter, Appless, 151
Lassiter, Lyman, 18, 44
Lauder, George, 159
LaVack, Carol Stein, 239
Lawrence, Skip, 179
Lee, Mary Ann, 81
Leimenstoll, Jo, 173
Lenoir County, 9, 11, 13, 25, 150–152, 248
Lenoir Hall Cafeteria, UNC-Chapel Hill, 55
Levister, Mike, 77
Lexington NC, 3, 4, 5, 156
Liberty Row, Fayetteville, *90*, 90–91
Liles, Joseph, 117
Little, Captain Daniel, 238
Little, Dr. Hannibal McDuffie, 237, 238
Little, Joshua Butler, 238, 246 (no. 38)
Little, Keith Kerley, *4*, *5*, 3–7, *8*, 7–9, 25, 37, 44, 68, 69, 110–111, 153, 156, 159, 185, 237–239
Little, Keith W., 4, *6*, 15–16, 22, 44, 62, 84, 110–111
Little Leisure 1, Morehead City (demolished), *8*, 8
Little Leisure 2, Morehead City (demolished), *135*, 135, 232
Little, Virginia "Jenny" White, 2, *3*, 3, *4*, 4, *8*, 9–11, *13*, 15–17, 19–22, 24–26, 28, 30, 36–37, 39, 43–45, 63–64, 84, 98, 110–111, 113, 122, 153, 156, 176–178, 217–218
Little-Stokes, Ruth, 84, 116, 130
Longleaf Studio, with Ruth Little at work, 212, *214*, 214
Lounsbury, Carl, 206, *207*, 207
Lowrey Building, Elizabeth City, 93
Lowry, Gayle, 222
Lyon, France, xi, 37, 39–42, 46–50, 53–54, 56, 84, *230*

*MAD* magazine, 60
Madonna Acres, Raleigh, *193*, 192–194
Mamie, 5, 28
Marin, Peter, 212
Market House, Fayetteville, 90, *158*, 158

Marshallberg, Carteret County, 205, 246 (no. 35)
McCauley Street, Chapel Hill, 55
Meredith College, Raleigh, 225, 103
Michael, Michelle, 185, 258
Michelangelo, 54
Mid-century Modernism, 191–192
Midyette, Carlton, 121
Miller, Jerry, 193
Miller, Tom, 181
Milton, Caswell County, 233–234
Minimal Ranch, *188*, 189
Modernist, 78, 182, 187–194, 196–197, 245 (no. 27)
Montague Building, Raleigh, 79–80
Montreal, Canada, 63–64
Morehead City, 8, 9, 12–13, 30, 135, 185–186, 204, 232, 248
Morrill, Dan, 107
Mount Hope Cemetery, Raleigh, 201, 246 (no. 33)

Nancy in Lyon, 41, 42, 54
National Art Interiors, Raleigh, 169
National Historic Preservation Act, 68–69
Naval stores, 89, 94
NC Agricultural Experiment Station Cottage, Raleigh, 182–183
NC Central University, Durham, 116
NC Gravemarker Survey, 96–97, 117–118, 144–145, 200–201, 248
NC Museum of Art, Raleigh, 31, 76
NC School of Science and Math, Durham, 116, 125, 174, 181
NC State Archives, Raleigh, 69, 70, 71, 75, 86
NC State Capitol, Raleigh, 25, 75, 76, 81, 83, 159, 201
NC State Historic Preservation Office, 69–71, 76–77, 86, 89, 93–95, 104, 140, 145, 152, 190, 234, 247
NC State Legislative Building, 76, 78, 245 (no. 25)
NC State University, ix, 24, 26, 28–30, 62, 77, 104, 137, 183, 187, 208–209, 212, 213, 222, 245 (no. 22), 246 (no. 36), 247, 248

New Bern, NC, 12, 146–147, 149, 164, 204, 209–210, 219, 244 (no. 16)
New Deal, 3, 68
Newport Preservation Society, Newport, RI, 62
Newport, RI, 62
*News & Observer*, Raleigh, 78, 102, 120, 242
Northwestern Insurance Office, Raleigh (demolished), 188
Nunn, Sam and Laura House, Orange County, *171*, 170–171

O'Neal, Ivey and Eliza House, Ocracoke, *139*
Oakwood Athletic Club, 101
Oakwood National Register Historic District, Raleigh, 86–88
Oakwood, Raleigh, 75, 77, 82–83, 85–88, 89, 98–103, *99*, 106
Oberlin Village, Raleigh, 213, 222–225, *224*
Ocracoke National Register Historic District, Hyde County, *138*, *139*, 138–140, 142
Ocracoke, Hyde County, 138–142, 164
Old Ugly (Pink House), 1407 Shackleford Street, Morehead City, *186*, 185–186, 232
Olmstead, Frederick Law, 92
Otis Redding, 27, 28, 57

Panic attack, xi, 41–42, 51–52, 58, 64, 84, 111, 113–115, 134, 153–155, 160, 164, 166–167, 169, 174, 197, 202, 219, 226–227, 231, 236, 240, 242, 244–245 (no. 22)
Parham, John and Roberta House, Oberlin Village, Raleigh, *224*, 224–225
Paris, France, 39, 47–48, 175
Parsons, Richard, 95, 121
Patterson, David, 123
Pendleton building, Elizabeth City, 93
Pezzoni, Daniel, 117
Piazza (porch), 10, 98, 100, 104, 114, 115, *120*, 120, 121, 125, 130, 133, 139, 183, 187, 189, 202–203, 205, 213, 240, 243 (no. 2), 248

Pinehurst, Moore County, 92
Piver House, 125 Ann Street, Beaufort, *206*, 206
Players Retreat, Raleigh, 77
Pope Air Force Base, Cumberland County, 7
Porch (see piazza)
Preacher room (see stranger room)
Preservation North Carolina Inc., 118–119, 224
Providence Preservation Society, Providence, RI, 62
Providence, RI, xii, 59–63, 90
Pruneau, Leslie, 212
Pullen Art Center, Raleigh, 212
Pullen, Richard S., 98

Que Sera Sera (song), 39

Raleigh Blue Printers, Raleigh, 169
Raleigh City Cemeteries Preservation Inc., 200, 201
Raleigh Historic Properties Commission, 80
*Raleigh Times*, 78, 79, 122
Ranch, 6, 133, 182, *188*, 188–189
Redford, Dorothy, 147–148
Renshaw, Jack, 62
Reudrich, Dean, 200
Rhode Island School of Design Museum of Art, Providence, 60
Rhone River, Lyon, 39
Rochester Heights, Raleigh, 192, 193
Romanesque Revival style, 63, 159, 180
Rosenwald, Julius, 199
Ross, Donald, 92
Roundabout Art Collective, Raleigh, ix, 212–214, 241
Russell School, 2001 St. Mary's Road, Durham County, *199*, 199–200

*S. S. France* ocean liner, 39, 53
San Malo, Brittany, 50–51
San Miguel, Mexico, 174–175
Sandhills region, NC, 89, 92, 136, 157
Sanford, Governor Terry, 143

Sayre, Thomas, 171
Scarborough, Al and Linda, 140–141
Scherr, Mary Ann, 213
School of Design (College) NC State University, 82, 101, 104, 187, 191, 193, 243 (no. 10)
Schultz, Professor Juergen, 60, 61
Schuster, Steve, 171
Sharpe, Bill, 204
Sharpe, Charles, 179
Shaw University, Raleigh, 144, 224
Shaw, Betsy, 200
Silver Spring, Maryland, 4
Simmons-Henry, Linda, 143
Simonet, Mademoiselle, 41
Sir Walter Raleigh Hotel, Raleigh, 85
Slane, Heather Wagner, 173, 184, 258
Small, Milton, 187–188, 245 (no. 27)
Smith-Cole House, Orange County, 171
Smith, Charlie, 78–79
Smith, McKelden, 104
Smith, Penne, 152, 258
Snow Hill, NC, 9, 11, 18, 26, 151, 195
Snyder Memorial Baptist Church, Fayetteville, 6
Soane River, Lyon, 39, 40
Soixante–huitards, 48, 49
*Somerset Homecoming*, 148
Somerset Place, Washington County, *148*, 147–148
Southeast Society of Architectural Historians, 202, 241, 245, 248
Southern Folklife Collection, UNC Chapel Hill, 70, 118
Southern Nonviolent Coordinating Committee (SNCC), 144
Southern, Kathleen, 116, 130, 195
Southern, Michael, 94, 104, 116, 234, 258
Spain, 50, 51, 54, 174, 175
Spanish Colonial Revival, 157
Split-Foyer, 189
Split-Level, 133, 187, 189, 192, 198, 222, 225
St. George, Robert, 123
St. Mary's College Chapel, Raleigh, 85

St. Mary's College, Raleigh, 24–32, 33
Staten, Ethel, 209–210
Stephenson, George, 71
Stone, Edward Durrell, 76, 245 (no. 25)
Story and a jump (Banker House), 139, 140
Stranger room (preacher room), 202, 248
Strevel, David, 209
Stronach Stables, Raleigh, 83
Stronach, Jimmy, 82, 83
Stronach, Pauline, 83
Stronach, William, 83, 201, 246 (no. 32)
Student Revolution of 1968, 48–49
Sugg, Francis Jr., 195
Sugg, Jefferson and Eva, 124
Sunflowers Restaurant, Raleigh, 244 (no. 20)
Swaim, Doug, 104, 247

Tarlton, Sam, 169
Tefft, Thomas, 62–63
The Capitol, Fayetteville, 197
*The Feminine Mystique*, 22, 128–129, 243 (no. 3)
Thomas Day Museum, Milton, 234
Thompson-Allen House, Raleigh, 86
Throckmorton, Karen, 223
Thurman, Jane, 200
Tilley, Nannie May, 171–172
Tilley, Roscoe, House, Durham County, 171–172
Tolbert, Lisa, 173
Toole, Clarence A., 144
Touart, Paul, 130
Trinity Park Historic District, Durham, 182, 245 (no. 23)
Tufts, James, 92
Tufts, James Walker, 92
Turco, Ellen, 157, 258

University of Georgia, 24, 243 (no. 4)
University of Lyon, France, xi, 39, 40, 41, 46, 47
University of North Carolina at Chapel Hill, 24, 26, 27, 29, 33–38, 54–56, 59, 61, 111–112, 113, 118, 143, 161, 184, 197–198, 209, 240
University of North Carolina at Greensboro, 25, 173
Upchurch, Britton, 133–134, 137, 174, 221, 226, 232, *235*, 241–242, 258
Upchurch, Virginia "Gia," 131–132, 137, 141, 174, 181, 218, 221, 227, 232, *235*, 241–242, 258
Upjohn, Richard, 85
Upton, Professor Dell, 110

Vass House, Raleigh (demolished), 75, 78
Velvet Cloak Inn, Raleigh (demolished), 85, 243 (no. 12)
Verdell, Emma headstone, 145
Vernacular Architecture Forum, 152–153, 191, 218, 234–236, 248
Vicki Villa, Elizabeth City, 93
Vietnam War, 6, 23, 30, 44, 156
Vieux Lyon, 39–40
*View from Dix Hill* (painting), *67*, *215*, 249
Virginia Dare Hotel and Arcade, Elizabeth City, 93

Wake Forest University, Wake Forest, 183–184
Wake Forest, NC, 183–185
Warehouse District (Depot District), Raleigh, 183, 245 (no. 24)
Warren, Henry, 235
Watauga County, 3
Watts-Hillandale, Durham, 181
Weaver, Ardath Goldstein, 78, 80–81
Webb, Harold, 193
Webb, Harold, House, 1509 Tierney Circle, Raleigh, *193*
Webb, Jim and John, 198
Weisz, Cheryl, 212–213
Westminster Arcade, Providence, xii, 61
White Rock Village, Caswell County, 235
White, Ruth Rouse, 10–12, *13*, 138
Whitney, Fred, 79
Williams, Ben, 31, 76

Williams, Cheryl, 223
Williams, F. Carter, 245 (no. 27)
Williams, Margaret, 31, 76
Willis, James, 135
Wilson, Chris, 153
Winters, John, 192
Woodson, Susan, ix–x, 209, 213
Wooten, Shade, House, La Grange, 243 (no. 1)
Works Progress Administration, 3
Wrenn, Tony, 71–72, 110
Wurster, William, 198
Wynne, Lucy, House, Oakwood, Raleigh, **99**, 98–102

Yancey-Womack House, Yanceyville, 235
Yanceyville, Caswell County, 233–235
Yeomans, David, 165–166
Yeomans, Eugene, 166
Young, Ailey, House, 184–185
Young, Allen, 184–185
Young, Ricardo, 185

# Acknowledgments

*The Book of Ruth* would not exist without the wise and ruthless but cheerful editing genius of Elaine Klonicki, Mary Lambeth Moore, Ann Lano, Kelly Lojk, and Nora Gaskin Esthimer, gifted writers all. Forbearing friends and family read and gave helpful feedback on early versions of the manuscript—Warren Davis, Gia Upchurch, Britton Upchurch, Carolyn Cobb, Don Arnold, Cate Chason, and Jennifer Martin. Dear colleagues Catherine Bishir and Michael Southern have walked beside me nearly every step of my career. Friends who have shared photographs, jogged my memory, and offered publishing advice include Ardath Goldstein, Linda Harris Edmisten, Susi Hamilton, Claudia Brown, Chandrea Burch, Bill Garrett, Will Boggess, Bill Price, Terry Eason, and Dave Wofford.

The younger colleagues, students, and field assistants whom I have nurtured brought more joy than they can know. Some names have escaped me, but I gratefully recall Mary Anne Lee Blackburn, Penne Smith, Michelle Michael, Kelly Lally, Ellen Turco, Michelle Kullen, Pat Dickinson, Todd Johnson, Jennifer Martin, Jenny Harper, Anna Quinn, Heather Wagner Slane, Sarah Lachenman, and Carrie Erfurth.

## About the Author

**Margaret Ruth Little**, principal of Longleaf Historic Resources, specializes in the study of the vernacular architecture, landscape, and decorative arts of the Upper South. After two stints in the NC Historic Preservation Office in Raleigh, she founded Longleaf Historic Resources, a consulting firm named in honor of the longleaf pine, the largest and strongest of the pine species indigenous to Little's childhood region of the Sandhills of North Carolina. Like the man-made resources that she studies, the longleaf pine is endangered. Her substantial works of art and architectural history of North Carolina include *Sticks and Stones: Three Centuries of North Carolina Gravemarkers*; *Carolina Cottage: A Personal History of the Piazza House*; *The Town and Gown Architecture of Chapel Hill, North Carolina*; and *Cameron Park, Raleigh, North Carolina: A Remote Retreat on Hillsborough Street*. She holds an MA from Brown University and a PhD from UNC-Chapel Hill. She creates paintings of North Carolina architecture and landscape and was one of the founders of the Roundabout Art Collective in Raleigh in 2011. Honors include:

- Robert E. Stipe Professional Award, Preservation North Carolina, 2002
- Named a highly respected observer of North Carolina's architectural heritage in *The Student Publication: Vol. 30 Continuum*, College of Design, NC State University, 2003
- Tar Heel of the Week, *News and Observer*, Raleigh 2010
- Best article on Southern architectural history for 2013: "Getting the American Dream for Themselves: Postwar Modern Subdivisions for African Americans, Raleigh, North Carolina," Southeast Society of Architectural Historians
- Award of Distinction for Preserving Oberlin Village History, Friends of Oberlin Village, 2021

www.ingramcontent.com/pod-product-compliance
Lightning Source LLC
Chambersburg PA
CBHW040108120526
44589CB00040B/2804